'Free Verse' as Formal Restraint

ALSO BY ANDREW CROZIER

Thrills and Frills. Selected Prose (Bristol: Shearsman Books, 2014) (ed. Ian Brinton)
An Andrew Crozier Reader (Manchester: Carcanet Press, 2012) (ed. Ian Brinton)
All Where Each Is (London: Allardyce, Barnett Publishers, 1985)
Utamaro Variations (with Ian Tyson. London: Tetrad, 1982)
Were There (London: The Many Press, 1978)
High Zero (Cambridge: Street Editions, 1978)
Duets (Guildford: Circle Press, 1976)
Residing (Belper: Aggie Weston's, 1976)
Pleats (Bishops Stortford: Great Works Editions, 1976)
Seven Contemporary Sun Dials (with Ian Potts. Brighton: Brighton Festival, 1975)
Printed Circuit (Cambridge: Street Editions, 1974)
The Veil Poem (Providence, RI: Burning Deck Press, 1974)
Neglected Information (Sidcup: Blacksuede Boot Press, 1972)
In One Side & Out the Other (with John James & Tom Phillips.
        London: Ferry Press, 1970)
Walking on Grass (London: Ferry Press, 1970)
Train Rides (Pampisford: R Books, 1968)
Loved Litter of Time Spent (Buffalo, NY: Sum Books, 1967)

ALSO BY IAN BRINTON
(ed.) *'An intuition of the particular': Some essays on the poetry of Peter Hughes*
        (Bristol: Shearsman Books, 2013)
Poems of Yves Bonnefoy 1 (Oystercatcher Press, 2013)
(ed.) *An Andrew Crozier Reader* (Manchester: Carcanet Press, 2012)
Brontë's Wuthering Heights, *A Reader's Guide* (London: Continuum 2010)
(ed.) *A Manner of Utterance, The Poetry of J.H. Prynne* (Exeter: Shearsman Books, 2009)
Contemporary Poetry: Poets and Poetry since 1990 (Cambridge Contexts in
        Literature; Cambridge: Cambridge University Press, 2009)
Dickens' Great Expectations, A Reader's Guide (London: Continuum 2007)

Andrew Crozier

'Free Verse' as Formal Restraint

*— an alternative to metrical conventions
in twentieth century poetic structure*

Edited by Ian Brinton

Shearsman Books

First published in the United Kingdom in 2015 by
Shearsman Books Ltd
50 Westons Hill Drive
Emersons Green
BRISTOL
BS16 7DF

Shearsman Books Ltd Registered Office
30–31 St. James Place, Mangotsfield, Bristol BS16 9JB
(this address not for correspondence)

ISBN 978-1-84861-396-6
First Edition

Contents

Introduction

The summary that Andrew Crozier provided in September 1972 for the thesis which he presented at the University of Essex in 1973 is quite clear in its sense of purpose and this is, of course, of no real surprise. One would do well to recall Michael Schmidt's comments about the glacial progress of Crozier's criticism that I quoted in my introduction to the Shearsman edition of *Thrills and Frills*: 'He is a magnificent critic, moving with the certainty of a glacier, gathering everything.' In the introductory summary Crozier wrote that his intention in writing the thesis had been to cast some light on the *prima facie* case that free verse, in abandoning the exercise of metre, had abandoned that principle of restraint upon which the creation of artistic form depends:

> This point of view contrasts with a general contention on the part of the exponents of free verse that their works possess form which is not only unique but which also bears an immediate relation to the significance of the work, a relationship felt to be "musical", although not in any directly analogical sense.
>
> It is this latter notion of form, implicit in Pound's concept of "absolute rhythm", which I have attempted to elucidate, and I have chosen to do so by considering a number of related earlier discussions of the way in which poetry and music have been thought to be related, rather than by a direct engagement with individual poems. I have been concerned, that is to say, not to undertake practical criticism, but to indicate a poetic theory whence the appropriate standards for such practical criticism can be supplied.

The summary concluded with references both to "the sensible qualities of natural language" and to "modern theories of perception and of nature" and it is perhaps these two thoughts which prompted Donald Wesling of John Muir College, University of California, (author of *Internal Resistances, The Poetry of Edward Dorn*, 1985) to write to Crozier in July 1974:

> "The sensible qualities of natural language": and yet, with the exception of the prose poem, free verse is divided into <u>lines</u>, which create equivalences superimposed on the natural language,

which coincide or don't coincide with sentences, which therefore supply additional conventions, which therefore profoundly qualify your term "natural language". In general, it may be you under-emphasize the role of the line.

Wesling went on to refer to Crozier's focus upon "modern theories of perception and nature" and suggested that he must be thinking here of A.N. Whitehead whose book *Process and Reality* had had such an influence upon Charles Olson:

> you're here thinking of such as Whitehead, I imagine, for "nature"; but having read in both these areas for a few years, I suspect your documented sense of modern theories of both perception and of nature is a bit thin. Gestalt psychology, directive state psychology, Heisenberg & Bachelard: that sort of thing brings us a bit closer to the present day, though of course the general lines of your account hold up very well.

In the letter Wesling went on to say that as far as he was concerned the constitutive date for modern concepts of form should not be placed around the end of the first decade of the Twentieth Century but at 1795 and that for him the Romantic break was the massive one; Modernism is merely the working-out of a whole new paradigm. He concluded by suggesting that Crozier most certainly had a book here, 'a sensible, lively, contentious, genuine contribution, the best thing on the subject we have so far… the book is there: an achievement: you should publish it soon.'

The official academic centre for Crozier's doctorate was the University of Essex where he had both studied and taught in the new Department of English and American Studies, founded there by his former teacher Donald Davie. Whilst there between the autumn of 1965 and the autumn of 1967 he not only started editing *The English Intelligencer* but also, along with Tom Clark, *The Wivenhoe Park Review*. The review continued under the title *The Park* when Crozier moved in 1967 to the University of Keele after he had taken up a lectureship there in the Department of American Studies. He remained at Keele until 1973, the date in which he was awarded his Doctorate, before moving on to the University of Sussex where he remained until his retirement. Throughout the time since he had left Cambridge he had kept in close correspondence with Jeremy Prynne and had organised the publication of *Brass* with Ferry Press in 1971[1].

Crozier's connection with Wivenhoe Park re-emerged in February 1972 when Prynne wrote to him about their mutual friend, Douglas Oliver, who had applied for admission to the literature course at Essex. Prynne was wondering at this point if there was anyone still at the university whom Crozier might have known and who might put in a word for this mature student. Crozier replied to say that 'My contacts with Essex have been minimal since I left the place… However, my current supervisor, Herbie Butterfield, seems to be fairly well disposed towards me, and I'll write to him about it. I suppose the one virtue of Essex would be that they might leave Doug alone.'

In March 2013 Tony Frazer wrote to me concerning Crozier's thesis, having heard about it from Kevin Nolan. He wondered if it was something 'that could be rescued'. It has been and I must acknowledge my debt to Jean Crozier for permitting it to be published. This edition of the thesis also contains the examiner's report written by J.H. Prynne whose concluding note to Crozier is itself of interest:

> "The analysis of the Williams poem is perceptive and convincing, but it makes no direct attempt to give a specific account of what a prosodic description would have given, i.e., some non-arbitrary indication of its line-divisions etc. If Crozier reasonably refuses to invoke any a priori formal expectations, he might also (reasonably) be expected to refer to just those features of poetic ordering which prosodic analysis would have dealt with, to shew that his own approach is (a) adequate, and (b) non-reductive."

Ian Brinton

Notes

[1] The details surrounding the publication of *Brass* can be found in an article 'Andrew Crozier and the Ferry Press' by Ian Brinton, *Tears in the Fence*, No. 55, Summer 2012.

'Free Verse' as Formal Restraint

Summary

My intention in writing this thesis has been to cast some light on the *prima facie* case that free verse, in abandoning the exercise of metre, has abandoned that principle of restraint upon which the creation of artistic form depends. This point of view contrasts with a general contention on the part of the exponents of free verse that their works possess form which is not only unique but which also bears an immediate relation to the significance of the work, a relationship felt to be "musical", although not in any directly analogical sense.

It is this latter notion of form, implicit in Pound's concept of "absolute rhythm", which I have attempted to elucidate, and I have chosen to do so by considering a number of related earlier discussions of the way in which poetry and music have been thought to be related, rather than by a direct engagement with individual poems. I have been concerned, that is to say, not to undertake practical criticism, but to indicate a poetic theory whence the appropriate standards for such practical criticism can be supplied.

Accordingly, I have first of all examined the kind of critical reservations to which free verse is susceptible, and I have in turn discussed the notions of restraint implicit in metre, together with its associated formal concepts. These suggest a notion of form as the product of two contending principles, in contrast to the notions of formality associated with free verse, which suggest, rather, the cooperation of several distinct principles working in a similar direction. These principles resolve themselves into issues concerning the melodic structure of the verse line, and the way it is shaped by real speech values.

I then turn to the question of antecedent exponents of a relationship between poetry and music; music here being a term which extends to deal with the construction of the verse line as an authentic unit. From the sixteenth century onwards, preoccupations of this type have concerned themselves both with the purely formal or technical organisation of verse, and also with the question of its expressive powers. A concept of universal harmony, of relationship by significant proportions, has underwritten critical speculation of this type, although its power to do so has diminished as the scope afforded to the notion of reason has been narrowed down to suggest that it is an exclusively mental quality. Thus my central narrative exhibits a decline in the coherence of speculation of this type from Campion's suggestion that the ear is a rational sense, to the agitation of the passions by mechanical association in Addison and Burke.

My final contention, therefore, that free verse embodies an authentic formal principle guided by the restraints imposed upon expression by the sensible qualities of natural language, and that such verse is amenable to criticism according to its own appropriate criteria, which I define, is sustained by an argument against such a restriction of rational function, together with the suggestion that modern theories of perception and of nature encourage us to understand a nature in which rational structure inheres, so that the restraints afforded by language to verse form are not merely arbitrary, but are consistent with potential meaning.

Chapter 1

Introduction:
Critical Reservations
About "Modern" or Experimental Poetry

It is generally acknowledged that round about 1908 English poetry began to undergo a series of radical changes and there exists by now a considerable critical literature charting and describing this process. By and large the various accounts given of "the new poetic" or "modernism" concern themselves with a range of potentially verifiable historical data: the formation of the Poets' Club, the publication of the Imagist "manifesto", the critical ideas of Hulme, Pound, and Eliot, and so on. These data provide an ambience against which the work of various poets of now established reputation can be observed; Yeats and Pound, Pound and Eliot, are seen to influence one another's work reciprocally, yet at the same time may be treated individually to present particular bodies of work which can be dealt with in a conventional critical way. It is difficult to avoid the impression that in most discussions of this complex and important period of poetic activity the idea of the "radical change" which so often serves as a premise to frame discussion is, in fact, held to be the feature of least importance.[1] It appears to be a rather elastic concept, allowed a fairly definite commencement, but with no real terminus, something which exerted its ghostly presence throughout the composition of Pound's *Cantos*, perhaps, but effectively redundant by the time *The Waste Land* was published. I am aware that from this point of view I may appear to be guilty of asserting a mere quality in the face of the superior claims of substance, by harping on the question of a radical change, its real nature, the extent to which it might be a gradual process, and whether such a process might not be still unfolding. One of the implications of such questions is that, unless "modernism" can be seen to be something which transcends the individual poetic achievement of a Pound or an Eliot, something therefore which can be generalised in terms of, for instance, common poetic procedures or attitudes of a sort which make a significant contribution to individual poetic achievement, I can see no point, given the advantage of half a century of hindsight, in attaching particular importance to the events of 1908 and thereabouts, no matter how radical or novel the actors in those events might have felt they were being. It would seem, rather, the proper critical task to reabsorb those events to the steady, evolutionary march of English poetry. There exists, after all, ample precedent for such a procedure in the secondary writings of T.S. Eliot.

The set of attention from which the argument of this essay derives reached back to 1963, when I was still an undergraduate, and takes as its point of departure an acceptance at face value of the premise that a radical and self-consistent transformation did occur in English poetry at the beginning of the present century. The idea of the self-consistency of these events is of particular importance, for I believe they need to be seen not as a single and absolute occurrence, but rather as a movement at work on a number of different and complementary fronts, possessing, moreover, important correlations with areas of knowledge and activity which are not normally regarded as falling within the scope of literary criticism. The idea of such a radical transformation possesses a certain inclusive interest by virtue of the way in which it can be made to offer both an explanation of how the poems to which the idea refers work at various different levels, and also an injunction that these levels, in any given poem, should work together in a complementary and consistent way. Such a formulation, which might amount to a poetics, since by extrapolation it might be held to apply normatively to any poem, is not, of course, anywhere explicitly worked out; nor, I think, is it to be found fully embodied in the work of any one poet. Indeed, various poets whom I regard as participating in this process of radical transformation have published statements which patently oppose the drift of my argument. What I am proposing here is, in fact, double-faced, both description and formulation, a projection of ideas about the present status of poetry in order to cast light upon the radical core (vortex might well be a more appropriate word to use in this context) of the events of 1908 and subsequent years—events to which, through my knowledge of them, I largely owe the ideas being entertained.

It should be clear by now that my diagnosis of the character of this process of radical change does not relate simply to ideas of formal poetic innovation on the one hand, and on the other to the revival or reaffirmation of certain poetic universals: twin purposes which some "Imagist" statements imply were the sum of the innovative concerns of that particular literary moment. I want to emphasise this from the start, since otherwise my working procedure might be taken to suggest an exclusive concern with the first of those propositions. What strikes me as a salient feature of the movement I am trying to define is not so much ideas about

1. Introduction — Critical Reservations

the "image" or the "ideogram", but something more fundamental still, the use of asymmetrical verse structures, a whole range of compositional strategies to which the title "free verse" has at best loosely, and in general uselessly been applied. My attention has focussed initially, therefore, on those areas of poetic activity which are referred to under such headings as prosody, metrics, rhythm, verse structure, and so forth. This is already in practice a sort of conceptual no man's land, in relation to which no set of descriptive terms can pretend to be critically neutral. I have found in particular that systems of metrical scansion fail to meet the case presented by the kind of poem which concerns me here. In effect, most prosodic or metrical <u>systems</u>, including their notational signs, turn out to offer what is essentially an account only of the examples they use as illustration. It seems to me more pertinent, rather than search for a complete account of rhythm as a feature of poems which can, by implication, be relegated to a subordinate position in the hierarchy of poetic effect, to see the study of prosody as an investigation of rhythm as something which makes a fundamental contribution to an <u>inclusive</u> poetic effect. From this point of view rhythm in poetry can be seen as something with a variable function rather than a specific modality or level.

Two related purposes are hereby brought into play: first, to offer terms for the perception of rhythmic activity in a poem, and second, to offer an account of the way rhythm cooperates in generating the total significance of the kind of poetry being dealt with here. In each case I have found that the analogy between poetry and music put forward so energetically by Ezra Pound could be illuminatingly followed back over four centuries of speculation about the ontological status of poetry. Moreover, whereas for Pound the analogy consisted chiefly in observed structural parallels between the temporal operations of poetry and music, so that he often seems to be offering little more than a sophisticated version of the Rhymers' Club obsession with the sung lyric, there is an important earlier literature of the relationship which opens up much fuller and more interesting possibilities. Thus, although for the Sixteenth Century theorist there was a potent nexus between poetry and music, as arts composed of time relationships, these issues were also bound up closely with the whole question of the availability and value of the vernacular tongue for literary composition; and while this temporal nexus is a recurrent issue, reappearing in a particularly interesting way in the work of Patmore and Hopkins in the middle years of the Nineteenth Century, the curve described by this fructive mental association of music and poetry is sufficiently encompassing to take in, during the Eighteenth Century, a series of comparisons between the sister arts in terms of their related expressive powers rather than their structural affinities.

For poetry which dispenses with a priori notions of form, or a given metrical base, the analogy between poetry and music offers a valuable model for our understanding of rhythmic presence and complexity. What it does not offer, however, and what should not be expected of it, is any explanation of how the rhythm which is defined in this way operates with and, perhaps influences other elements in the poem—syntax, grammar, reference, and so forth. How it does this is the question of determining importance, and needs to be approached from a different direction, that of the general ideas one has of the nature and purpose of poetic discourse. If it can be assumed that there is a significant correlation between formal metrical schemes and statement in the form of a sentence which can be parsed throughout according to agreed grammatical procedures, it should be possible to invert such an axiom to apply to a case whereby, if the conventions of former apparatus are altered it will follow that the conventions in the latter may alter in a significant way also, so that one will find, not the abrogation of the grammatical laws necessary for meaningful and verifiable discourse, but a transformation both of the world which is implied in any particular instance of verbal structure, and by the same token a transformation of the rules for organising language which are to be inferred from any such implied world. This means that a poem might effect a transformation of the culture of which it was in part an expression. The intellectual underpinnings of this argument, obviously enough, are not to be drawn from literary history, but derive instead from such disciplines as linguistics, anthropology, and metaphysics. I feel very simply that these matters lie outside my competence; indeed many of the specific issues to which I might refer are controversial within their proper fields, and it will therefore be with reluctance that I refer to my superficial reading in such matters. Where I do so I hope it may be not to put forward a point to sustain my argument, but rather to indicate the broad-ranging reference which I think poetry entails. Many of the poets whose work I shall be discussing have, in fact, made excursions into these fields in the course of commenting on the nature of their poetic activities, and so it should be possible to register these extra-literary concerns as a metaphor for the scope claimed on behalf of the poetry I am discussing. In this way, I believe, the argument can be made to remain within the traditional territory of the literary critic.

I wish now to discuss briefly the ideas of two poets who have written extensively about the mode of discourse of modern poetry and its relation to prosodic structure, since the arguments they put forward run counter to ideas which must remain implicit during much of my subsequent argument.

In his book *Articulate Energy, An Inquiry into the Syntax of English Poetry* Donald Davie asks "What is Modern Poetry?", and suggests that it is a derivative of _symbolisme_, a special way of organising symbolic events to such an end that, in a phrase taken from Marshall McLuhan, "syntax becomes music."[2] What Davie understands by music here is not very much to the point, although he appears to harbour a rather dim judgement of it, suggesting elsewhere in the book that in poetry "music" or "sound" is a property which enables the poet to spin his work out to the detriment of sense. By syntax, however, Davie means something quite precise—it is the syntax which satisfies the demands of the logician and the grammarian, and also of the "folk", "authentic" syntax in fact.[3] Against this he sets a "modern" usage of syntax, or pseudo-syntax, which makes of it merely an "emptied form", which can harbour, nevertheless, "presented" experience. (There is a strange elision in the topics Davie is dealing with at this point, from symbolic event and _paysage intérieure_ to a modern use of syntax as a handy convention to provide a presentational framework for concrete experience, which is what I take him to be discussing subsequently.) Davie makes considerable play with the distinction between "presentation" and "description", while at the same time deprecating it as a point of controversy. The crux of his argument, however, involves a passage of Coleridge's in which, as Davie sees it, an analogous distinction is drawn between the "imageable" and the "conceivable".[4] What Coleridge is intent upon, in this distinction between different modes of mental projection, is an oblique attack on the sensationalist axiom that nothing can be in the mind which was not first in the senses; the "imageable", that is to say, standing for the processes of tangible sensory experience.[5] Coleridge is recommending what amounts to an operational procedure which will discover for the transcendental notions about the presence of innate ideas ("the conceivable") their proper station in mental life. For Davie, however, "This is the Coleridge who admonished Wordsworth that the best part of human language comes from the allocation of fixed symbols to internal acts of the mind." Allowing for the apparently pleonastic condition of internal here, these acts of the mind appear to embrace both the power of generalisation and conceptualisation, together with the formal rules of logic and grammar, which seem to have been endowed with a stiff immutability at this point.

The phrase does not however, as Davie uses it, refer to either involuntary or mechanical mental activity, or that range of mental states and processes which for convenience's sake only can be denoted by the term irrational.

I am not happy about the particular grounds upon which the argument about pseudo-syntax is conducted, nor, I think, is Davie himself, for he does not seem prepared to offer any answer to the question which he originally posed.[6] What in fact appears to be at stake for him here is not simply the bleak future for formal syntax (which I should prefer to denote by the term "grammar") and the conceptual impoverishment of symbolic presentations; of much greater importance must be the notions about knowledge, truth, and meaning in relation to poetry which are brought into play by his argument. The goal of modern poetry, it seems to me, entails the accomplishment of a self-verifying and self-validating discourse, which does not need to refer to an ostensive reality separate from itself in order to establish the possibility of its own existence. This sort of proposition can, of course, easily be corrupted to turn into a case made for language as an absolutely expressive system, a kind of poetic hermeticism which cancels at a stroke a further modern goal, the return of poetry to a direct presence in the world, and it is this easy tendency which must, I imagine, have been at the back of Davie's mind as he wrote the passage I have been discussing. But by using Coleridge's term the "conceivable" to conflate two distinct notions, the transcendent idea, which manifests itself to the poet through nature, and the concept, the complex idea formed internally by the mind out of the simple ideas of sense data, Davie has implicitly left the poem bifurcated uneasily between natural and human worlds, neither one nor another. (It is as though, for Davie, "presented" experience can only occur in a singular manner, reminiscent of the atomism of Locke's sensationalism. And that a complex or gestalt can never be "presented" to experience with the same "directness". I should imagine that modern theories of perception would undercut any notion that the minutiae of sense data possessed a superior intensity as knowledge.)

Davie's argument, in effect, only shelves the important questions about the relation between poetry and language, and between language and human experience. Davie seems to assume a radical discontinuity between the natural and the human worlds, but because in this respect he is only typical of an anthropocentric culture, he is not required to make the assumption explicit, and it is difficult to hold him to the point for the purpose of discussing an assumption about the relationship between these two "worlds" which is, I believe, basic to the poetry I am going to discuss. This assumption is, crudely stated, that there exists no radical discontinuity

1. Introduction — Critical Reservations

between the human and natural worlds, but that, on the contrary, man exists as part of a nature to which he owes his fullest existence. (It is a point of view put forward with particular emphasis by Charles Olson in his essays "Human Universe" and "Projective Verse".[7]) If man, and, what is more to the point in the context of the present argument, language also are part of the natural world (it should be noted, in passing, that such a view need not commit one to the assumption that language is therefore simply a mechanical operation, devoid of intentional structure) then it should follow that what Davie means by his concept of "pseudo-syntax"—a conventional form drained of rational structure since it only contains bare and undiscriminated, therefore meaningless and presented, experience—is nothing more than a discrimination of sensibility. Whatever its character as syntax, any manifestation of linguistic organisation is nevertheless meaningful, since linguistic apprehension and rendering of experience need not require any logically prior and separate act of evaluation, the point being that the notion of priority at work here, non-verbal experience giving way to evaluated verbal expression, has become tautological. (Again, this view does not commit one to the naïve view that the structure of language is somehow mimetic of the perceived relations of the external world; on the contrary it is a view which should be able to utilise Chomskyan notions about the "deep structure" of grammar.) I am sure, to draw into discussion at this point a poet whose work implies that view about man in his relation to nature of which I have suggested Charles Olson is an exponent, that this is one of the implications of William Carlos Williams' axiom "No ideas but in things"—a praxis of naming which carries the thing named over into the act of discourse, which suppresses, in other words, the need for the middle ground of a lexicon of generic concepts, or words, which mediate between simple naked facts and our ability to discriminate between one such fact and another. It is not that I dispute whether, in certain circumstances, words exercise such a character of generic abstractness; or that the situation of the lexicon possesses this kind of logical middle ground; what I do question is the view that all operations in language stem from and have their functions defined by such a source. However, in trying to clarify these reservations I have allowed myself to run on a bit too fast, leaving unexamined the assumption which I have suggested underlies Davie's argument at crucial points. This assumption about the separation of man and nature is explicitly advanced by Yvor Winters in his important book *Primitivism and Decadence, A Study of American Experimental Poetry*, first published in 1937.

§ § §

Winters' book is important historically because it was the first coherent critical account of what he chose to call experimental, rather than modern, American poetry. In a sense Winters had answered Davie's question "What is Modern Poetry?" twenty years before it was put, and even though Winters' term begs the question of the comparative value of the poetry he is dealing with, his book remains unsurpassed as an attempt to grapple with the implications of the intentions and working principles of modernism. And, even while disagreeing fundamentally with Winters' final judgements, one is impressed by the accuracy and justice of Winters' early recognition of the central area of attention for the critic of modern poetry. His generous interest, however, is undercut by a set of assumptions about language and poetry which make him unable beyond certain limits to understand the coherence and validity of the procedures of the poetry he writes about. The question of logical procedure, around which battle-lines were finally drawn up in an acid exchange of footnotes between Winters and Pound[8], a commitment which Winters reaffirmed in the title given to his volume of collected criticism *In Defence of Reason*, is, I feel, at least as a starting point, misleading as a means for scrutinising Winters' ideas about the relationship between language and poetry.

The real value of poetry for Winters lies in its ability to embody the life of reflexive consciousness: he makes this quite clear both at the beginning and at the end of *Primitivism and Decadence*.

> The conception which I am trying to define is a conception of poetry as a technique of contemplation, of comprehension, a technique which does not eliminate the need of philosophy or of religion, but which, rather, completes and enriches them.[9]

Poetry is different from both philosophy and religion because it is essentially personal; Winters' two terms for the subject matter poetry has to deal with are "motive" and "feeling".

> It will be seen that what I desire of a poem is a clear understanding of motive, and a just evaluation of feeling; the justice of the evaluation persisting even into the sound of the least important syllable. Such a poem is a perfect and complete act of the spirit;

       1. Introduction — Critical Reservations

it calls for the full life of the spirit; it is difficult of attainment, but I am aware of no good reason to be contented with less.[10]

These normative concepts are elaborated into an analytical procedure by the application of the idea that language possesses two complementary qualities, the denotative and the connotative. These qualities possess the attributes of functions in language, but their separate areas of operation are not, it seems, to be completely discriminated: the denotative function of a word possesses ontological priority, and all other features of language are relegated, of necessity it seems, to the category of connotation. Winters' commitment to the denotative functions of language leads him in two directions: towards a view of poetry as an ostensive gesture on the part of the poet, in which he refers to his experience, and also towards a standard for poetry which, because it eschews the idiosyncrasy of connotation, directs the reader's attention to an order of general truth. I shall mention later on how these tendencies, in appearance contradictory, lead Winters to place the highest value in poetry on the lyric; meanwhile it is important to note how Winters reconciles the contradiction in his view of language as abstraction.

> ...language is a kind of abstraction, even at its most concrete; such a word as 'cat', for instance, is generic and not particular. Such a word becomes particular only in so far as it gets into some experiential complex, which qualifies and limits it, which gives it, in short, a local habitation as well as a name.[11]

This is slightly odd in its implication that there is a name for the word "cat", and suggests that although for Winters experience is nameless at first, it is sufficiently vivid to present him with entities that can only be fitted back into the dimension of experience by being given a name. In fact Winters was probably dreaming of the Cheshire Cat, for how else except in having an unique case before the mind is it possible to confuse the activity of naming a category and naming an object? It should be clear that what Winters means by denotation is the function of referring to a word's place in the generic lexicon; to refer "cat" to an actual beast in the shrubbery, say, is the function of connotation, so that all experience is suffused with emotional colour. What I want to draw particular attention to, however, is Winters' use of the phrase "experiential complex", which very tellingly indicates the reflexive nature of poetic energy as Winters understands it.

The phrase itself would be tautological if Winters were simply referring to the idea of a poem as an instance of <u>complexity</u> to be <u>experienced</u>; it has to be a complex that refers back to experience, as if the only cats in a poem are to be those the poet has met, although he has to look the thing up in his bestiary before he can recognise it. Never, in Winters, does one find the suggestion that language is an originary human faculty with which it is possible to go out into a world of primary experience.

For Winters, therefore, the business of the poet is to bring together his rich but incoherent experience and his copious but ineloquent language. Stated thus baldly it seems an impossible project, since one is presented with categories so much at variance as to be incompatible. And even if one were to modify the category of language in such a way as to make it the possession of the poet, the equation still ignores the important ways in which, so linguists tell us, the structure of language influences the way we experience things. But for Winters language possesses no inherent structure, it is simply words arranged in patterns of conventional usage, and is given structure by the poet's careful discriminations in correlating the simplicities of his generic lexicon with the complexities of his connotational experience. The structure of language, that is to say, is borrowed from a nature on which generic concepts have been imposed, and the relations between these categories generate (have generated, perhaps in some ideal history) the formal rules of grammar which express an established and, necessarily correct understanding of nature, but nature which is now elevated from experience. Winters' pseudo-ontological statement about language, in fact, exemplifies a profoundly felt cultural prejudice, and as such is immensely impressive.

To characterise Winters in these terms is to say more than that he dislikes some sorts of poetry—a common enough verdict on Winters the critical eccentric—because it explains why he thinks that experimental poetry must inevitably be second-rate. Experimental poetry by definition has abandoned the proven means of success. Language is not only a kind of abstraction, it is also stiff and unexpressive. It is only when words are given their local habitation by being used in a certain kind of context that they gain power (although they do so in an essentially mechanical way).

> …many writers have sought to seize the fluidity of experience by breaking down the limits of form, but… in so doing they defeat their own ends. For, as I have shown, writing, as it approaches the looseness of prose and departs from the strictness of verse, tends to lose the capacity for fluid or highly complex relationships between

words; language, in short, reapproaches its original stiffness and generality; and one is forced to recognise the truth of what appears to be a paradox, that the greatest fluidity of statement is possible where the greatest clarity of form prevails.[12]

Language is most fully charged with meaning when it is subject to traditional checks because those checks are themselves the structure of human reality. The most complex relationships between words appear at points of variation within a clear (i.e. traditional) form. Winters' argument about the relationship of rational structure, traditional form, and significant variation can be reduced to a simple proposition, but its bases are complex, as I have already in part shown. I want now to sketch in the remaining parts of his argument as they relate specifically to his major injunctions to poets.

As I suggested in my discussion of the primacy which Winters accords to the function of denotation, his argument moves in two directions, each veering away from the particularities of subjective experience. Poetic activity is seen by Winters as always following after the event (to which it refers), to which it is related as perception is said to be related to experience.

> …a poem in the first place should offer us new perceptions, not only of the exterior universe, but of human experience as well; it should add, in other words, to what we have already seen.[13]

One is right to be disturbed, surely, by this insistent separation of the exterior universe from human experience, of that which is experienced from what is perceived of it. Winters' increment to perception takes place, in effect, as an abstraction of, and not an addition to, a phenomenal world which can exact perception of itself, and the poem as such is left finally separate from the world, and never an object of experience in its own right.

Winters' other direction involves the programmatic control of experience. He makes this function explicit in his comments on Allen Tate's sonnet The Subway, to which I shall refer at length in a moment. Control is tied up with the creation of poetic form.

> …the creation of a form is nothing more nor less than the act of evaluating and shaping (that is, controlling) a given experience.[14]

The particular importance of this control of experience however is its function as a control of the emotions. Metre offers a means by which the poet controls emotion (specifically his own emotion, and by extrapolation the reader's) by being able to vary it.

> The nearer a norm the writer hovers, the more able is he to vary his feelings in opposite or even many directions, and the more significant will be his variations.[15]

The necessity for this control and direction of feeling occurs because feeling is concerned with the unformalised natural world of connotation, as I have already suggested. Winters spells the danger out.

> ...all feeling, if one gives oneself (that is, one's form) up to it, is a way of disintegration; poetic form is by definition a means to arrest the disintegration and order the feeling, and in so far as any poetry tends towards the formless, it fails to be expressive of anything.[16]

For Winters, then, feeling is primarily mechanical and instinctual, and requires to be checked because its relationship to its occasion is such that it takes man away from himself into nature, and is a process of self-annihilation. There is no sense in what Winters says that feeling, in the sense of particular feeling or feelings, is connection with an object or situation of objects, might occupy its appropriate space and time, might in fact be discrete. Like connotation in language, feeling is a secondary quality of perception (while being somehow primary to experience—where feelings come from, their psychology in other words, is never fully explained) with the power to carry all before it in headlong flight down a single infinite perspective of monomania and madness.

Just how feeling and perception, connotation and denotation, paraphrasable content and formal construct came together in the poem is suggested by Winters in his discussion of Allen Tate's sonnet, to which I have previously alluded. This passage needs to be quoted in full and at length because, while clear in its parts, the way in which the parts are made to fit together is not made quite clear.

> If one takes, for example, Mr. Allen Tate's sonnet, The Subway, and translates it into good scholarly prose, using nothing but the rational content of the poem as a reference, one will find the author saying that as a result of his ideas and of his metropolitan

environment, he is going mad. Now as a matter of fact, the poem says nothing of the sort:

> Dark accurate plunger down the successive knell
> Of arch on arch, where ogives burst a red
> Reverberance of hail upon the dead
> Thunder, like an exploding crucible!
> Harshly articulate, musical steel shell
> Of angry worship, hurled religiously
> Upon your business of humility
> Into the iron forestries of hell!
>
> Till broken in the shift of quieter
> Dense altitudes tangential to your steel,
> I am become geometries—and glut
> Expansions like a blind astronomer
> Dazed, while the wordless heavens bulge and reel
> In the cold revery of an idiot.

The sonnet indicates that the author has faced and defined the possibility of the madness that I have mentioned (a possibility from the consideration of which others as well as himself may have found it impossible to escape) and has arrived at a moral attitude toward it, an attitude which is at once defined and communicated by the poem. This attitude is defined only by the whole poem, not by the logical content alone; it is a matter not only of logical content, but of feeling as well. The feeling is particular and unparaphrasable, but one may indicate the nature of it briefly by saying that it is a feeling of dignity and of self-control in the face of a situation of major difficulty, a difficulty which the poet fully apprehends. This feeling is inseparable from what we call poetic form, or unity, for the creation of a form is nothing more nor less than the act of evaluating and shaping (that is, controlling) a given experience. It should be obvious that any attempt to reduce the rational content of such a poem would tend to confuse or even eliminate the feeling: the poem consists in the relationship between the two.[17]

Clearly, what the poem says is not the paraphrasable content, and a modification of its content is offered, derived from certain felt implications of the poem's form. It is quite clear, then, that by "form" Winters means something possessing an existence independent of a particular poem, perhaps a kind of generic abstraction akin to words themselves. But also, in the passage quoted, Winters has suggested some kind of relationship between connotation and form, and we can understand the parallel in terms of the control form exercises over connotation. But since neither the form nor the connotation are to be found in the rational, paraphrasable content, they are presumably derived from a common or similar source. I do not think this kind of scrutiny of the passage is worth pursuing into even deeper confusion; what I want to point out is the central equiv-ocation which occurs about the idea of "feeling", which is not given a definite location, but seems variously to be the poet's (Tate's?) feeling, the feeling expressed in the poem, and the feeling the reader has. This marks the failure of Winters' scheme to confront the moral stance of the poem in its resolution of the problem, which Winters himself diagnoses, How does the poet face madness? Answer: With dignity and self-control. This strikes me as a most serious moral evasion. If the world posited by the poem really does have the power to drive men mad, and Tate has avoided madness by deploying a moral attitude implicit in the form he uses, then his avoidance of the implications of the world referred to by the poem, which is by definition not a personal world, has been merely a matter of private, one might add privileged, adjustment. It might be argued that the control exercised in the poem by its form is not exclusively poetic, that in fact the poem is an instance of control. The implication of such a view is, anyway, that the social causes of madness are to be met and resisted by non-social energies. Tate, as he occurs as the voice of the poem, does not enter the world it posits, because the solution to the problem stated in the poem is borrowed, and the avoidance of madness takes place outside the world of the poem, or in the space that occurs between the poem and the separate meaning of its form as something possessing its own existence, the sonnet form. What I am left with, given Winters' reading of the poem, is a sense of the extreme irresponsibility of poet and poem towards the world referred to by both. Of course Winters does not see this as irresponsibility because he thinks of poetry as an aid to meditation and as a process that heightens perception as the attention is submitted to the exigencies of a difficult form. It is possible, indeed, to argue that irresponsibility of this sort is endemic to Winters' point of view, since it places the greatest value on the poetic lyric, as containing the optimum of personal connotation together with generic denotation.

1. Introduction — Critical Reservations

My comments on Tate's poem are not concerned with it as a particular case, but as an occasion for the kind of argument Winters makes to justify his view of poetic convention, and should stand or fall irrespective of the particular merits of the poem. What I am arguing is that one is rightly suspicious of the moral advantages offered to the poet, according to Winters, in cooperating with formal and "rational" a priori shapes. With this kind of reservation in mind it is possible to look more circumspectly at his strictures of what he calls "pseudo-reference" and "qualitative progression", the typical forms of decadent poetic organisation and feeling. These two procedures are closely related, both being seen as "retaining in our language coherence of feeling, but as far as possible reducing rational coherence"[18]. Pseudo-reference retains the form of rational and syntactical coherence, and is thus closely related to Davie's pseudo-syntax. Qualitative progression dispenses even with these traditional forms, and is the form par excellence of Pound's *Cantos*. It is unnecessary to comment fully on all aspects of these twin concepts, since, in their dependence on Winters' dualism of denotative and connotative language, to do so would entail going over many of my foregoing comments. I have also, in passing, commented on Davie's notion of pseudo-syntax, and it is possible, therefore, to take Winters' two concepts together without doing him a severe injustice.

Feeling is excessive in pseudo-reference and qualitative progression because paraphrasable statement is insufficiently modified by formal structure, either syntactical or metrical. One thus has the form either of reverie or of random conversation. Winters cunningly overstates his case with his either/or structure, and confuses the issue with what should be, for him, a redundant qualification in his use of "random". He has elsewhere made it clear that poetry is a form of interior discourse, and so the idea of conversation should be enough to register his disapproval. But he needs to balance conversation against the less-arguable and light-weight randomness of reverie, remembering, no doubt, Tate's own description of the form of the *Cantos* as conversation in an essay published only six years earlier.[19]

Unlike pseudo-reference, however, qualitative progression can possess an implicit rational structure, but such structure cannot be sustained at any length without being made explicit. The notion of levels of discourse within a poem, indicated here, is unexceptionable, but Winters falsifies it by again applying his restrictive formal dualism, as a real category independent of context, using the terms implicit and explicit as analytical rather than descriptive, much in the way he uses the terms denotation and connotation.

It should be clear then that from the point of view of the criticism of Winters being advanced here the idea of qualitative progression, the method of the *Cantos*, as merely a progression of analogous feeling-states, is one which obscures the possibility of there being other means of progression and coherence at work in the poem. Winters is always ready to recuperate value from the experimental writing he is discussing, but does so by the application of terms which falsify the essential values and quality of the work. Thus there is free verse which is fine, but it turns out not in fact to be free, but to contain a dissimulated metrical substructure. The whole idea of freedom is in fact a metaphysical red herring. Is it a case that a poem is rescued from a bogus and deleterious freedom by the operation of an implicit metrical structure, and that whatever other rhythmical features it may possess offer nothing that can be perceived as structural? It is clear why this should be the case for Winters, since for him the poem cannot be experienced directly by the reader, it is not that kind of an object. I think, on the other hand that there are alternative non-metrical structures, and that these link up in a significant way with moral and philosophical standpoints which Winters does not share. The next chapter will discuss some of the ideas about non-metrical verse formations put forward by their exponents, the modern poets. But by way of concluding these introductory remarks, I should like to put forward a view of language diametrically opposed to that offered by Winters. This occurs in Louis Zukofsky's essay "Sincerity and Objectification, With Special Reference to the Work of Charles Reznikoff".

> …distinct from print which records action and existence and incites the mind to further suggestion, there exists, tho it may not be harboured as solidity in the crook of an elbow, writing (audibility in two-dimensional print) which is an object or affects the mind as such. The codification of the rhetoric books may have something to do with an explanation of this attainment, but its character may be simply described as the arrangement, into one apprehended unit, of minor units of sincerity—in other words, the resolving of words and their ideation into structure. Granted that the word combination "minor units of sincerity" is an ironic index of the degradation of the power of the individual word in a culture which seems hardly to know that each word in itself is an arrangement, it may be said that each word possesses objectification to a powerful degree; but that the facts carried by one word are, in view of the preponderance of facts carried

by combinations of words, not sufficiently explicit to warrant a realization of rested totality such as might be designated in art form.[20]

The objectification which each word carries to a powerful degree, and writing which is an object or affects the mind as such: these propositions can carry morals and structures appropriate to themselves, with a fidelity to experience and the modes in which we undergo experience which need not relegate the world we inhabit to a dangerous transcendence, threatening madness and death.

§ § §

At the beginning of this introduction I referred in passing to poetry's ontological status, but in fact this strategic denomination will not carry my argument far enough. My disagreement with Winters and Davie, which is the more acute for the indebtedness I feel to their work, amounts to a more complex description of the operations which can be traced back to *symbolisme*, together with a more generous assessment of their value, and to sustain these views what needs to be proposed is a sense of the poem as an instance not of being but of action.

Notes

[1] See, for instance, C.K. Stead, *The New Poetic*, London 1964. Stead's account of his subject is largely given over to an evaluation of the orthodox poetic climate at the beginning of the 20th Century, a point of view from which the Georgian poets emerge as radical innovators, together with a pedestrian discussion of T.S. Eliot's work as the definitive achievement of modernism. Stead's account of Imagism, for example, follows the lines established by Burne and Coffman, presenting it as a coherent movement with a literal history and determinate aesthetic criteria.

[2] Donald Davie, *Articulate Energy, An Enquiry into the Syntax of English Poetry*, London 1955, pp. 150-151.

[3] The argument which I am paraphrasing here runs throughout Davie's book; for a summary of his position, however, see *Articulate Energy*, op.cit., p.148.

[4] Ibid., p. 153. The passage in question from Coleridge is quoted by Davie from Herbert Read's *The True Voice of Feeling, Studies in English Romantic Poetry*,

London 1947, n.p. 179, and comes from one of Coleridge's notebooks published in Alice B. Snyder's *Coleridge on Logic and Learning*, Yale 1929.

[5] Cf. my discussion of the effect of language on the passions in Burke in Chapter 6, below.

[6] In his paper "Pound and Eliot: A Distinction", in *Eliot in Perspective, A Symposium*, ed. Graham Martin, London 1970, however, Davie appears to have withdrawn his notion of pseudo-syntax entirely.

[7] Cf. Charles Olson, *Human Universe and Other Essays*, San Francisco 1964.

[8] See Yvor Winters, *In Defence of Reason*, London 1960, pp. 57-58.

[9] Ibid., pp. 21-22.

[10] Ibid., p. 150.

[11] Ibid., pp. 17-18.

[12] Ibid., pp. 22-23.

[13] Ibid., p. 17.

[14] Ibid., p. 20.

[15] Ibid., p. 130.

[16] Ibid., p. 144.

[17] Ibid., pp. 19-21

[18] Ibid., p. 40.

[19] Tate's essay "Ezra Pound" was first published in *The Nation* in 1931, and is reprinted in his *The Man of Letters in the Modern World, Selected Essays: 1928-1955*, London 1957.

[20] Louis Zukofsky, "Sincerity and Objectification, With Special Reference to the Work of Charles Reznikoff", *Poetry* XXXVII, v, (Feb. 1931), p. 274.

Chapter 2

The Concept of Metre
and the Relation of Prosody to Meaning

The forms we perceive are susceptible to the functions and purposes we expect of or attribute to the events or entities to which we are referring the idea of form in the first place. Some sort of statement along these lines concerning the relativism and contextual dependence of the perceptual process should be sufficiently commonplace not to arouse question except on matters of detail. In the previous chapter I discussed the circumstance in which two of the most interesting and sympathetically-disposed critics of modern poetry, both with impeccable academic training, found that implicated with this kind of poetry is a qualifying proportion of qualities which are irreconcilable to their notion of what constitutes the best poetry. Qualities, that is to say, to which they can attach no intrinsic purpose or value equivalent to those of other qualities which modern poetry has ignored. A conventional response to such a critical impasse—interest which cannot fulfil itself in approbation—is for the critic to transfer his attention from the texts which furnish the occasion for his deliberations, and then direct terms of intellectual and moral censure towards their authors. The idea that the writer is either a fool, a charlatan, or involved in a conspiracy to undermine the art of letters, is uttered with dissimulated discretion, but its occurrence is sufficiently frequent to be typical. The critic performs a methodological volte-face and in effect takes up the role of polemical journalist for a threatened cause. Winters and Davie are only marginally susceptible to this pathology in those works which I have just discussed, and the point from which I wish to start now is not that they were wrong according to their own terms, but that their terms are inappropriate in the first place. They observed a set of phenomena with the expectation that they should perform in ways which are at variance, it is going to be my contention, with the very modes upon which those phenomena depend for their existence. This argument is deliberately question-begging for the time being in order to draw certain issues out into the open. I have already suggested ways in which the Winters-Davie position makes certain assumptions about the nature of language. I now wish to consider their ideas about poetic form, not from the point of view of the purposes which form might serve (to subdue feeling for instance), but from the prior issue of its ontology. The idea of form per se is one which mediates between the idea of form as something purposive and functional, and the idea of form as the description of definite "objective" features of a particular poem (or class of poems). Even though it is axiomatic that the processes involved in the perception of form are selective, since it is possible to distinguish between processes of selection which are natural or biological (neurological, for instance), and others which are cultural (learnt), the relationship between form in its conceptual aspect and form as a matter of description is a difficult one. It might be supposed that it is possible to postulate alternative modes or concepts of formal function to those advocated by Winters and Davie, alternatives which will fit the case presented by modern poetry, discovering it to possess an achieved and complex formality of its own.

Form is a word with no single hard and fast lexical definition: for a start, it can function either as a verb or as a noun. The O.E.D. lists fifteen different usages of the substantive form of the word, the first and fourth of which are of particular relevance to the notion of form in a work of art. Form can be "the visible aspect of a thing", a meaning which has a clear relevance to the transactions we have with a work as we experience it directly and for itself—the staple of New Critical procedures. (It is worth noting the two-fold optical bias given by this definition, explicit in <u>visible</u> and implicit in <u>aspect</u>; I shall come back to the question of the sensory bias implicit in conventional notions of form when I discuss theories of metre.) Form in this sense is a limiting factor, and by implication refers only to individuals—it may explain the specific character of an object, but is unable to account for an object's history or genesis, or to suggest ways in which it may have affiliations to a class of similar or even formally identical objects. If the critic is going to concern himself with any of the latter questions he may turn to the fourth usage of form, which the dictionary designates <u>philosophical</u>. This form is variously an essential principle (as in scholastic philosophy), the objective conditions for the existence of an object (as in Bacon), and the subjective factor of knowledge which gives reality to a thing (as in Kant). The philosophical distinctions in each case are basically locational, each of the three meanings suggesting a way in which form is to be understood as an inherent type of activity, not synonymous with the sensory configurations of a particular object. This sense of the word, also, is etymologically closer than the previous one to the Indo-European root given for Form by Skeat in his *Etymological Dictionary of the English*

Language, DHER, to hold, maintain. It is closer, as well, to the function of the word as a verb.

The distinction between these two senses of form is not one between the particular and the generic. The form perceived of an object depends on the philosophical view of form held by the perceiving individual, even though the knowledge he has of an object's form may appear to derive entirely from the object itself. One well-established way out of the difficulty which presents itself when objective data are taken to be synonymous with the knowledge of form (the difficulty being that such an identification endows any demarcated contingency with formal properties—a device of framing, of course, which some contemporary artists do take to be an adequate definition of their activity) is to hypostasise a catalogue of forms on the basis of given data. There is an ideal sonnet-form, say, which is a fiction designed to enable us to recognise whether a certain poem is or is not a member of the class "sonnet" and, if it is found to be a member of this class, to say how well it observes the rules for that class of object. This is at best a vulgarisation of Platonism, one in which sensory data are no longer felt to be inherently untrustworthy, or insufficiently trustworthy in themselves.

Such a view of form is posited on ideas of completion and execution. Form becomes a matter of the given work's internal relations: symmetry, proportion, but not scale. It is a form which stops short at the work's peripheries. It relegates formal considerations to a level at which they can be merely assumed (nowadays consigned to the attentions of the linguistic critic), or transformed into the idea of genre, thus releasing the critic to attend to his "real" business of discussing "meaning", and making him the artist's peer. ("Formalist" criticism is merely the inversion of this convenient arrangement; the critic remains the artist's peer, although he has substantially reduced the kind of scope and relevance to which the artist's work can lay claim.)

It should be sufficiently clear therefore that the idea that an object's form is in a sense a property of the object incorporates a philosophical premise about the nature of form in general. That is to say, that although we know the form from the object, what we know in this way can only be known as form by referring to a form-type independent of the object, which offers a model for that object's existence and completeness. The objective characteristics of the object are basically featureless and undifferentiated. This premise is easily confused with the critical practice of giving attention to a poem in isolation, and is vigorously opportunistic in its attempts to appropriate such pragmatic gestures as a form of disguise. In fact, however, such pragmatic tactics are entirely in keeping with the view that, put in extreme terms, an object is the property of the form it contains or exemplifies. (This is not a restatement of the premise, which I have just been discussing, that form is a class or type, needless to say.) I am not, at this point, interested to argue either case; it is always possible that there are others to be made. What I propose, rather, is to look at the ideas about a poem's formal properties which Yvor Winters advances, and to see what are the philosophical premises about form which they imply. It should be understood that, on the philosophical level, ideas of form do not relate exclusively to the aesthetic domain, but have concomitants for the ordinary world also. The critic who sees literary forms as the hypostasised versions of human fictions is likely to see, in ways which will be rather more complex, the world of natural forms as an attribute or function of mind also.

§ § §

The word form itself is not terminologically basic to Winters' exposition of his argument in *Primitivism and Decadence*. The word only enters his expository vocabulary about half-way through the book, when he comes to discuss the idea of Qualitative Progression, and his use of the word suggests that it is quasi-synonymous with the idea of structure, and of coherence also. Up to this point Winters' taxonomy of compositional procedures has been primarily concerned with rhetorical and logical procedures.

> Since one of the means to coherence, or form, is impaired, form itself is enfeebled. In so far as form is enfeebled, precision of detail is enfeebled, for details receive their precision from the structure in which they function just as they may be employed to give that structure precision; to say that detail is enfeebled is to say that the power of discrimination is enfeebled.[1]

Form here is one of the desiderata of a poem rather than an analytic concept of a particular modality of poetic ontology. Form as a given referent need only enter the discussion, as far as Winters is concerned, as something susceptible to the influence of the poetic practices, experienced as detail and structure, which Winters has been enumerating. Rather than be an

2. The Concept of Metre and the Relation of Prosody to Meaning

attribute of the poem as we directly know it, form becomes an element in our secondary knowledge of the poem—our deduction that the poem possesses form enables us to recognise the detailed or local features of the poem, but these features are not features of the form, they occur against the matrix of complete or unitary form which we carry away from our experience of the poem as one of its qualities (perhaps even its primary quality) but not as one of its effects. Our experience of a poem's form, therefore, can never be referred directly to the poem; we can say that it is, but what it is we have to refer to a separate concept. The completeness of a poem's form, in this case, and also notions of formal variation, both have to refer to an extrinsic concept of form. It is impossible to imagine an incomplete sonnet, and formal variations within the poem do not occur in relation to a form the poem has created for itself. Those poetic gestures which otherwise might be regarded as creative of form are in fact to be understood as recognition features by which the poem indicates the class of form to which it belongs. Winters' view of form draws into the poem significant and, one assumes, semantically determinant features from a specifically non-poetic source.

This source is what is referred to by Winters' terms structure and convention. Structure, form, and detail all depend on the existence and observation of convention. Like many of Winters' key concepts, this one has a very definite upward and downward valency. At the upper level, convention very obviously refers to the idea of an agreement between poet (s) and reader (s) to accept certain rules to apply to poems. But at the lower level, which is also that of critical application, convention is felt to be something which emerges in a natural way from language itself. This is a quite intelligible strategy for enforcing the observance of conventional standards, and fosters the idea of spontaneity and inevitability of response in the reader. These are political acts.

Winters' first step towards absorbing the power of the natural to the idea of the convention is to be seen in his insistence that what he calls the denotative power of words is in itself a matter of arbitrary convention. In poetic language the primary convention is that of metre; it is not synonymous with convention, just as structure is not quite synonymous with form, for metre can have an influence upon convention. But as far as the critical analysis of poetry is concerned the predominant convention to be dealt with is a metrical one. The whole concept of metre is based on a supposition which Winters rarely makes explicit, that is: that the poetic line is neither a semantic nor a syntactic unit, but a unit of measurement.

This is not to say that the poetic line may not afford syntactic or semantic units in specific cases, according to the theory I am stating, but that the semantic and syntactic are not in themselves organisations susceptible to measurement, although they may embody other linguistic features that are measurable. This is a statement of the obvious but not, I believe, of the meaningless. What metre measures is some phonetic series occurring in language; phenomena which are not special to poetic language, that is to say, except as they are incorporated into some systematic usage. Any sort of metrical scheme involves the observation of natural linguistic phenomena, but in the process of measuring them as part of a recurring series they are transformed by a process which isolates them from various other phenomena with which they normally occur. As a formal construct, therefore, a metrical scheme is arbitrary to a very high degree.

Winters' section entitled "General Theories of Metre" offers a usefully concise list of the phonetic elements which metre can deal with.

> The poetic line, as I understand the subject, has at one time or another been constructed according to four different systems of measurement: the quantitative, or classical system, according to which a given type of line has a given number of feet, the feet being of certain recognised types and being constructed on the basis of the lengths of the component syllables; the accentual, or Anglo-Saxon, system, according to which the line possesses a certain number of accents, the remainder of the line not being measured, a system of which free verse is a recent and especially complex subdivision; the syllabic, or French, system, according to which a line is measured solely by the number of syllables which it contains; and the accentual-syllabic, or English, system, which in reality is identical with the classical system in its most general principles, except that accented and unaccented syllables displace long and short as the basis of constructing the foot, and that pyrrhic and spondaic feet seldom occur and might in fact be regarded as ideally impossible because of the way in which accent is determined, a matter which I shall presently discuss.
>
> Mechanically perfect meter, were it possible, would be lifeless; meter of which the variation is purely accidental is, like all other manifestations of pure accident, awkward and without character. There are in English accentual-syllabic meter the following principles of variation, if no others:[2]

Winters then lists four such principles: Substitution, Quantity, Varying Degrees of Accent, and Sprung Meter. He discusses the way in which accent is determined under the third of these headings.

> Accent, like quantity, is unlimited in its variations. In practice, the manner of distinguishing between an accented and an unaccented syllable is superior, I believe, to the manner of distinguishing in classical verse between a long syllable and a short. In English verse, a syllable is accented or unaccented wholly in relation to the other syllables in the same foot, whereas in classical verse each syllable is arbitrarily classified by rule, and its length is in very small measure dependent on the context.[3]

There is a terminological confusion here, in that Winters fails to distinguish between accent, a prosodical notion, and stress, a linguistic one. This confusion comes about partly because Winters is comparing a metrical system, the quantitative, based on a natural phonetic phenomenon (in theory at least) with one based on a conventional hypostasised phenomenon known as accent. I do not want to become involved in a discussion on the nature of accent here. Suffice it to say that the structural linguist observes four levels of stress in English phonetics, in other words all syllables possess stress to a certain degree.[4] The notion of accent, on the other hand, is comparative, and depends on the absence of accent in syllables adjacent to accented ones. Accent does often occur in conjunction with normal phonemic stress, but does not require to do so[5]. In terms of the description of a line a quantitative metre obviously offers the fullest account of what takes place within it at the phonetic level, since it is continuous despite the fact that it is also exclusive, whereas accentual metres are discontinuous and comparative. But the purpose of metrical analysis is not to describe the line at all, but to analyse it into equivalent units. Winters' comments on Quantitative Variation, although of interest, are in fact digressive, and motivated presumably by a responsiveness to phonetic qualities excessive in terms of the accentual schema Winters professes. The purpose of metrical convention in fact is not to describe or even measure an instance presented by a given verse line, but to reduce it to terms which correlate with what it is, to all intents and purposes, an a priori metrical schema, the schematic character of which will be primary, and the metrical purpose to which it is designed secondary.

Metre, then, can be see as a kind of grid, to which the metrist assigns ontological priority, superimposed upon and to an extent determining the occurrence of an item of natural language which is specialised for metrical purposes. Winters's views are, in essence, the same as those expressed by the majority of subsequent writers on metre, although he is not concerned with metre as a study in itself. W.K. Wimsatt and M.C. Beardsley, in their frequently cited article "The Concept of Meter: An Exercise in Abstraction" give five "traditional, or classic" principles of English metre, concluding:

> Since poems have other patterns than their meter… it is possible for the poet to work out an interplay between the metrical pattern and other patterns. But the interplay cannot be analysed and discussed without discriminating the metrical pattern as such from the other patterns.[6]

These other patterns will include phonetic patterns not accounted for by the metrical pattern. The same pattern of interplay is described by Roman Jakobson with his discrimination between verse design and verse instance.[7] Linguistically-oriented critics such as Jakobson are more frank than Winters, they admit that the concept of metre (i.e. the concept of verse design in general) is dependent on the evidence of verse instances; there is a tacit selectivity in the operation of their theories, which contain no prospective element. They are not part of poetic theory, but the application of linguistic theory. Critics of this type are able to describe the qualities of the interaction between verse design and verse instance, between a poem and its metre, only by a number of poorly-defined and largely suggestive designations of effect: counterpoint, tension, elegant variation, and so on. These qualities by and large can constitute no more than the effects of a larger poetic discourse, they will be forms which correspond to or in some way imitate the ostensible level of discourse, or at the worst become merely pleasing devices. Winters is superior as a critic because of his insistence that the metrical convention play a more dynamic role in the overall poetic effect; his word for interplay, variation, is more specific, and he is clear in his insistence that its occurrence is meaningless if it is accidental.

To cast one's mind back to Winters' disposition towards the idea of Nature is the best way of making his theory of significant variation intelligible. Conventional metrists do not assume a destructive nature as a determinant of the metrical conventions they describe, they are too scientific for that. The way in which nature opposes art is therefore a convention which Winters adds to the convention of metre in the account he gives of its operations. For the run-of-the-mill metrist, metre is nothing more than a concept co-incident with the idea of poetry. He is unable to dissociate the two ideas. Winters, clearly, is able to entertain the notion of poetry independent of the idea of metre, since for him poetry is in part at least defined by the ends it serves, although he maintains that the best poetry will be that which makes use of the best metre. A cause and effect relationship no doubt. What metre offers, from Winters's point of view, is a formal restraint upon the natural qualities of language equivalent to the restraint which, he insists, denotative meaning exercises over the contextual specificity of connotative meaning. Language as denotation follows nature in stiff and arbitrarily referential imitation, and is energised, made fluid and supple, by the conscious artifice of metre. The correspondence, therefore, is not a simple one of:

metre: denotation: : natural language quality: connotation

but rather to be understood as a field in which forces transect one another. Natural language, Winters seems to be saying, has minimal formal significance; it requires a metrical intervention to raise language's casual phonetic characteristics to perceptual and formal relevance.

Winters' objections to non-metrical poetry, therefore, can best be articulated on two grounds. First, that without an imposed or assumed metrical pattern it is impossible to perceive figures of formal rhythm in actuality. They will partake of the unlimited—and therefore meaningless—variability of accent and quantity, as he sees their occurrence in natural language. Second, that the relation between actual rhythmic features and the underlying metre—the phenomenon of variation—is significant because it indicates a conscious human intervention and choice, for which non-metrical verse has no equivalent. It is not enough merely to employ a convention, the poet must make his use and understanding of it explicit. It should be clear that although these two functions relate to a common set of phenomena they are not logically connected; the first relates to metre only in its conventional aspect, the second to a complex of notions concerning the function of reason in nature which were discussed in the course of the preceding chapter. I have arguments with the second of these issues which I shall be putting forward in the final chapter of this essay. For the time being I should like to consider whether it is possible to dissociate, as my terminology just has, the ideas of metre and of rhythm, and see if it is possible to envisage alternative modes of poetic organisation on the basis of attention to the full range of phonetic items in language without reducing them to selective metrical sets. The identification of ideas of form in poetry with the idea of metre entails a philosophical view of form which will lead the reader to attend to phonetic phenomena in poems only as constituents of a metrical pattern, and to see form as something which moves towards a defined state of completion. An alternative philosophical view of form might lead the reader to attend to phonetic phenomena as formal items in their own right, and allow him to perceive by way of an enlarged field of sensory response other forms of organisation than those of equivalence and symmetry. It is for this reason that it is still worthwhile to examine the polemics of the initiators of free verse in English, and to attempt to discover what they intended their innovations to mean. Despite Hrushovski's comment, that writings of this period "although of considerable historical interest, have almost no structural value"[8], if one follows the axiom with which this chapter begins, and its elaboration in terms of variable philosophical premises for the idea of form, it is likely that statements of intention can be read as an indication of formal principle. (This can be taken, in part at least, as a critique of the methods of Structuralism.)

§ § §

Since 1954 when T.S. Eliot wrote in his introduction to *The Literary Essays of Ezra Pound* that "the situation of poetry in 1909 or 1910 was stagnant to a degree difficult for any young poet of today to imagine"[9], that "XXth Century revolution in poetry" for which Pound was "more responsible... than any other individual"[10] has become a notably well-worn critical notion. The salient formulations of Pound's early essays, and also those of Hulme and Ford and several other poets, have been cited with such frequency that they have become quasi-talismanic. They are familiar to many more readers than are acquainted at first hand with the contexts from which they are taken. Does anyone try to understand what Pound meant by "the musical phrase" and "an absolute rhythm" as orders of poetic composition, rather than accept them as vague statements of value, a poet's license with explicit language? Eliot's pamphlet *Ezra Pound: His Metric and Poetry*, together with his essay "Reflections on <u>Vers Libre</u>", both published in 1917, quickly initiated a process by which the reader is discouraged from examining Pound's own terse and often enigmatic pronouncements for meaning by virtue of Eliot's opportunistic insistence that there is no distinction between free and strict verse forms, an identical principle of mastery applying to each. Eliot discusses the music of Pound's verse at some length, but comments upon it purely as a quality of achievement in a way which precludes it from being thought of as a formal or structural element. Eliot's critical writing, of course, envisages a different audience to that which Pound had in mind for "A Few Don'ts"; he is easily persuasive because he speaks a more familiar language. The idea of metre is always comfortingly alluded to, any line of verse can be scanned, although it might be made up of entirely dissimilar feet; so metre is not really an issue of paramount importance. If one looks at the different kinds of statement about metre made by Eliot at different stages in his essay on *vers libre* it becomes clear that his sense of what metre amounts to does not possess the clarity of the matrix and variation theory which I have just discussed; sometimes metre is spoken of as being <u>in</u> the line of verse, at others the reader is imposing it himself. Eliot's pleasant figure of metre hiding behind the arras to nudge the inattentive reader is a fair description of some of his own poetic practices, and is the explanation of a man for whom metre exists in a casual relation to the discourse it is associated with, something bought ready-made at the store, but it dismisses irrevocably from mind the Poundian insistence on an exact correspondence of particular emotion and rhythm in a single-minded expression of sincerity via technique. Pound's "absolute rhythm" suggests a formal restraint in poetry which will be creative of its own achievement; it is a restraint not derived from an autonomous art-world but from sources which provide the whole of art's activities with a context. For Eliot the absence of freedom from the production of successful art is axiomatic, but the nature of the restraints which operate seems endlessly variable, derivative of the scale of "good verse, bad verse, and chaos" with which he concludes his essay. These qualitative distinctions are not perceived as functions of the exercise of restraint; the concept is not able to explain their occurrence. In the following stages of my argument the last thing I wish to find myself involved in is a recapitulation of the well-known history of the "XXth Century poetic revolution", and several episodes in the popular account will therefore be passed over quickly or else ignored. It is the formal conception of their art evinced by the pioneers, by Pound in particular, which I wish to discuss.

Earlier in this chapter I described a theory of metre according to which the customary English pentameter line is to be seen as a unit which owes its existence to the operation of a conventional sensory selectivity on the part of readers of verse—their attention is focussed on the phenomenon of pairs of accented and unaccented syllables, to the number of five pairs, and ignores other phonetic phenomena, in a way more "natural", but not taken into account by the metrical scheme in the reader's head. Of course, since he shares a community of cultural values with the reader this scheme will exist in the poet's head also, and therefore the scheme will tend to be realised as if it were actually in the verse or poem which he is composing. But as Eliot implies, the metre or restraint of any poem will be undetectable to ears not accustomed to it. It is not in the verse in any intrinsic or structural sense. One might suppose therefore that the poet who is concerned to search out new rhythms or new metres will begin by making a census of those phonological qualities which might variously be put to service: as well as accent and number of syllables per line, that is to say, he will also consider the uses of quantity, pitch, timbre, and the variations of stress which accentual theory reduces to a simple binary system. Such a reductive ontology was not Pound's method, however, since he recognised, one supposes, that all these phonological items do not occur naturally in isolation but in combination. A single syllable will combine all four qualities, pitch, stress, quantity, and timbre in a unique way. It might be attractive at this point to say that Pound's ideas about poetic ontology start off from the idea of the word or the phrase rather than the syllable, but the evidence suggests instead that he conceives of a hierarchy of simultaneous structure: just as the syllable is composed of distinct phonological items, so the word can be a combination of sylla-bles, the phrase a combination of words, each element moving towards increasing significance in which the natural phonological items continue to play a necessary and increasingly complex role.

> I believe in an ultimate and absolute rhythm as I believe in an absolute symbol or metaphor. The perception of the intellect is given in the word, that of the emotions in the cadence. It is only, then, in perfect rhythm joined to the perfect word that the twofold vision can be recorded... The rhythm of any poetic line corresponds to a particular emotion.[11]

Thus meaningful poetic discourse, from the point of view of such an ontology, is never separable from the world of natural events upon which it is predicated. The natural phonological items continue busily at work even when discourse has become entirely conceptual. This kind of mul-tivalency of linguistic operation, in which phonological, semantic, and syntactic levels are all bound together, seems a characteristic also of the Image to which Pound refers frequently. The Image, that is to say, requires to be seen as a configuration in the natural world, a perception on the part of the poet, and a discrete entity realising itself within the poem. When Pound talks about prosody as "the articulation of the total sound of the poem" it is just such a simultaneous and continuous multivalency of process which I believe he has in mind.[12] The same can be said of his idea of the timelessness and contemporaneity of all poetry, a world liter-ature, advanced in the "Praefetio ad Lectorum Electum" to *The Spirit of Romance*. "Art is a fluid moving above or over the minds of men."[13] The rules of poetry, as far as any exist, are not conventional, cannot be based on the study of historical sets. The balance which will weigh Theocritus and Yeats against a common scale has a measure which transcends any system of data. There is a mystery beyond which the purely technical and descriptive consideration is unable to penetrate.

Pound's engagement with the idea of poetic ontology or activity, there-fore, does not start from technical or objectively verifiable evidence. Like Yvor Winters, he proposes an end or purpose for art, and as in Winters the end he envisages is contemplative and static. But instead of locating the end in human response, to which the poem ultimately subsists in a pragmatic relationship, Pound invests the end in the enduring existence of the work of art itself. The work participates in the mystery of its final evaluation. Pound's early point of view seems suspiciously close to the aestheticism of Pater, whom he cites occasionally at this stage in his career, but the direction of his own thought is sufficiently distinct. The corroboration which Pater offers for the habit of contemplation of the work of art as a vessel for intense experience is offset by the way in which Pound offers a correspondence for art's enduring character in an equally enduring characteristic of responsive human psychology. What this set of belief produces, in effect, is a doubling of the concept of art: there is art as an end-conditioned activity, that end being in a sense also synonymous with the work of art. A single hypostatisation of the eternal as opposed to the multiple hypostatisations of disparate forms. This enables Pound to adopt what strikes me as his characteristic critical gambit, to posit the basis of artistic ontology in certain definite and characteristic affects. The arts according to this view constitute a common system, but different arts by virtue of their means have distinctive capacities for dealing with or expressing specific states or modalities of feeling and experience. Fun-damental poetic criteria therefore will be those which are peculiar to the specific virtues of a verbal art. In his two best known formulations of poetic principles, which taken together exemplify that doubling of the concept of art which I suggest is basic to Pound's cast of mind, one predicated on the technique of composition, the other on the details of experience, Pound offers a tripartite pattern of functions.

Pound's three Imagist principles were first mentioned by F.S. Flint in his article "Imagisme" which appeared in *Poetry* in 1913, where they immediately preceded Pound's own "A Few Don'ts by an Imagiste". These three principles were reprinted by Pound as part of "A Retrospect" in *Pavannes and Divisions*, published in 1918, and are sufficiently well known not to require quotation here in full. These three injunctions about the art of composition can be helpfully correlated with the three "kinds of poetry" which Pound discriminates in "How to Read" in 1929. The temporal lapse between these two formulations is not, in fact, as great as might appear, for Pound clearly distinguishes his three kinds of poetry in a review of the *Others* anthology which he published in the *Little Review* in 1918, although he had not, at this point, hit on his special term for the imagistic function.

> In the verse of Marianne Moore I detect traces of emotion; in that of Mina Loy I detect no emotion whatever. Both of these women are, possibly in unconsciousness, among the followers of Jules Laforgue (whose work shows a great deal of emotion.) It is possible, as I have written, or intended to write elsewhere, to divide poetry into three sorts; (1.) melopoeia, to wit, poetry which moves by its music, whether it be a music in the words or an aptitude for, or suggestion of, accompanying music; (2.) imagism, or poetry wherein the feelings of painting and sculpture are predominant (certain men move in phantasmagoria; the images of their gods, whole countrysides, stretches of hill land and forest, travel with them); and there is, thirdly, logopoeia or poetry that is akin to nothing but language, which is a dance of the intelligence among words and ideas and modification of ideas and characters. Pope and the eighteenth century writers had in this medium a certain limited range. The intelligence of Laforgue ran through the whole gamut of his time. T.S. Eliot has gone on with it. Browning wrote a condensed form of drama, full of things of the senses, scarcely ever pure logopoeia…

These two contributors to the "Others" Anthology write logopoeia. It is, in their case, the utterance of clever people in despair, or hovering upon the brink of that precipice.[14]

This is an exceptionally interesting passage in Pound's criticism, and has not, as far as I can tell, been commented upon before. One finds Pound secure in his established interest, the music of verse, the image, and at the same time reaching out to respond to an unfamiliar quality. Despite the tone of omniscience ("I have written, or intended to") it is clear that Pound's whole attention is directed to a phenomenon which, if not of fundamental novelty, he had at least thought sufficiently rare not to command an explicit place in his taxonomy of verbal art. He is compelled, in fact, to revise his previous notion of "verbalism" as he had applied it to the work of Laforgue in his "French Poets" issue of the *Little Review* the month before. Pound's comments on Laforgue in the *Little Review* are taken more or less intact from the essay "Irony, Laforgue, and Some Satire" which he had published in *Poetry* in the previous year. Verbalism at this stage in Pound's perception is akin to rhetoric, the commodity which it has been his whole purpose and that of the other proponents of *vers libre* to circumvent. "The function of *vers libre* was to strip poetry of rhetoric…" was how Flint put it in 1912.[15] Pound said of Laforgue:

> One may discriminate between Laforgue's tone and that of his contemporary French satirists. He is the finest wrought; he is most "verbalist". Bad verbalism is rhetoric, or the use of cliché unconsciously, or a mere playing with phrases. But there is a good verbalism, distinct from lyricism or imagism, and in this Laforgue is a master. He writes not the popular language of any country, but an international tongue common to the excessively cultivated, and to those more or less familiar with French literature of the first three-quarters of the nineteenth century….
>
> Verbalism demands a set form used with irreproachable skill. Satire needs, usually, the form of cutting rhymes to drive it home.[16]

When he reprinted this in *Make it New* Pound noted that he subsequently applied the term logopoeia to the phenomenon of verbalism; in fact, as the review of the *Others* anthology demonstrates, he did so within a comparatively short time. In his 1918 essay "Swinburne Versus His Biographers" we find Pound using the term <u>melopoeic</u>, to contrast in an interesting way with verbalist qualities.

> Moderns more awake to the value of language will read him with increasing annoyance, but I think few men who read him before their faculty for literary criticism is awakened—the faculty for purely literary discrimination as contrasted with melopoeic discrimination—will escape the enthusiasm of his emotions, some of which were indubitably real. At any rate we can, whatever our verbal fastidiousness, be thankful for any man who kept alive some spirit of paganism and of revolt in a papier-mâché era, in a time swarming with Longfellows, Mabies, Gosses, Harrisons.
>
> After all, the whole of his defects can be summed up in one— that is, inaccurate writing; and this by no means ubiquitous.[17]

It was presumably in contrast to the established term melopoeia that Pound was inspired to coin his neologism. I think it involves no distortion of Pound's thought to equate melopoeia with the third of the Imagist principles, "to compose in sequence of the musical phrase", and to equate the image itself or phanopoeia with the first principle, "direct treatment of the thing". The second principle is framed negatively, and is the least explicit of the three: "To use absolutely no word that did not contribute to the presentation". It is obviously subordinate to the principle which precedes it, and implies certain beliefs about diction and concrete reference which are amplified in the "Don'ts", "Go in fear of abstractions". Logopoeia in a good sense corresponds to this principle and makes up some of its deficiencies; at the same time by focussing on some of the ambiguities in Pound's notion of the Image it redresses an imbalance, pairing itself with melopoeia as an aspect of a purely verbal art. Pound's 1929 definition of logopoeia shows him not to have developed the idea much since 1918.

> LOGOPOEIA, "the dance of the intellect among words", that is to say, it employs words not only for their direct meaning, but it takes count in a special way of habits of usage, of the context we <u>expect</u> to find with the word, its usual concomitants, of its known acceptances, and of ironical play. It holds the aesthetic content which is peculiarly the domain of verbal manifestation, and cannot possibly be contained in plastic or music. It is the latest come, and perhaps most tricky and undependable mode.[18]

The quotation marks do not set off a poetic formula, but acknowledge, in a way that is rare for Pound, an act of self-quotation (although new intelligence has become intellect). One can assume that with the acknowledgement of the intellect's <u>dance</u> among words Pound has cut loose from the requirement, in relation to Laforguian verbalism, that the mode entails a strict form.

One of the most interesting ideas put forward by Hugh Kenner in his recent book *The Pound Era* is that, even when he was initially involved with the idea in the course of his advocacy of the work of Richard Aldington and H.D., Imagism was for Pound a retrogressive movement. Kenner represents Pound's natural development along the lines of an aesthetic of virtuous language, *le mot juste*, in cooperation with a sinuous and musical verse technique, the *motz el son* of the Provençal poets whom Pound had studies since his undergraduate days, and from this point of view the static and reductive insistencies of Imagism are indeed a diversion from the poet's coherent development, to which he subsequently returned with his engagement with Vorticism and the Chinese ideogram. I am not certain that Pound's association with Vorticism offers a more central version of the essential character of his poetic development; his typically Vorticist writings indeed, as they are collected in his memorial volume for the sculptor Gaudier-Brzeska, engage with poetic concerns only at a remove, and moreover, the essential Vorticist concern with the aesthetic quality of intensity possesses clear parallels in the work of Hulme and with Imagism in general. Like the first Imagist principle of direct treatment of the object, in which propositions about diction and syntax are transformed in practice into a proposition about subject matter, intensity is a quality which does not contain within its definition a prescription for its achievement. And whereas in painting and sculpture movement is an illusion which by its manifestation in the observer's response intensifies his perception of the work, in poetry movement is an actual quality of a work, whether it be good or bad. So while the short-lived Vorticist movement may have proved a valuable corrective and even escape route for Pound in the short run, I cannot think that in longer terms it would have had any determining effect on his work, even had the movement not been cut short by the outbreak of war.[19] A proposition such as Kenner's, however, has the merit of absolving the critic of the need to become absorbed in the history and factional squabbles of the Imagist movement. At the same time it is no longer necessary to maintain the fiction of collecting and evaluating "representative" Imagist poems. The movement can, without distortion, be seen to best advantage as a curiosity of literary history, which intersects as crucial points with important issues in modern poetic theory. None of the four poets of long-term distinction who were associated with Imagism (I refer, in addition to Pound, to William Carlos Williams, H.D., and D.H. Lawrence) can be fruitfully discussed as though Imagism were a factor of definitive importance in their work. The one serious injustice in this point of view concerns its oversight of the poetry of F.S. Flint, and here the situation is anomalous to a considerable extent as a result of his abandonment of poetry in the early 1920s.[20] I propose therefore to devote the remainder of this chapter and most of the next to a consideration of those issues of poetic theory which, I have just suggested, can be usefully substituted for a historical approach to the "XXth Century poetic revolution".

§ § §

In Poundian terms the two major issues are logopoeia and melopoeia. More general issues such as the rhetorical and rational structure of poetic discourse, or the large-scale intellectual and formal coherence of the *Cantos*, say, can be dealt with in terms of such theoretical issues. I have already suggested that the notion of the Image under the heading of direct treatment of the thing can be absorbed into the question of logopoeia; in a good sense, also, "the dance of the intellect among words" can be seen to absorb the other aspect of the thing directly treated, the thing as subjective. I am sure that Pound's eventual somewhat cool placing of Hulme, in his article "This Hulme Business", does not reflect a personal animus, but implies a recognition on Pound's part that Hulme's distinctive contribution to poetic theory was a specialised form of the French symbole which, from the point of view of Pound's own development was, if not irrelevant, at least subsumed to a larger and more complex theoretic construct.[21] Hulme's Image, I have suggested, operates at the level of diction, and it is no coincidence that the writer whose role in influencing the course of his ideas Pound advocates as a counter to the claims made for Hulme, Ford Madox Hueffer, was also concerned with issues of diction. I shall deal with these issues in the next chapter, and for the time being wish to consider Pound's contribution to the theory of versification through his concept of melopoeia, and to set this, briefly, alongside the theories of his contemporaries who were also involved in the movement towards *vers libre*, free verse, or cadence, as it was variously known.

As I have discussed the notion of form so far, the idea of rhythm has been subsumed to the idea of metre, rhythm being understood as an effect precipitated as we refer the verse instance of a poem to its verse design, to use Jakobson's terms. From this point of view, when we speak of rhythm in relation to poems we are referring to a unique event which occurs when a poem is "performed", but which by virtue of its uniqueness cannot be employed as a concept in poetic theory.[22] Pallister Barkas makes such a reservation about the value of rhythm quite clear: "The word 'Prosody' means the system of rules followed by the poet in composing. Whatever cannot be reduced to rule cannot be part of it".[23] Since rhythm is not the kind of experience which can be reduced to rule, as metre can be, prosody does not concern itself with rhythm. Pound's belief in an "absolute rhythm" as a central factor in his poetic theory, on the other hand, clearly ordains a poetics in which qualities are primary and not mediated by rule or convention. They are experienced directly. Whatever Pound means by absolute rhythm, and the term is not original to him, it suggests, by its implicit refusal of metrical contrast or doubling, a way of understanding his employment of free verse.[24] In the Introduction to his Cavalcanti translation, written in 1910, from which I quoted earlier in this chapter, in which Pound first adumbrates the idea of absolute rhythm, he proceeds to comment on the relation of our sense of rhythm to our "ideas of swiftness or easy power of motion", and then goes on as follows:

> Rhythm is perhaps the most primal of all things known to us. It is basic in poetry and music mutually, their melodies depending on a variation of tone quality and of pitch respectively, as is commonly said, but if we look more closely we will see that music is, by further analysis, pure rhythm; rhythm and nothing else, for the variation in pitch is the variation in rhythms of the individual notes, and harmony the blending of these varied rhythms. When we know more of overtones we will see that the tempo of every masterpiece is absolute, and is exactly set by some further law of rhythmic accord. Whence it should be possible to show that any given rhythm implies about it a complete musical form—fugue, sonata, I cannot say what form, but a form, perfect, complete. Ergo, the rhythm set in a line of poetry connotes its symphony, which, had we a little more skill, we could score for orchestra. *Sequitur*, or rather, *inest*: the rhythm of any poetic line corresponds to emotion.[25]

This passage is of very great interest, despite its rather off-hand but vague grandiosity, for in it Pound combines two ideas which subsequently he tended to treat separately: the relation of rhythm to pitch or tone, and the relation of pitch and rhythm, through their correspondence with tone as we see from this passage, to emotion. What Pound is suggesting here is that musical pitch, and by extension the tone of language, are functions of tempo and rhythm, and vice versa.

Pound's interest in free verse is best understood as an outgrowth of his study of Provençal poetry. For him it was not initially a formal or technical necessity, as it was, I shall argue, in the case of Hulme, but an expressive one. John Hummell notes that "the quantitative determinant in Provençal poetry is not based on the phonology of the language itself. It derives from the fact that troubadour poetry was, virtually all of it, written to be sung."[26] The focus of Pound's mind at this early point in his career was the question of the relationship between words and music in song. His sense of the interaction of the various phonological characteristics of language with musical tones was constantly changing, and we find him coming back to it, for instance, as late as 1927 in his essay on George Antheil. The musical element which seems to have especially caught his attention is tone, and we find him asking himself the question whether there might not be exigencies of vowel tone to be observed in language itself.

> …the other limb of melody is the pitch and pitch-variation, and upon this our sole query is to be whether there is in speech, as there is in music, "tone-leading". We know that certain notes played in sequence call for other notes, for a "resolution", for a "close"; and in setting words to music it is often the hunger for this sort of musical apparatus that leads the musician away from the rhythm of the verse or makes him drag out the final syllables. What I want to get at is this: in the interpreting of the hidden melody of poetry into the more manifest melody of music, are there in the words themselves "tone-leadings"? Granted a perfect accord of word and tune is attainable by singing a note to each syllable and a short or long note to short or long syllables respectively, and singing the syllable accented in verse on the syllable accented in the music, is there anything beyond this. Does, for instance, the voice really fall a little in speaking a vowel and nasal, and is a ligature of two notes one half-tone lower than the other and the first very short, a correct musical interpretation of such a sound

2. The Concept of Metre and the Relation of Prosody to Meaning

as "son", "um", "cham"? And are there other such cases where a ligature is not so much distortion as explication.[27]

It was the exactness with which precision of observation coincided with rhythm and tone and rhyme in the work of Arnaut Daniel, in particular, that impressed Pound when he was writing the series of essays under the title "I Gather the Limbs of Osiris" which were published in *The New Age* in 1911 and 1912. Exactness which made for an intensity which was not available in the conventional metrical norm with its reduction of formally useful sensuous response. This can be taken as a statement not of judgement but of fact if intensity is understood as a matter of the number of elements brought simultaneously into play. The absolute quality of rhythm in which Pound believed suggests a way in which these elements might lock together in an unique occasion. One of the things which interested Pound in the musical settings for Provençal poetry was the way in which only the tonal value of notes was indicated. Their temporal value was not indicated by the notation, and barring as we understand it today was not employed.

> We do not know whether the first neumes indicated a rise or fall of voice by definite gradations of pitch, or whether they indicate simply rise or fall. The music of the troubadour period is without bars in the modern sense. There are little lines like them, but they mean simply a pause, a rest; the notes do not register differences of duration—i.e. halves, wholes, quarters are written alike. One reads the words on which the notes indubitably depended; a rhythm comes to life—a rhythm which seems to explain the music and which is not a "musician's" rhythm. Yet it is possible to set this rhythm in a musician's rhythm without, from the poet's feeling in the matter, harming it or even "altering it", which means altering the part of it to which he is sensitive; which means, again, that both poet and musician "feel around" the movement, "feel at it" from different angles.[28]

As Pound develops and repeats his concept of "absolute rhythm" it is the correspondence between emotion and rhythm which he constantly emphasises. Music does not offer a mere analogy or way of enforcing an *a priori* interest in quantitative metre, which is rather what Hummell suggests, but a way of engaging rhythm in a temporal series in which it is locked by the parallel progression of tones. Pound's definition of melody in his *ABC of Reading* as "a rhythm in which the pitch of each element is fixed by the composer" suggests a loosening of the natural and involuntary, and therefore expressive relationship between rhythm and tone which Pound had thought of earlier.[29] In *The Treatise on Harmony* and *Antheil*, published in 1927, Pound offers his conception of this relationship in perhaps its clearest terms. The early students of harmony, he says, "thought of music as travelling rhythm going through points or barriers of pitch and pitch-combinations"[30]. And of the relation of pitch and time he says:

> ...we must emphasise the relation of raga, tala, and harmony. Any note can follow any other, any ten notes can follow each other in any order you like, but if their arrangement, I mean their tala, their tone sequence, is of any interest it will lock their time intervals, i.e. their individual durations and the rests between them.[31]

At one point in the Osiris essays Pound comments on the canzon of Daniel in relation to the Platonic melos, "the union of words, rhythm, and music (i.e. that part of music which we do not perceive as rhythm)," and then remarks that Daniel "bears to the technique of accented verse of Europe very much the same relation that Euclid does to our mathematics."[32] The implication of Pound's train of thought here must be that, for him, rhythm was still very greatly determined by accent, and that the way in which quantity might be a constituent of rhythm (rather than something which transpired between or was marked by accents) had not yet clearly presented itself to him.

In the "Credo" which he published in the *Poetry Review* in 1912, Pound returns to the idea of absolute rhythm.

> I believe in an "absolute rhythm", a rhythm, that is, in poetry which corresponds exactly to the emotion or shade of emotion to be expressed. A man's rhythm must be interpretative, it will be, therefore, in the end, his own, uncounterfeiting, uncount-erfeitable.[33]

A number of ideas are compressed within this passage, which focusses on the question of what it is that is to be expressed or interpreted. Whereas emotion or shade of emotion can have that specificity which we associate with the idea of the Image or moment of experience, the thing presented, the personal rhythm which Pound goes on to talk about, suggests something more akin to his idea of the characteristic virtue which makes a work of art endure. It is possible to suppose that as rhythm moves beyond the

2. The Concept of Metre and the Relation of Prosody to Meaning

expressive to the interpretative it will carry a signature, in other words that the interpretation of emotion will testify to authority, but the passage is too ambiguous for me to suggest this with total conviction. The third occasion on which Pound adduces his faith in an absolute rhythm is the essay on Vorticism which he published in 1914 in the *Fortnightly Review*, in which he suggests that the rhythmic correspondence to emotion subsists in a "toneless phrase", in other words the way in which he previously implied a connection between vocal pitch, tone, and emotion is no longer being considered. At the same time Pound proceeds, as he did in his "Credo", to deal with the question of symbolism.

> I said in the preface to my Guido Cavalcanti that I believed in an absolute rhythm. I believe that every emotion and every phase of emotion has some toneless phrase, some rhythm phrase to express it.
> (This belief leads to *vers libre* and to experiments in quantitative verse.)
> To hold a like belief in a sort of permanent metaphor is, as I understand it, "symbolism in its profounder sense. It is not necessarily a belief in a permanent world, but it is a belief in that direction.
> Imagisme is not symbolism. The symbolists dealt in "association", that is, in a sort of allusion, almost of allegory. They degraded the symbol to the status of a word.[34]

What happens to Pound's term "absolute rhythm", it seems to me, is a process of transformation from a point at which it marks a quality of supreme intensity to a point at which it implies a means of composition. The toneless phrase of emotion will acquire tone (and also intellectual precision) from the verbal and musical context in which it occurs, but as an explanation of the concept of absolute rhythm we now find a situation in which accents occur vertically against a principle of duration or elapsed time. Such an idea yields up the notion of the musical phrase as it was formulated in 1913. A phrase is musical rather than metronomic when the beats (or stresses) and time intervals which a metronome counts regularly and mechanically are distributed in some other way. Pound comes back to this sense of composition at the conclusion of his essay "The Tradition", published in 1913, and it is clear that the idea he is putting forward is not conceived at all as one of metrical regularity and variation, since the irregularities of time we find are not variations on a rule but a principle of composition derived from an emotional source. In the musical phrase, perhaps, the occurrence of stresses is measured by the time intervals.

> As to quantity, it is foolish to suppose that we are incapable of distinguishing a long vowel from a short one, or that we are mentally debarred from ascertaining how many consonants intervene between one vowel and the next.
>
> As to the tradition of *vers libre*: Jannaris in his study of the Melic poets comes to the conclusion that they composed to the feel of the thing, to the cadence, as have all good poets since....
>
> No one is so foolish as to suppose that a musician using "four-four" time is compelled to use always four quarter notes in each bar, or in "seven-eights" seven eighth notes uniformly in each bar. He may use ½, one ¼, and 1/8 rest, or any such combination as he may happen to choose or find fitting.[35]

Pound's discussion of rhythm and the attentions exercised by the poet in his pursuit of the musical phrase (which are elaborated in valuable detail in "A Few Don'ts by an Imagiste") suggests that in a sense he is trying to replace the notion of form by that of technique. I find this an exceptionally interesting possibility. Comparison is without doubt a valuable activity, but we too easily equate the notion of species with that of class. If it is possible to imagine a poem the form of which is so closely bound up with the facts of its existence that it is impossible to predicate the independent existence of the form, then it is possible to see a way in which technique can become a definition of a philosophical premise about form, the way an object comes to be itself. Our comparisons would then be made between objects which, despite superficial dissimilarities of outline, were embodiments of identical techniques. I shall come back to this question in my final chapter when I discuss the relation of restraint and freedom, fixed and variable elements, in poetic theory. From this point of view one sense of Eliot's comments on free verse, that it is not a form, confirms Pound's insight. Free verse is a technique. (Eliot simply did not take his insight any further than was necessary for his immediate limited ends.) To say that a poem is written in free verse, that is, will contribute little to our understanding of its form because we will know nothing about the kind of phonological properties and the arrangement of them which contribute to the poet's shape. In free verse these decisions and the relation of fixed to variable elements, if not perhaps a matter of the poet's discretion, are related to his expressive impulse, are not a matter of convention or formula: "technique is the only gauge and test of a man's lasting sincerity" is how Pound put it in 1912.[36]

If Pound had been alone in his advocacy of _vers libre_ the main current of his ideas, as I have presented it here, would be much easier to grasp. But Pound had made his own way to _vers libre_, and at a crucial point in his development allied his preoccupations to the activities of another group of poets, whose interest in _vers libre_ set off from quite different premises. For T.E. Hulme, the centre of this group, free verse was a form, the exigencies of which derived from his notion of the organic life and death of forms in cultural history, a notion similar to the ideas about the currency of language which are the effective determinants of his poetic theory. "All possible tunes have been played on the instrument" of a form which needs to be replaced.[37] In his article "The History of Imagism", published in _The Egoist_ in 1913, F.S. Flint is concerned to establish the chronological priority of Hulme's ideas.

> At that time [1908], I had been advocating in the course of a series of articles on recent books of verse a poetry in _vers libre_, akin in spirit to the Japanese. An attack on the Poets' Club brought me into correspondence and acquaintance with T.E. Hulme; and, later on, after Hulme had violently disagreed with the Poets' Club and had left it, he proposed that he should get together a few congenial spirits, and that we should have weekly meetings in a Soho restaurant.

And so forth.

> I think that what brought the real nucleus of this group together was a dissatisfaction with English poetry as it was then (and is still, alas!) being written. We proposed at various times to replace it with pure _vers libre_, by the Japanese _tanka_ and haikai; we all wrote dozens of the latter as an amusement; by poems in a sacred Hebrew form, of which "This is the House that Jack Built" is a perfect model; Joseph Campbell produced two good specimens of this, one of which, "The Dark" is printed in "The Mountainy Singer"; by rhymeless poems like Hulme's "Autumn", and so on. In all this Hulme was ringleader. He insisted too on an absolutely accurate presentation and no verbiage; and he and F.W. Tancred, a poet too little known, perhaps because his production is precious and small, used to spend hours each day in search of the right phrase.[38]

Flint's purpose here is obviously to suggest that Hulme anticipated the three Imagist principles as they were formulated by Pound, and the polemic only serves to create confusion between the ideas of the two men. Just how different Hulme's sense of *vers libre* is from Pound's is to be seen from a passage towards the end of Hulme's "A Lecture on Modern Poetry", which was delivered to the Poet's Club in 1908.

> This new verse resembles sculpture rather than music; it appeals to the eye rather than to the ear. It has to mould images, a kind of spiritual clay, into definite shapes. This material, the ὕλη of Aristotle, is image not sound. It builds up a plastic image which it hands over to the reader, whereas the old art endeavoured to influence him physically by the hypnotic effect of rhythm.[39]

This and other passages in the same lecture demonstrate how narrow was Hulme's sense of the music of verse, its rhythmical properties: they are narcotic, and lull the mind. The conception is fundamentally similar to Davie's own version of music in *Articulate Energy*. Free verse is a necessity for Hulme not because it offers a rhythmical resource but because it enables the poet to escape from rhythm, and to communicate his ideas in a modern way. The intensity Hulme sought in poetry was not one of dense verbal and musical effect, but an intensity of perception expressed in images which represent the way in which we experience the world. For Hulme the fabric of experience was a matter of the intense impressions of a discontinuous world, and these impressions could only be registered adequately by means of a vivid visual image which is pre-intellectual. For all Hulme's pretence of objectivity and classicism, his "modern" reflects an acute form of idealism and is "definitely and finally introspective and deals with expression and communication of momentary phases in the poet's mind."[40] The preposition by which the mind's activities are related to the external world is of some interest.

The "entirely empirical nature of the old rules" which "cramp" the modern writer needed to be overcome.[41] Like Flint, Hulme found inspiration in French *vers libre*.

> There were certain impressions which I wanted to fix. I read verse to find models, but I could not find any exactly suitable to express that kind of impression, except perhaps a few jerky rhythms of Henley, until I came to read the French *vers libre* which seemed exactly to fit the case.[42]

It is clear that *vers libre* offered two things for Hulme: an emancipation from dead form which enabled the poet to play his new tunes, and at the same time a model for the combination of impressions or images. The image was a non-intellectual form of apprehension, which became significant only when encountered in combination with other images in novel ways; the mode of fancy, as opposed to imagination, which creates new and effective metaphors according to the theory outlined in "Romanticism and Classicism". Free verse suggested to Hulme a way of combining images line by line, and is, for him, basically a means of syntactical organisation.

> The length of the line is long and short, oscillating with the images used by the poet; it follows the contours of his thoughts and is free rather than regular; to use a rough analogy, it is clothes made to order, rather than ready-made clothes.[43]

> Say the poet is moved by a certain landscape, he selects from that certain images which, put into juxtaposition in separate lines, serve to suggest and to evoke the state he feels. To this piling up and juxtaposition of distinct images in different lines, one can find a fanciful analogy in music. A great revolution in music when, for the melody that is one dimensional music, was substituted harmony that moves in two. Two visual images form what one may call a visual chord. They unite to suggest an image which is different to both.[44]

This musical analogy is the exact opposite of Pound's interest in melody, of course. One might remember what Pound said in *The Treatise on Harmony*: "The early students of harmony were so accustomed to think of music as something with a strong lateral or horizontal motion that they never imagined any one, any one could be stupid enough to think of it as static; it never entered their heads that people would make music like steam ascending from a morass."[45]

I think we must come to understand Imagism as a confluence of Hulmean and Poundian notions of linear organisation and image. Hulme's notion of the image is fundamentally epistemological, and demands a certain kind of expression; Pound's image is psychological, and is only one among other ways of presenting experience in poetry.[46] It has been suggested by Sir Herbert Read that Hulme's Image prefigured the Poundian ideogram, but, as I shall argue in the next chapter, such an identification falsifies both ideas.[47] The various prefaces to the three Imagist Anthologies published under the aegis of Amy Lowell represent a dilution and obfuscation of the ideas I have been discussing, and need not be given much serious attention. They add nothing to poetic theory.

NOTES

[1] Yvor Winters, op. cit., p. 61.

[2] Ibid., pp. 106-107.

[3] Ibid., p. 108.

[4] See, for example, G.L. Trager and H.L. Smith Jr., *An Outline of English Structure*, Norman, Oklahoma, 1951. The Trager-Smith, or structural-linguistic approach to metrical analysis is now regarded as somewhat old-fashioned by transformational linguists. Nevertheless, their phonological prescription is of relevance to the point I am making here.

[5] See, Roger Fowler, "What is Metrical Analysis?" Anglia, 86 (1968), p. 302 et. seq. for examples of Pope's use of iambic pentameter in which "ictus" can only be inferred from the metrical set of the verse.

[6] In PMLA, LXXIV, (Dec. 1959), pp. 585-598. Quoted from their abstract in *Style in Language*, ed. Thomas A. Sebeok, Cambridge, Mass., 1960, p. 194.

[7] See Jakobson's "Concluding Statement: Linguistics and Poetics" in Sebeok, op. cit., pp. 350-377. For a fuller account of the theory of metrical interplay see the "Editorial Introduction" to the section on Metrics in Seymour Chapman and Samuel R. Levin (eds.), *Essays of the Language of Literature*, Boston 1967.

"The further inference... is that one has to do with two systems in every performance of a poem, the metrical system (with its events and prominences) and the supra-segmental system of English (with its stresses, intonations and junctions, however they are analysed). These co-existent systems are given different names: meter vs. performance, (traditional) meter vs. "rhythm" (potential or core), meter vs. its actualization, abstract frame vs. actual instance etc... despite the variation in terminology, the principle is the same, and the solidarity of view inspires confidence in the validity of the distinction." Op. cit., pp. 69-70.

[8] Benjamin Hrushovski, "On Free Rhythms in Modern Poetry", in Sebeok, op. cit., n. p. 176.

[9] *The Literary Essays of Ezra Pound*, London 1954, p. xiii.

[10] Ibid., p. xi.

[11] *The Sonnets and Ballate of Guido Cavalcanti*, London 1912; quoted from Ezra Pound, *Translations*, enlarged edition, NY 1963, p. 23. Eliot's two early essays are reprinted in his *To Criticize the Critic*, London 1965.

[12] See Pound's 1940 footnote to his essay "T.S. Eliot" (1917), *Literary Essays*, p. 421.

[13] Ezra Pound, *The Spirit of Romance*, New Directions edition, NY (n.d.), p. 7.

[14] Ezra Pound, "A List of Books", *The Little Review*, (March, 1918), p. 57.

[15] F.S. Flint, "Contemporary French Poetry", *Poetry and Drama*, I, viii, (August, 1912), p. 359.

[16] Ezra Pound, "French Poets", *Make it New*, London 1934, p. 172.

[17] *Literary Essays*, pp. 292-293.

[18] Ibid., p. 25.

[19] In 1917 Pound was engaged in controversy with the fag-end of Imagism and militant free-versifiers, and had turned with Eliot to the "sculptural" rhymed quatrain of Gaudier. Pound's interest in the rhymes of Arnaut Daniel is to be recalled. Eliot's two essays are a reflection of this affirmation of technique as against freedom. For a discussion of Pound's views on the strictness involved in the practice of *vers libre* see my discussion of melopoeia below.

[20] Flint published three books of poems, none of which has been reprinted. The last and best of the three, *Otherworld: Cadences* was published in 1920.

[21] "This Hulme Business" was published in *The Townsman* in January 1938, and is reprinted as Appendix I in Kenner, *The Poetry of Ezra Pound*, London 1951. Pound's renewed interest in Hulme at this late date (Hulme was killed in 1917, his *Speculations* published posthumously in 1924) was the result of his correspondence with Michael Roberts concerning the latter's proposed study of Hulme, eventually published in 1938.

[22] See note 7, above. I have ignored the matter of the relation of a poem's performance, whether read aloud or silently, to its written or printed form. In a sense it is true that the sensible auditory and articulatory features which are assumed in any use of a concept such as melopoeia are not realised until given life in performance, and that at the same time no one performance can be taken to furnish a standard of measurement. The distinction, however, between our knowledge of a poem as a printed form and our knowledge of it in performance is an unimportant one, since by talking about the phonological characteristics of a poem we are referring to something which is identical both in performance and when shut up between the pages of a book. It is, anyway, only by thinking of a poem in such a way that we are able to envisage its complete existence independent of any performance situation.

[23] Pallister Barkas, *A Critique of Modern English Prosody (1880-1930)*, (Studien zur Englischen Philologie No. LXXXII), Halle 1934, p. 37.

[24] Barkas quotes R.M. Alden in *Introduction to Poetry* (1909) using the term "Absolute Rhythm" to denote an unvarying norm which is never actually found in real sounds. Kenner, op. cit., cites Remy de Gourmont in *Le Latin Mystique* to show that "absolute rhythm" was used by the Gregorian musicians to refer to the relation of the anterior and posterior morphologies of words and syllables.

[25] Quoted from Pound, *Translations*, op. cit., pp. 21-22.

[26] John Hummell, "The Provençal Translations", *Texas Quarterly*, X, iv, p. 48.

[27] Ezra Pound, "I Gather the Limbs of Osiris, X: On Music", *The New Age*, (Jan 8, 1912), p. 344.

[28] Ibid., p. 344.

[29] Ezra Pound, "Treatise on Metre", *ABC of Reading*, London 1934, p. 198.

[30] Ezra Pound, *Patria Mea, and the Treatise on Harmony*, London 1962, p. 80.

[31] Ezra Pound, *Antheil*, Paris 1924.

[32] Ezra Pound, "I Gather the Limbs of Osiris, IV: A Beginning", *The New Age*, (Dec. 21, 1911), p. 179.

[33] Quoted from *Literary Essays*, p. 9.

[34] Quoted from *Gaudier Brzeska: A Memoir*, new edition with additional material, NY 1961, p. 85.

[35] T.E. Hulme, "A Lecture on Modern Poetry", in Michael Roberts, *T.E. Hulme*, London 1938, p. 260.

[36] Ezra Pound, "I Gather the Limbs of Osiris, IX: On Technique", *The New Age*, (Jan 25, 1912), p. 298.

[37] "A Lecture on Modern Poetry", op. cit., p. 260.

[38] F.S. Flint, "The History of Imagism", *The Egoist*, II, 5, pp. 70-71.

[39] "A Lecture on Modern Poetry", op. cit., pp. 269-270.

[40] Ibid., p. 265.

[41] Ibid., p. 260.

[42] Ibid., p. 259.

[43] Ibid., p. 263.

[44] Ibid., p. 266.

[45] Ezra Pound, *Patria Mea, and the Treatise on Harmony*, London 1962.

[46] In *The New Age under Orage*, Manchester 1967, Wallace Martin makes a similar point with less precision, saying that Hulme's image, derived from Bergson, is intellectual, whereas Pound's, derived from Freud via Hart, is intensive.

[47] See Herbert Read, op. cit., pp. 101-138.

Chapter 3

Prose and Speech as Criteria for the Organisation of Poetic Discourse

If we are able to assume a prosody which is open to the full range of phonological possibilities in language it follows that we must refer our sense of rhythm, not to an artificially induced "poetic" experience such as recurrence of accents, but to something which, if not actually common speech, we must feel to be present in the experience of articulated sounds. Ever since Coleridge, in Chapter XVII of *Biographia Literaria*, took Wordsworth to task for his propositions that poetry should employ "a selection of the REAL language of men," and that "between the language of prose and that of metrical composition, there neither is, nor can be, any essential difference," the question of the relation of poetry to speech has been a difficult and unresolved issue.[1] The distinction between poetry and prose is customarily felt to have the force of antithesis, and a natural connection between prose and speech tends to be assumed as a matter of course. We see this implicit in the passages from the Preface to the second edition of the *Lyrical Ballads* quoted above. Molière was able to discover an amusing stroke of wit by making such a tacit assumption dramatically explicit when, in *Le Bourgeois Gentilhomme*, M. Jourdain discovers that he has been talking prose for forty years. It is possible to sense that Molière's joke has an historical significance, to see such a "natural" bracketing of rational speech and prose as the concomitant of the development of scientific prose in the latter half of the Seventeenth Century, together with an allied attack on the licences of poetic fancifulness, but all such speculation is beside the immediate point. Less open to question is the way in which the mere exercise of a vernacular tongue does not immediately issue in a mature and comprehensive prose style, as we can discover if we consider the development of English prose style in the Sixteenth Century.[2]

Whatever its history, the basis for the tacit connection of prose and speech is fairly obvious: the informal and pragmatic character of day-to-day discourse is paralleled in the purposive and unpatterned discursiveness of prose, the form men customarily turn to when they need to communicate with one another in writing. Poetry, on the other hand, is written in a pattern which draws attention upon itself, called verse. Custom ordains a less clear distinction between poetry and verse than it does between prose and poetry for, while it is possible to say of a piece of writing that it is verse without being poetry, the reverse proposition, that a piece of writing may be poetry without being in verse, encounters a problem which T.E. Hulme was aware of when he formulated his aesthetic of a line-by-line articulation of concretely apprehended and expressed images.

> The criticism is sure to be made that when you have abolished the regular syllabled line as the unit of poetry, you have turned it into prose. Of course this is perfectly true of a great quantity of modern verse. In fact, one of the great blessings of the abolition of regular metre would be that it would at once expose this sham poetry.[3]

Hulme is able to turn the tables on the conventional argument and the sham metrical poetry which it defends in this neat fashion by virtue of his sense of the direct, physical apprehension that is a prerequisite of effective communication between men, rather than a manipulation of abstract verbal tokens on a board or grid of conventional but arbitrary grammatical relations. "Freshness convinces you, you feel at once that the artist was in an actual physical state. You feel that for a minute. Real communication is so very rare, for plain speech is unconvincing. It is in this rare fact of communication that you get the root of aesthetic pleasure."[4] An interesting corollary to this, and a little remarked phase of Hulme's thought, is that ordinary language, what Hulme calls "plain speech", places a limitation on experience; the relation between experience, impression, and the images drawn from one's experience is not a direct and automatic one, but is in some way mediated by language. It is a pity that Hulme did not develop this idea, for it would have taken him in the direction of linguistic discoveries made by Sapir and Whorf in the Twenties. In Hulme's sense, "language" is not the same as what, in a different context, we might mean by natural language. For Hulme language as one finds it is always a degraded, secondary product. In the following passage it is not clear how much is a straightforward exposition of Bergson, and how much is authentic Hulme, but that is not a very important issue. It is the fit of the ideas which Hulme adduces that makes his work of value.

> Language, as we have said, only expresses the lowest common denominator of the emotions of one kind. It leaves out all the individuality of an emotion as it really exists and substitutes for it a kind of stock or type of emotion. Now here comes the additional

observation which I have to make. As we not only express ourselves in words, but for the most part think also in them, it comes about that not only do we not express more than the impersonal element of an emotion, but that we do not, as a matter of fact, perceive more. The average person as distinct from the artist does not even perceive the individuality of their own emotions. Our faculties of perception are, as it were, crystallised out into certain moulds. Most of us, then, never see things as they are, but see only the stock types which are embodied in language.

This enables one to give a first rough definition of the artist. It is not sufficient to say that an artist is a person who is able to convey over the actual things he sees or emotions he feels. It is necessary before that that he should be a person who is able to emancipate himself from the moulds which language and ordinary perception force on him and be able to see things freshly as they really are.[5]

If we compare this final phrase, "to see things freshly as they really are", with the argument, mentioned in the previous chapter, that the task of the artist is to render his impressions, we discover the contradiction at the heart of Hulme's system. He is concerned to put forward an aesthetic which has an epistemological basis, but fails to explore fully the nature of the two poles which of necessity define any epistemic transaction. We can understand this shortcoming, I think, in terms of a desire to absorb into this transaction, by isolating its aesthetic character, psychological entities to which Hulme did not wish to attach significant importance. This is reflected, surely, in his exclusive interest in a single sensory modality, the optical, which is also the most "objective" of the sense and holds, in a way of speaking, the world away at more than arms' length. However, the point I want to make is that Hulme's animadversions about language, and his ideas that the aim of art is to communicate the artist in "an actual physical state", provides him which the means to distinguish between prose and poetry in a non-technical fashion, without reference to structure or medium, since for him language is susceptible to processes of degradation and ossification through usage which reduce it inexorably to a system of abstract counters and signs unless it is deliberately and continuously renewed by the coining of novel visual analogies.

Poetry as an abstract thing is a very different matter, and has its own life, quite apart from the metre as convention.

To test the question of whether it is possible to have poetry written without regular metre, I propose to pick out one great difference between the two. I don't profess to give an infallible test that would enable anyone to say at once: "This is, or is not, true poetry", but it will be sufficient for the purposes of this paper. It is this: that there are, roughly speaking, two methods of communication, a direct and a conventional language. The direct language is poetry, it is direct because it deals in images. The indirect language is prose, because it uses images that have dies and have become figures of speech.

The difference between the two is, roughly, this: that while one arrests your mind all the time with a picture, the other allows the mind to run along with the least possible effort to a conclusion. Prose is due to a faculty of the mind something resembling reflex action in the body. If I had to go through a complicated mental process each time I laced my boots it would waste mental energy; instead of that, the mechanism of the body is so arranged that one can do it almost without thinking. It is an economy of effort. The same process takes place with the images used in prose. For example, when I say that the hill was clad with trees, it merely conveys the fact to me that it was covered. But the first time that expression was used was by a poet, and to him it was an image recalling to him the distinct visual analogy of a man clad in clothes; but the image has died. One might say that images are born in poetry. They are used in prose, and finally die a long, lingering death in journalists' English. Now this process is very rapid, so that the poet must continually be creating new images, and his sincerity may be numbered by the number of his images.[6]

The implications of Hulme's argument are not, perhaps, entirely clear unless it is remembered that a non-technical distinction between prose and poetry of the type he is making must apply to what we <u>ordinarily</u> mean by prose as well as to poetry. If the distinction between prose and poetry is a matter of the ends they serve and the uses of language appropriate to those ends, then the strictures which Hulme makes about prose do not necessarily apply to our usual sense of what prose is. Hulme never set his mind to the question of large scale literary structures, confining his attention to the possibility of combining immediately-felt images in consecutive lines of verse. He does not appear to have taken any account of the necessary linear and temporal character of such combinations, and the main distinction for him between verse and prose in the ordinary sense seems merely to be that the line can function as a kind of supplementary demarcation of the image. The theorist interested in the possibility of an extended literary composition which would fulfil Hulmean criteria would have to take into account the Bergsonian ideas concerning intensive manifolds, and that duration which is real time because it embodies real and not counter experience, both of which were appropriated by Hulme, together with Hulme's own sense of a discontinuous, cindery universe. Against these he would have to set the kind of impression which Hulme maintained it was the task of the modern artist to express, working out the possible relationships between an impression (of Canadian prairies, say, which constituted one of Hulme's typically modern experiences) and the images which combine to express it. In *Articulate Energy* Donald Davie argues that the intensive manifold is an anti-syntactic concept, and that in his employment of it Hulme is characteristically modern. Davie sets against this Fenellosa's argument, which is syntactic in Davie's terms, that the kinetic transfer of energy in language, through an active verb, is the core of meaning and also a figure of universal grammar, corroborated by nature. It is an interesting comparison, but to my mind a misleading one. It is the sensory exclusiveness of Hulme's image, the insistence on visual analogy, which causes it to be asyntactic in Davie's sense, reliant on metaphoric constructions which are more or less appositional. The lack of sensory resourcefulness behind Hulme's prose-poetry distinction allows one to feel that the distinction is the usual technical one, but the flaccidity of Hulme's sense of the possible resources of word combination need not at all be accounted for in terms of the intensive manifold. That aspect of Bergson's philosophy, the world as it really is which certain forms of language distort by explanation is, as I suggested earlier, unassimilated and contradictory in Hulme. We can understand, perhaps, just what his teleological distinction can amount to if we consider the use which Hulme's editor, Herbert Read, put it to in his own critical work.

> Poetry is creative expression; Prose is constructive expression....
> By creative I mean <u>original</u>. In Poetry the words are born or reborn in the act of thinking. The words are, in Bergsonian phraseology, a becoming; they develop in the mind *pari passu* with the development of the thought. There is no time interval between the words and the thought. The thought is the word and the word is thought, and both the thought and the word are Poetry.

"Constructive" implies ready-made materials; words stacked round the builder ready for use. Prose is a structure of ready-made words. Its "creative" function is confined to plan and elevation—functions these, too, of Poetry, but in Poetry subsidiary to the creative function.[7]

This lacks Hulme's indignant contempt for "prose", but it is probable that Read had thought more carefully than Hulme about the nature of individual words. The suggestion that the absence of interval between word and thought is an absence merely of temporal interval is to my mind excessive, and suggests Read's subsequent psychological theories of creativity, which attempt to annexe the unconscious to a single mode of spontaneous behaviour. What this lack of interval between word and thought might amount to I shall suggest later in this chapter; for the time being I wish simply to note the suggestion of the integrity or autonomy of poetry as distinct from prose which Hulme and Read both have at the back of their minds.

The most extreme statement of the prose-poetry distinction probably occurs in F.S. Flint's Preface to his final collection of poems, Otherworld, which he dedicated to Read. Flint opens his Preface with the observation that "There is only one art of writing, and that is the art of poetry; and, wherever you feel the warmth of human experience and imagination in any writing, there is poetry, whether it is in the form we call prose, or in rhyme and meter, or in the unrhymed cadence in which the greater part of this book is written."[8] What Flint does is to take over the substance of the prose-poetry distinction as made by Hulme, while jettisoning the terminology. Flint is quite fierce in his rejection of rhyme and metre, what he calls the "tyranny of the dead", as viable poetic means. "Swinburne gave the *coup de grâce* (and the *coup de Jarnac* too) to English rhyme and meter."[9] Like Hulme, his procedure is to make the line the basic unit of verse, only it is organised around the idea of the cadence rather than around the individual image. Flint's cadence is a less precise version of Pound's absolute rhythm, but as in Pound it is defined by its emotional function. Flint defines poetry in general, "Clarity and sincerity of speech and purpose are the perennial qualities of all good poetry," and then goes on to draw a distinction between two sorts of writing which is technical.

For the poets such as I have in mind, there are the two forms, which are really one, the first being prose and the second I have called unrhymed cadence. The one merges into the other; there is no boundary line between them; but prose, generally, will be used for the more objective branches of writing—for novels, plays, essays and so on—and poetry in this form is accepted with so much goodwill that I have some misgiving in applying to it its rightful name; cadence will be used for personal, emotional, lyric utterances, in which the phrasing goes with a stronger beat and the words live together with an intenser flame. If you ask why cadence should not be printed as prose, the reply is that the unequal lines mark the movement of the cadence and the tempo...[10]

The distinction is technical in a very crude and accepted sense; Flint clearly does not wish to bother himself with the intricacies of phonological resources which a line of verse can command, although his remarks about movement and tempo imply that he knows something of these matters. The relegation of verse to "personal, emotional, lyric utterances" is something which Pound must have deplored, and proceeds from the literal identification of verse and speech. It suggests that poetry is in essence the simulacrum of spontaneous, passionate speech, which soon exhausts its initial impetus; whereas I would maintain that a non-metrical verse offers the resources for exemplifying the complex, flexible movements of unprepared and unrehearsed <u>thought</u> brought over into speech.

Within the compass of such an idea of primary writing, creative of its own meaning, as we have seen it argued variously by Hulme, Read, and Flint, it is possible, as Flint himself does in an off-hand way, to look again at the technical distinctions between prose and verse. While I have suggested a prosody which involves the utilisation of the full phonological range of language, it need not follow that the whole spectrum of phonological items should be used in the same ratio at all times; and thus it is surely possible, without adducing a blueprint, to imagine a "prose" in which account is taken of the phonological properties of a discourse as it proceeds, without using them simply as a patterning device. This sort of prose will not be expository in the sense that it will not be referring at all points to a pre-conceived and objectively-referring plan, which I would call a rhetorical discourse, but need not thereby, I would contend, find itself employing an empty syntax. Davie's syntax employs abstract concepts, but if these can possess a reality equivalent to that of the generic concepts of language such as table or chair, then I would argue that they must possess a reality which is prior to the possible operational utility which such abstract concepts offer. Davie's view of syntax, as he often states it, seems to validate syntax, or rather authenticate it, in terms of its operational pay-off. But real is not operational. Thus, from the point of view I am advancing, what the faculty for verbal invention may be led to in prose by phonological impulse could be real and occur in syntactic relationships in a genuine way. This polemic excursion is simply by way of introduction to Pound's advocacy of what he called "The Prose Tradition in Verse", an impressively clear formulation in its refusal to be drawn into any controversy about "poetry".

§ § §

From the standpoint of "The Prose Tradition" prose is an antidote to rhetoric, to poetry in which forms of metre and diction, supposedly special to poetic emotion, are allowed to operate to the detriment of meaning. This is a more fortunate notion than the idea that sound alone operates against the demands of sense. Prose in this sense offers correctives of diction and word order (which metrical imperatives can easily distort from a "natural" sequence), but is not necessarily an adjunct of speech. We need not feel too far away from Coleridge when we come across the following argument in "I Gather the Limbs of Osiris", both on account of its sense of the inadequacies of common speech, and on account of the notion of poetic pleasure it implies.

> And the only way to escape from rhetoric and frilled paper decoration is through beauty—"beauty of the thing, certainly, but besides that, beauty of the means". I mean by that that one must call a spade a spade in form so exactly adjusted, in a metric itself so seductive, that the statement will not bore the auditor. Or again, since I seem to flounder in my attempt at utterance, we must have a simplicity and directness of utterance, which is different from the simplicity and directness of daily speech, which is more "curial", more dignified. This difference, this dignity, cannot be conferred by florid adjectives or elaborate hyperbole; it must be conveyed by art, and by the art of the verse structure, by something which exalts the reader, making him feel that he is in contact with something arranged more finely than the commonplace.

There are few fallacies more common that the opinion that poetry should mimic the daily speech. Works of art attract by a resembling unlikeness. Colloquial poetry is to the real art as the barber's wax dummy is to sculpture. In every art I can think of we are dammed and clogged by the mimetic; dynamic acting is nearly forgotten; the painters of the moment escape through eccentricity.[11]

The anecdote about Ford Madox Hueffer rolling on the floor when Pound brought his *Canzoni* to him at Geissen in 1911 is well known; the critical perspicuity of Hueffer, the master of English prose, saved him three years' work, Pound subsequently averred.[12] Prose in this context is *le mot juste* (which Wordsworth neglected in his advocacy of the real speech of men)[13]; French clarity and precision; Flaubert and Maupassant. But the conception of poetry into which Pound wishes to incorporate these qualities is still a transcendent one, the form musical rather than verbal. It was not until Pound brought his mind to bear on the Image, and the relation of art to the data of experience, that he began to see that *le mot juste* might do more than possess a contextual rightness, but could be situationally and expressively right also. From here the step to speech is but a short one.

When in 1913 Pound wrote, in his series of addenda to Flint's note on Imagisme in *Poetry*, that "An 'Image' is that which presents an intellectual and emotional complex in an instant of time," and that "the natural object is always the <u>adequate</u> symbol," he came as close to Hulme as he ever was to, but he is explaining Hulme's ideas in terms of their expressive capacities.[14] No account is offered of the poet's sources of power. He is told to "Go in fear of abstractions,"[15] and also that "your rhythmic structure should not destroy the shape of your words, or their natural sound, or their meaning."[16] The latter instructions are no more than the reservations which Pound insists, throughout the "Osiris" essays, are to be observed when setting words to music, but here they are given a prominence equal to that of precepts which previously received particular emphasis. This whole passage of "Don'ts" is interesting, but not really very instructive if one is trying to elucidate the shape of Pound's thought. No idea appears to be holding together the Hulmean antagonism to abstractions and the Poundian absorption in rhythmic phenomena. Pound's essay "The Prose Tradition", published in *Poetry* in the following year, is largely taken up with a review of Hueffer's *Collected Poems*, and adds very little to the achievement of Pound's thought on these matters, apart from repeating several times that poetry should be as well written as prose. What Pound might mean by this is not clear from the context which the article supplies, but it is possible to supply a gloss from a series of articles which he published the year before in *The New Freewoman* under the title "The Serious Artist".

> Good writing is writing that is perfectly controlled, the writer says just what he means. He says it with complete clarity and simplicity. He uses the smallest number of words. I do not mean that he skimps paper, or that he screws about like Tacitus to get his thought crowded into the least possible space. But, granting that two sentences are at times easier to understand than one sentence containing the double meaning, the author tries to communicate with the reader with the greatest possible despatch, save where for any one of forty reasons he does not wish to do so.[17]

This is essentially a rhetorical conception of prose and good writing, similar to that put forward by Coleridge which I shall discuss later in this chapter. It certainly owes very little to Hueffer's own prose style, which rather tends to fit the case allowed for in Pound's final qualifying clause. Although he draws attention to Hueffer's Preface in "The Prose Tradition in Verse", Pound says very little about it, and his most substantial comment on the text of the *Collected Poems* is to say that they are "gracious impressions, leisurely, low-toned."[18] The necessary synthesising of all these jostling precepts does not take place until January 1915, in a letter Pound wrote to Harriet Monroe, and is put into effect around the idea of the expressive capacities of speech. Pound starts off from his maxim that poetry should be as well written as prose, and that "Its language must be a fine language, departing in no way from speech save by heightened intensity," and then proceeds, by way of a series of admonitions, to the heart of the matter.

> Objectivity and again objectivity, and expression: no hindside-beforeness, no straddling adjectives (as "addled mosses dank"), no Tennysonian-ness of speech; nothing—nothing that you couldn't in some circumstance, in the stress of some emotion, actually say. Every literaryism, every book word, fritters away a scrap of the reader's patience, a scrap of his sense of your sincerity. When one really feels and thinks, one stammers with simple speech; it is only in the flurry, the shallow frothy excitement of writing, or the inebriety of a metre, that one falls into the easy—oh, how easy!—speech of books or poems that one has read.[19]

The question of the relation of prose and speech has hardly been settled in this outburst, but at least we can discern from it the direction in which the "Prose Tradition" had taken Pound. The lynch pin of the whole argument is to be found in a phrase which Pound makes further use of in his Preface to the *Poetical Works of Lionel Johnson*, later that same year.

> His language is a bookish dialect, or rather it is not a dialect, it is a curial speech and our aim is natural speech, the language as spoken. We desire the words of poetry to follow the natural order. We would write nothing that we might not say in actual life—under emotion.[20]

Nothing that you could not or might not say is a directly expressive proposition. Pound has turned his whole position on the matter of "curial speech" right around since 1912. The ghost of colloquial vulgarity has been exorcised; natural speech, the language <u>as spoken</u>, is a matter of sequence and response, articulation caught up with the concrete experience of existence, rendering itself in an appropriate language, which now possesses some of the specificity of dialect. By extrapolation from this, Pound's clearest formulation of these issues, we can see that natural speech is one of the class of natural objects, and so we can propose a theory whereby the fullest potential recognitions of speech in poetry operate gracefully between melopoeia and logopoeia.

The influence of Hueffer's Preface must have been real enough, I think, in precipitating this sudden coherence of Pound's thought around the motif of natural speech. It is an impressive document, prolix, indirect, very witty, in which Hueffer formulates his characteristic aesthetic purpose: "I may really say that for a quarter of a century I have kept before me one unflinching aim—to register my own times in terms of my own time."[21] He notes the prevalence in English letters of a literary poetic diction in which a word such as "procession", for instance, which can capture a whole range of human existence, religious, military, etc., is proscribed because it is unpoetic, and suggests that this has the effect of excluding certain aspects of life from poetic treatment. The implication of this proposition is that contemporary life is overlooked by poetry and, as a result, the capacity of poetry for the realisation of distinct emotional states is abandoned. "Modern life is so extraordinary, so hazy, so tenuous with, still, such definite and concrete spots in it"; and this is, par excellence, "the Crowd—the Crowd blindly looking for joy or for that most pathetic of all things, the good time."[22] This is all quasi-Hulmean, but dense with a resourceful knowledge and experience which Hulme is entirely without, and leads up to a superb paragraph in which Hueffer spells out the way in which natural objects can be natural symbols.

> …the business of poetry is not sentimentalism so much as the putting of certain realities in certain aspects. The comfrey under the hedge, judged by these standards, is just a plant—but the ash-bucket at dawn is a symbol of poor humanity, of its aspirations, its romance, its ageing and its death. The ashes represent the sociable fires, the god of the hearth, of the slumbering, dawn populations; the orange peels with their bright colours represent all that is left of a little party of the night before, when an alliance between families may have failed to be cemented, or being accomplished may have proved to be a disillusionment or a temporary paradise. The empty tin of infant's food stands for birth; the torn up scrap of a doctor's prescription for death. Yes, even if you wish to sentimentalize, the dustbin is a much safer card to play than the comfrey plant. And, similarly, the anaemic shop-girl at the Exhibition, with her bad teeth and her cheap black frock, is safer than Isolde. She is more to the ground and much more touching.[23]

Hueffer is of course dealing with the processes of symbolisation rather than the manner in which natural objects or images are to be presented with symbolic force. Much of what he says is written more or less as an oblique commentary upon various Poundian texts, but in doing so proclaims a vigorous independence which Hueffer's current disclaimers of any real commitment to or aptitude for the writing of poetry, although ironic, sustain in a paradoxical way. Hueffer's comments on language are particularly interesting.

> But it is better to see life in terms of one damn thing after another, vulgar as is the phraseology or even the attitude, than to render it in terms of withering gourds and other poetic paraphernalia. It is, in fact, better to be vulgar than affected, at any rate if you practise poetry.[24]

> The actual language—the vernacular employed—is a secondary matter. I prefer personally the language of my own day, a language

clear enough for certain matters, employing slang where slang is felicitous and vulgarity where it seems to me that vulgarity is the only weapon against dullness.[25]

These attitudes never fully permeate Pound's arguments in favour of the prose tradition. We need to distinguish, I think, between two ways in which speech qualities can function in a poem. The use of the quality of speech utterance as an expressive resource among other resources at the poet's command, which is the emphasis Pound gives throughout his discussion of this subject, is a matter which can be dealt with at Pound's preferred level of technique. The "resembling unlikeness" Pound spoke of in 1912 is not so very unlike this. Against such an expressive use of speech qualities we may set Hueffer's sense of speech as a substantive criterion, actual, contemporary, non-imitative and non-resembling. It is possible to see in this traces of an earlier dramatic form of poetic structure, the persona rearing its head some time after Pound had abandoned it as a determining imaginative convention, but such a regressive tendency is offset by the way in which speech is a non-resembling mode implies a poetics based on the direct and sincere utterance of the poet and all that is in his mind.

Such a distinction within the aesthetic criterion of speech parallels a distinction which needs to be drawn, as I suggested towards the end of the previous chapter, between the Hulmean image and the Poundian image or, as it was later to become, the ideogram. Both images are intensive structures. Hulme's is conceived in terms of an intensity of experience, occasional and unitary, which demands expression in poetry, but a poetry which will, so as not to traduce the modality of the source experience, ordain for itself an equivalent intensity of expression. This intensity will be structural. Pound's image, on the other hand, is in itself the primary intensive unit, presenting a complex which may be quite scattered and heterodox in its source impulses. Pound never loses contact with an artistic impulse towards transcendence, which will lift and liberate the reader, freeing him from temporal and spatial limits. Hulme's notion of the poet in a "physical state" is the exact converse of this. Fenellosa's ideogram, from this point of view, was exquisitely opportune for Pound, and gave him more than a straightforward corroboration of widely-held theories pertaining to concrete particulars, for it implied a method whereby disparately derived elements could be combined in a significant, "instantaneous", and potentially large-scale sequence. By about the time he left London for Paris Pound had more or less completed his development as a poetic theorist. Although he continued to be active as a critic, the manner in which he did so was different. He was no longer mulling over ideas, allowing them to develop without much appearance of deliberate guidance, often in response to the dense artistic milieu of which he was a part; instead he repeats himself, elaborates ideas from his earlier phase, presenting his discoveries in technique now as the substantive elements of poetry, rather than as a means of deploying and organising such elements. The ideogrammatic method presents itself, in Pound, not just as an equivalent means for expressing the essential character of one's experience, but as a universal grammar equivalent to the structure of the world. (This is quite unlike anything Hulme ever thought. For him the only unity the world possessed was to be sought in the consciousness of an individual. Pound sets off from a similarly idealist position, but by a process of hypostatisation has more or less converted it to the substance of the rational universe of the Enlightenment). Technique as an expressive means is geared to the intrinsic structures of human experience and communication-systems; Pound's ideogram is an intellectual postulate for incorporating the world. The implications of such a method which serves also as a structure enabled Pound to recuperate the vague and tenuously mystical propositions of his very first poems, "The Tree", for instance, and "La Fraisne", and to transpose them into a cosmology of the timeless, the recurrent, and the metamorphic. What happens in the *Cantos*, and makes them such an interesting work, of major importance, is that the ideogram as a structural device is married with the whole range of compositional techniques which Pound had earlier isolated and defined. Pound's prosody is one which consists of the articulation of all natural phonological objects, the total sound of the poem, real time, real stress, real singing, and resists the intellectual tendency of the *Cantos* towards a condition of contingent absolutism. These realities are, in a sense, symbols equal in weight to the Tempio or the Bank, and while they do not shape the overall form of the *Cantos*, they do shape each passage, and thereby sustain the complete structure. I do not want to allow myself to be drawn into the argument about the overall structure and intellectual coherence of the *Cantos*, the relation of the parts to the whole, since such is not in the least my concern in this essay, but I would maintain, and it is the purpose of this essay to advance demands of this sort for any reading of a poem, that the large issues of form cannot be properly discussed without taking into account the question of the poem's prosody, all the way down to the level of the individual syllable.

§ § §

Given the ideogram as a quasi-syntactic device, sustained in sequential language by a resourceful prosody, it is clear that Pound turned his back on speech as a syntactic and constitutive function of a poem; a syntactic function in the sense that it organises meaning, "one damn thing after another" in Hueffer's sense. Yet speech as such is nothing if it is not a matter of words presented in sequential order, as Coleridge recognised in passing in his censure of Wordsworth. "We do not adopt the language of a class by the mere adoption of such words exclusively, as that class would use, or at least understand; but likewise by following the <u>order</u>, in which the words of such men are wont to succeed each other. Now this order, in the intercourse of uneducated men, is distinguished from the diction of their superiors in knowledge and power, by the greater <u>disjunction</u> and <u>separation</u> in the component parts of that, whatever it be, which they wish to communicate."[26]

Coleridge goes on to talk of the want of what he terms "surview" in the discourse of the uneducated, and it is clear that the order he is talking about is a rhetorical one, that induced in his discourse by a man who can "foresee the whole of what he is to convey."[27] The point Coleridge is at pains to make is that the organisation of a poem such as "The Thorn" is dramatically inappropriate in terms of the supposed narrator of the poem. Coleridge assumes that there is a natural scale of organisational complexity in language, which functions as an index of a speaker's knowledge and power. I, on the other hand, would propose a distinction between a superinduced rhetorical order of argument or exposition, and a natural speech order in which no interval occurs between the sequence of words and the perception they embody. Direct and immediate expression in this sense does not mean that word order and syntax precede perception, or vice versa, but that the two are coterminous. This in turn does not commit one to a theory of spontaneous and momentary expression, but means that however a given form of words is arrived at, just so is the condition of their author's perception. We do not see the man behind the words, with the message mediating between him and us; rather, the man is in his words, is his words even.

This kind of distinction between modes of ordering language is obviously similar to the distinction between prose and poetry made by Hulme, but it has a much older pedigree. In his prose treatise *De Vulgari Eloquentia* Dante, who inherited Arnaut Daniel's care for the individual qualities of words, the combed and the shaggy, makes just such a distinction in a remarkable way, relating it not merely to the uses but also to the acquisition of language.

…we say at once that we call the Vulgar Tongue that to which children are accustomed by those who are about them when they first begin to distinguish sounds; or, to put it more shortly, we say that the Vulgar Tongue is that which we acquire without any rule, by imitating our nurses. We afterwards have another secondary speech, which the Romans called Grammar. And this secondary speech the Greeks also have, as well as others, but not all. Few, however, acquire the use of this secondary speech, because we can only be guided and instructed in it by the expenditure of much time, and assiduous study. Of these two kinds of speech also, the Vulgar Tongue is the nobler, as well because it was the first employed by the human race, as because the whole world makes use of it, though it has been divided into different forms of utterance and words. It is also the nobler as being natural to us, whereas the other is rather of an artificial kind; and it is of this nobler form of speech that we intend to treat.[28]

It is like William Carlos Williams' speech of Polish mothers. Dante himself adds "we have for the most part given the name of poets to those who write verse in the Vulgar Tongue."[29] The order of natural language (which should not be confused with any notion of the natural order of language) is not merely conventional or casual, but carries with it a quasi-genetic power, in which the individual is put in touch with his most intimate and immediate, primary life. Dante's distinction is both like and unlike Hulme's, for he does not offer intensity of experience as a privileged and occasional moment of contact with a special reality, the prairie or the illuminated city; nature is not placed <u>over there</u>, but is felt close to, things are natural to us. Like Wordsworth but unlike Coleridge, Dante does not invent arbitrary distinctions for a non-technical purpose. Speech in the sense that I am trying to describe here can enter poetry as an element of technique, or as an expressive means, but it is also, and fundamentally, like to poetry in what it does. Pound was never sure how his absolute rhythm was able to be expressive of emotion, never clear as to whether it was something in the reader or something in the poem that brought about a response to the congruence of toneless phrase and emotion. If the inter-relationship is more than merely casual then some correspondence is implied between the qualities of poetry and those of speech. The correspondence may be one of identity, as in the extreme theory put forward by Flint, or it may derive from some more submerged parallels in structure, so that it is possible to conceive of poetry as possessing a dependent but separate existence from speech. In "The Serious Artist" Pound contemplates briefly how far back such a correspondence will take us.

> You wish to communicate an idea and its concomitant emotions, or an emotion and its concomitant idea, or a sensation and its derivative emotions, or an impression that is emotive, etc. etc. etc. You begin with the yeowl and the bark, and you develop into the dance and into music, and into music with words, and finally into words with music, and finally into words with a faint adumbration of music, words suggestive of music, words measured, or words in a rhythm that preserves some accurate trait of the emotive impression, or of the sheer character of the fostering or parental emotion.[30]

From this point of view the correspondence has its seat in a phylogenetic source which the poet is able to tap. It is of interest to set beside this a musicologist's theories concerning the source of rhythm. In <u>Rhythm and Tempo</u> Curt Sachs suggests that musical rhythm has its ultimate source in body movements. He controverts the affective theory of dance, that it is inspired by the power of music, and maintains that the rhythmic patterns of dance music are derived from the patterns of the dance which it accompanies.

> Organized in regular patterns, motor impulses pass from the moving limbs to the accompanying music, only to revert from voices, clappers, and drums as a stronger stimulus to the legs and torsos of those who dance. For in Heusler's words, "the recurrence of equal sections of time stimulates our muscle sense." Often, music seems to be in the lead: melody begins, and the dancers follow as if obeying the rhythm and tempo imposed on them by the singers and players. This is quite customary among North American Indians. Actually, the musical introduction only anticipates the usual rhythm and tempo of the well-known, often performed movements of the dancers.[31]

Over against the phylogenetic and archetypal emphasis of Pound, with its emphasis on the position of the individual in a racial or cultural history, we may set an ontogenetic correspondence, which places the individual in touch with his personal growth, his immediate and temporal environment. Ontogeny recapitulates phylogeny in the sense that the embryo passes through the morphological stages of development appropriate to is species, but racial memory in this sense is incorporated into physiological process. Again, we are shown a rhythmic source which lies outside language itself, and exists in dialect as the product of the diastolic rhythm of the heart-beat and the sum of local particulars of landscape and climate and work. Herbert Read discusses some of the implications of a view such as this in a passage which he added to the text of *Form in Modern Poetry* (1932) when he reprinted it as part of his *Collected Essays in Literary Criticism*.

> If, then, we are to substitute for the concepts of measure (that is, for regular, accented feet) a concept of rhythm dependent on nothing but its own innate rightness as tested by the ear, we must enquire more closely into the nature and origins of such rhythms. How are they come by? The conventional metrist will say that at any rate in the case of Shakespeare and Milton, and even in the case of Arnold, they are variations on the basis of a regular measure. But this is casuistry, for all rhythm, even the rhythm of prose and speech, is only perceptible by contract to a hypothetical norm of reality—a uniform temporal beat or simple iambic sequence. Certainly all free verse of rhythmical structure is related to such a norm or basis. But actually no rhythms are consciously constructed by a system of normal measurements: they are rather spontaneous sense perceptions. And any comparative study of rhythms reveals the fact that they are relative. They vary from age to age and from language to language. Chinese and Polynesian rhythms are perceptible to us, but they are foreign to our habits. English rhythms have a good deal in common with Germanic rhythms, but both are quite different from French or Spanish rhythms. Even within the limits of our own language, if we observe carefully purely local dictions, we find surprisingly different rhythms. A man from Newcastle and a man from Hull speak in entirely different <u>tempi</u>. But we must beware of a loose connotation of the word "rhythm", which is best kept for aesthetic effects. We can, however, resort to the word "idiom", so aptly used by Daniel. A living language analyses into idioms: idioms are the live organisations of speech—words are molecules and letters atoms. Now this organic unit, this idiom, is instinct with

rhythm: it has irrefrangible intonation, and poetic rhythm is but the extension and aggregation of these primary rhythms. Even measured, regularly accented verse is successful only in so far as it makes use of or accommodates itself to these idioms. Free verse, which includes the slightest as well as the widest divergence from regular pattern, is but the free use of these idioms.

Idioms arise out of the contacts of daily life. They are the response of the human organism to the elements around it. They reflect the speed of life, the pressure of life, its very essence. Idioms are the vocal chimings-in of man in the rhythm of life, and have their parallels in the beating of drums and the dancing of limbs. All the arts are built up from these primary elements, and their reality, their actuality, depends on this strict relation. To build up poetry with dead idioms is like living a life of dead habits and obsolete manners.[32]

One wishes that Herbert Read had desisted from using the word "rhythm" in a loose fashion somewhat earlier in this passage. It might appear at first sight that Read is putting forward the argument which runs counter to the one which I was advancing in the previous chapter, but in fact the simple norm of which he talks is a pre-metrical standard. When Read says that poetic rhythms are not "constructed by a system of normal measurements", but are "spontaneous sense perceptions" he is not of course ruling out the composition of metrical verse, but insists that it is the verse instance which will be the product of sense perception, and not the verse pattern. It is when he talks about idiom, however, that Read becomes seriously interesting; idiom here is not a matter of local variations of diction merely, but the whole feel and pulse of a local speech. If the idioms of Newcastle and Hull are so distinct and yet contain in themselves the bases of authentic poetic rhythms, the question we must ask ourselves is how these idioms are measured or registered in verse. We can assume, that is, that Read is not discussing regional or dialect literature, and that the problem takes place within a common written convention. This is a problem in part of perception, which I shall attempt to deal with in the final chapter of this essay, which it is important to register for the time being because it suggests ways in which the issues of speech quality in poetry are not to be understood as exclusively technical and formal.

§ § §

If speech contains within itself the insistence that we consider the matter of speech communities and environments, the poet who opens up these issues to the fullest is William Carlos Williams. Long before he discovered the concept of the American idiom, Williams had his finger on the complexities at issue in his insistence on what he called "contact". In the Prologue to *Kora in Hell*, dated 1918, in a long article "Belly Music" published as a supplement to the final issue of *Others* in 1919, and in his "Comment" on the first issue of his own magazine *Contact*, published in the second issue in 1921, Williams prods at his own impatience with the domestic American artistic and critical milieu, and at the same time elaborates, in a very indirect way, his own sense of the grounds and present needs of American art. The localism which Williams at times seems to be advocating is a quite different affair to the nativism of a poet like Sandburg; the intrinsic value of American subjects is in no way part of Williams' argument. For Williams, in each of these articles, only that art which is new is of value. Like Pound, and like Hulme in some respects, Williams' notions of poetic structure are based on the notion of accuracy of perception, and the expression of the individual character of objects. "The true value is that peculiarity which gives an object a character by itself."[33] Where Williams differs from Pound and Hulme though, and this is a point of the utmost importance, is in shearing off from the idea of expression the function of communication. This has the effect of short-circuiting, so to speak, the epistemic or perceptual transaction, which instead of taking place between two poles, and applying to the poem a message-bearing criterion, is now located in that faculty for which Williams appropriated the name of the imagination. For Williams there was an antagonism between the functions of the senses and those of the imagination which created the necessity for a ragged, discontinuous form of discourse. Williams describes a perceptual phenomenon rather like the notion of "drift" which communications engineers today use to describe intensity fluctuations of biological transducers (the kind of phenomenon, that is, which would explain the non-conscious or inattentive lacing of boots which Hulme mentions.)

> The associational or sentimental value is the false. Its imposition is due to lack of imagination, to an easy lateral sliding. The attention has been held too rigid on the one plane instead of following a more flexible, jagged resort. It is to loosen the attention, my attention since I occupy part of the field, that I wrote these improvisations....

The imagination goes from one thing to another. Given many things of nearly totally divergent natures but possessing one thousandth part of a quality in common, provided that be new, distinguished, these things belong to an imaginary category and not in a gross natural array. To me this is the gist of the whole matter. It is easy to fall under the spell of a certain mode, especially if it be remote of origin, leaving thus certain of its members essential to a reconstruction of its significance permanently lost in an impenetrable mist of time. But the good thing that stands eternally in the way of really good writing is always one: the virtual impossibility of lifting to the imagination those things which lie under the direct scrutiny of the senses, close to the nose. It is this difficulty that sets a value upon all works of art and makes them a necessity. The senses witnessing what is permanently before them in detail see a finality which they cling to in despair, not knowing which way to turn. Thus the so-called natural or scientific array becomes fixed, the walking devil of modern life. He who even nicks the solidity of this apparition does a piece of work superior to that of Hercules when he cleaned the Augean stables.[34]

That which is permanently before the senses does not exclude the inventive imagination; the two have to find a means to co-exist. It is of interest to set this dialectical pairing alongside the idea, which Williams set out in a letter to the *Egoist* in response to Dora Marsden's "Lingual Psychology" articles, of complementary male and female psychologies, the one abstract and tending to drunkenness, the other real and of the earth.[35] Williams incorporates into the Prologue to *Kora in Hell*, as part of his argument, some of the "Improvisations" from the main text.

> The virtue of strength lies not in the grossness of the fiber but in the fiber itself. Thus a poem is tough by no quality it borrows from a logical recital of events nor from the events themselves but solely from that attenuated power which draws perhaps many broken things into a dance giving them thus a full being.[36]

> Rich as are the gifts of the imagination bitterness of world's loss is not replaced thereby. On the contrary it is intensified, resembling thus possession itself. But he who has no power of the imagination cannot even know the full of his injury.

VIII. No. 3. Those who permit their senses to be despoiled of the things under their noses by stories of all manner of things removed and unattainable are of frail imagination. Idiots, it is true nothing is possessed save by dint of that vigorous conception of its perfections which is the imagination's special province but neither is anything possessed which is not extant.[37]

In <u>Others</u> Williams makes it clear that it is not the object which interests him; it is necessary, but it is the registration of an object's impact in the mind that testifies in art to its presence. A man writes "to free himself, to annihilate every machine, every science, to escape defiant through consciousness and accuracy of emotional expression."[38] It is not that "these things make a damned bit of difference to any one, especially to a poet, but because they stick unconsciously in a man's crop and pervert his meaning unless he have them sufficiently at his fingers' tips to be ware of them."[39]

BUT has he a vision into the desolate PRESENT. Love, yes, but love as it is affected by the violence of present day thought: music, yes, but music as it is affected by the present day revelations concerning the dead or living idolatries of yesterday. I don't give a damn about airplanes and airplane poetry but I do give a damn about the distraught brain that must find its release in building gas motors and in balancing them on cloth wings in its agony.[40]

I am not one damned bit interested in socialism or anarchy but I am interested and deeply interested in the brain that requires socialism and anarchy and brings it on, just as I am interested in morbidity—a release, an assertion, a necessary release an imperative assertion.[41]

Under the pressure of these ideas about poetic resources and the means of their expression, which he must struggle to define, Williams does not need to give any explicit attention to the question of idiom, which is for all practical purposes able to be subsumed by the idea of free verse.[42] Where he comes closest to such explicit attention is at the crux of his sense of the difference between American and European poetic means. After remarking that Pound is "the best enemy United States verse has. He is interested, passionately interested—even if he doesn't know what he is talking about," Williams goes on to characterise the potential of the

American context, for which there is no "associational or sentimental value," and which is thus new.

> The accordances of which Americans have the parts and the colors but not the completions before them pass beyond the attempts of his thought. It is a middle-ageing blight of the imagination.[43]

Williams's impatience with Pound, and his total rejection of Eliot and all that he stood for as he saw it, is not at this point a rejection of Europe, but a rejection of any search after old values, even if in renewal. In Williams' view it is not value (or intensity) which is primary; by the same token beauty is a distraction, the mere singing of peasants. It is a new object that alone can create the conditions in which value can flourish, and it is in this respect that the difference of Williams' position to that occupied by Hulme and Pound is most acute. So for Williams, in his "Comment" on the first ten page number of *Contact*, necessities become quite clear. Starting off from the instance of Joyce's writing, which "forces me, before I can follow him, to separate the words from the printed page, to take them up into a world where the imagination is at play and where the words are no more than titles under the illustrations", Williams can say that Joyce's is a classical method without traducing his own demand for novelty.

> It is a reaffirmation of the forever-sought freedom of truth from usage. It is the modern world emerging among the living ancients by paying attention to the immediacy of its own contact; a classical method.

> And in proportion as a man has bestirred himself to become awake to his own locality he will perceive more and more of what is disclosed and find himself in a position to make the necessary translations. The disclosures will then and only then come to him as reality, as joy, as release. For these men communicate with each other and strive to invent new devices. But he who does not know his own world, in whatever confused form it may be, must either stupidly fail to learn from foreign work or stupidly swallow it without knowing how to judge of its essential value. Descending each his own branch man and man reach finally a common trunk of understanding.[44]

Williams's insistence on locality (not localism) becomes in his poetry and other imaginative writings, a means of resisting the crass depredations of the ordinary environment, which is only transformed when it is lifted to the imagination. The usual comparison of Williams's view of place and Eliot's dictum that "Place is only place" needs to be reversed if we are to understand the emphasis of Williams's earlier views.[45] In *Four Quartets* Eliot's places are all special, dense with a history which reaches down into the present-day of the poet's imagination, whereas for Williams, in the passage just quoted, place is wherever a man happens to be, and possesses no special qualities except those which reside in the imaginative perception of it.

§ § §

In this and the previous chapter I have attempted to articulate an argument about the nature of free verse, suggesting that its structure is best understood as one which proceeds along complementary axes of musical and speech progressions, and that these can be seen as technical devices which interact to generate a potentially infinite variety of verse conventions. The one, poetry as an art of rhythmical composition, embodies a tendency to develop to the detriment of the qualities of poetry as speech, while at the same time providing various means for ensuring the formal integrity of the verse line; the other, poetry as speech, offers a non-musical and natural restraint to purely rhythmic qualities, and suggests ways in which poetry can literally be a direct mode of expression, without interval between word and thought. The metrical conventions of traditional English verse have the capacity to obscure such organisational features from the perception of the unprepared reader. In the following chapters I shall discuss a number of the theoretical statements about English prosody which have been made since the mid-Sixteenth Century which, I believe, can be of use in dismantling an inherited metrical conditioning of an incomplete literary history.

NOTES

1   The point at issue here is that of word order rather than that of diction.

2   See, for example, R.F. Jones, *The Triumph of the English Language*, Stanford 1952.

3   "A Lecture on Modern Poetry", op. cit., p. 268.

4   T. E. Hulme, "Romanticism and Classicism", *Speculations*, ed. Herbert Read, London 1924, p. 136.

5   "Bergson's Theory of Art", ibid., p. 166.

6   "A Lecture on Modern Poetry", op. cit., pp. 268-269.

7   Herbert Read, *English Prose Style*, London 1928.

8   F. S. Flint, *Otherworld: Cadences*, London 1920, p. v.

9   Ibid., p. viii.

10 Ibid., pp. xi-xii.

11 Ezra Pound, "I Gather the Limbs of Osiris, XI", *The New Age*, (Feb 15, 1912), p. 370.

12 Ezra Pound, "Ford Madox (Hueffer) Ford: Obit", *The Nineteenth Century*, CXXVI, (August, 1939), p. 179.

13 *Literary Essays*, pp. 371-377.

14 Ezra Pound, "A Few Don'ts by an Imagiste", *Poetry*, I, vi, pp. 200, 201.

15 Ibid., p. 201.

16 Ibid., p. 204.

17 Ezra Pound, "The Serious Artist, III. Emotion and Poesy", *The New Freewoman*, I, 10, (Nov., 1913), p. 194.

18 *Literary Essays*, p. 375. Hueffer's Preface is substantially based on a series of articles entitled "The Poet's Eye" which he contributed to *The New Freewoman* during 1913.

19 *The Letters of Ezra Pound*, ed. D.D. Paige, London 1951, p. 91. Excerpts from this letter were published as *Correspondence* in *Poetry* VII, pp. 321-322.

20 Quoted from "Lionel Johnson", *Literary Essays*, op. cit., p. 362.

21 F. M. Hueffer, *Collected Poems*, London 1913, p. 13.

22 Ibid., pp. 15, 16.

23 Ibid., p. 17.

24 Ibid., p. 20.

25 Ibid., p. 28.

[26] Samuel Taylor Coleridge, *Biographia Literaria*, ed. J. Shawcross, London 1907. II, pp. 43-44.

[27] Ibid., p. 44.

[28] Dante, *De Vulgari Eloquentia*, English translation by A.G. Ferrers Howell, London 1890, p. 2.

[29] Ibid., p. 55.

[30] Ezra Pound, "The Serious Artist, III. Emotion and Poesy", op. cit., p. 194.

[31] Curt Sachs, *Rhythm and Tempo*, London 1953, pp. 38-39.

[32] Herbert Read, *Collected Essays in Literary Criticism*, London 1938, pp. 54-56.

[33] W. C. Williams, *Kora in Hell* (1920), quoted from Williams, *Imaginations*, NY 1970, p. 14.

[34] Ibid., p. 14.

[35] *The Egoist*, (August, 1917), pp. 110-111.

[36] *Imaginations*, op. cit., pp. 16-17.

[37] Ibid., p. 18.

[38] William Carlos Williams, "Belly Music", *Others*, V, 6, (July 1919), p. 26.

[39] Ibid., p. 27.

[40] Ibid., p. 30.

[41] Ibid., p. 31.

[42] Cf. Ibid., p. 30: "I ask in Christ's name where is someone who knows something about free verse who will point out its excellencies over any other sort in those departments where it possesses such excellencies. Where is an analyst to state the perfections that can be achieved in free verse and no other way? When this has been done, when some ONE American critic has BEGUN to think, then and then only will any man have a right to say that I am a good or a bad poet."

[43] *Imaginations*, pp. 26-27.

[44] William Carlos Williams, "Comment", *Contact* (2), (Jan. 1921), no page numbers.

[45] The expression "Place is only place" occurs in "Ash Wednesday". Cf. Charles Tomlinson's Introduction to *William Carlos Williams, A Critical Anthology*, Harmondsworth 1972, p. 30, for a statement of the usual view of the differences between Williams and Eliot in this respect.

Chapter 4

The Influence of Humanist Notions of Organisation on Sixteenth Century Poetics

In the three previous chapters I outlined two complementary notions about poetic form which, I suggest, activate and define the use made of free verse by its most deliberate and technically alert practitioners. First, that the primary form of poetic organisation (but not necessarily the primary motive, it should be made clear perhaps) is a combination of the phonological qualities of language in patterns which are shaped by adherence and response to natural linguistic features. Second, that the criteria by which such combinations are made are to be discerned embedded deep in the idioms of language, the daily habit of speech. While both of these functions can be reduced to convention (as *occus*, for instance, in the case of metrical verse—the same natural linguistic phenomena underlie both metrical and non-metrical verse), neither can ever be fully accounted for by a single convention, since the establishment of a convention entails the special and exclusive emphasis of selected phonological qualities to serve as the basis for its pattern. In England in the Sixteenth Century, when the vernacular language was struggling to establish itself as the basis for all regular literary and intellectual discourse, in response at least in part to the Reformation and the attendant desire to translate religious texts, there existed no formal convention for poetry. Various attempts were made to establish a coherent structure for the English poetic line from 1540 onward and these can be examined in such a way that they illuminate in a useful, although sometimes oblique way the problems of poetic theory which are brought about when free verse is widely and successfully written.

Dante represents the commonplace medieval view of poetry in *De Vulgari Eloquentia* when he remarks that "we have for the most part given the name of poets to those who write verse in the Vulgar Tongue; and this we have doubtless ventured to say with good reason, because they are in fact poets, if we take a right view of poetry, which is nothing else but a rhetorical composition set to music."[1] This medieval conflation of poetics and rhetoric was a general European phenomenon, which endured well into the Sixteenth Century. A treatise on poetics would to a considerable extent be taken up with a discussion of rhetoric, as is the case for example with J.C. Scaliger's *Poetices Libri Septem* (1561) and George Puttenham's *The Arte of English Poesie* (1589), both of which pay special attention to the various schemes and tropes which fall under the heading *Elocutio*, (Puttenham refers to this as "ornament", and he devotes more than half of his text to it) according to the five-fold division of the *Rhetorica ad Herennium*.

At the same time the art of rhetoric was in a similarly confused state, its sphere of activity transferred from oratory to writing, and its subject matter confused with logic, grammar, and dialectic—a situation which was "reformed" by the intervention of Pierre de la Ramée who, by a process of rationalisation, deprived rhetoric of those operations (*Inventio, Dispositio*, and *Memoria*) which it had shared with logic, and reduced its scope to those two functions (*Elocutio* and *Pronunciatio*) which are in a sense secondary to knowledge.[2] The way in which, in a situation where poetry was understood as versified rhetoric, the treatment of versification was subordinated to the discussion of rhetoric, and tended to be conceptual rather than practical, is typified in the comments of Richard Wills in *De Re Poetica* (1573).

> The origin of metrical form is from God the Creator, in that He created this universe and whatever is contained in its sphere with a fixed design, as it were by measure; to such an extent that Pythagoras has asserted that there is a harmony in celestial and earthly things. For how could the universe exist, unless it were governed by a fixed order and established harmony? Again, all the instruments we use are made with certain proportions—that is, by measure. If this happens by other things, how much more so with language, which gives expression to all things.[3]

Wills is offering a Platonic defence against the tendency of one aspect of Humanist learning to denigrate poetry as an activity which is not directly concerned with knowledge, and he does so in part by adducing a distinction between versifiers (those, citing Horace's *Satires*, Book I, X, "For whom to close a verse with six feet is enough") and poets, who are protected by the muses who are, according to Plato, the interpreters and servitors of the Gods. Dante's definition of poetry as a rhetorical composition set to music suggests more than simply a contingent addition to eloquent words if it is possible to sense behind his idea of music the resources offered by a belief in a cosmic or divine harmony. Wills draws on a correspondence of this sort to explain the basis of the pleasure that is derived from poetry.

Since poetry is speech drawn together, as it were, by a fixed law of measure—in which there is not only a bond of feet, but also a rhythm and harmony—it comes about that there is a wonderful pleasure in the art. The ears of the audience are spellbound by this and their spirits softened, because of the affinity which music has with the human soul.[4]

A similar appeal to pleasure is the basis of Sidney's initial argument in *The Defence of Poesie*. When Sidney notices the discredit into which poetry has fallen "which from almost the highest estimation of learning, is falne to be the laughing stocke of children,"[5] he is making a conventional complaint which already has a pedigree more than half a century long. In *The Boke named the Gouernour* (1531) Sir Thomas Elyot makes a similar complaint from a position which he defends, like Sidney, by an appeal to classical authority.

For the name of a poete, wherat nowe (specially in this realme) men haue suche indignation, that they use onely poetes and poetry in the contempt of eloquence, was in auncient tyme in high estimation: in so moche that all wysdome was supposed to be therein included, and poetry was the first philosophy that euer was knowen: wherby men from their childhode were brought to the raison howe to lyve well, lernynge therby nat onely maners and natural affections, but also the wonderfull werkes of nature, mixting serious mater with thynges that were pleasaunt: as it shall be manifest to them that shall be so fortunate to rede the noble warkes of Plato and Aristotle, wherein he shall finde the autorie of poetes frequently alleged: ye and that more is, in poetes was supposed to be science misticall and inspired, and therefore in latine they were called <u>vates</u>, which worde signifyeth as moch as prophetes. And therefore Tulli in his Tusculane questyons supposeth that a poete can nat abundantly expresse verses sufficient and complete, or that his eloquence may flowe without labour words wel sounyng and plentuouse, without celestiall instinction, which is also by Plato ratified.[6]

To be fully understood this Humanist agitation about the status of poetry needs to be seen partly in the context of a parallel controversy about the expressive resources of the English language: whether it was copious enough for accurate translation; whether it could be used for an eloquent, or merely for an accurate language; how and whether it should borrow words, and so on. Elyot is aware of these questions, as he makes clear in the Preface to his treatise *Of The Knowledge whiche maketh a wise man* (1533).

> His highnesse benignely receyuynge my boke whiche I named the Gouernour, in the redynge therof sone perceyued that I intended to augment our Englyshe tongue, wherby men shulde as well express more abundantly the thynge that they conceyued in theyr hartis (wherefore language was ordained) hauynge words apte for the pourpose: as also interprete out of greke, latyn, or any other tonge into Englyshe, as sufficiently, as out of any one of the said tongues into an other. His grace also perceyued, that through out the boke there was no terme new made by me out of a latine or French worde, but it is there declared so plainly by one mene or other to a diligent reder, that no sentence is therby made derke or harde to be understande.[7]

Elyot's position on this controversy is a typically moderate one, indeed the genuine advocate of inkhorn terms is a phenomenon difficult to actually discover, so that he seems to be a straw man invented for polemic purposes as much as anything.

Whatever position the protagonists in the controversy adopted, however, none of them assumed that the English language could be taken for use simply as it was found. Even such an ardent advocate of the self-sufficiency of the English language as Richard Mulcaster, in his *The First Part of the Elementarie* (1582), argued that language needed to be reduced to rule by discipline and art, and that this took place at "som one period in the tung, of most and best account, and therefore fittest to be made a pattern for others to follow…. Such a period in the English tung I take this to be in our daies, for both the pen and the speche."[8] The humanist who undertook to defend poetry against the charges of his more adamant colleagues felt unable to turn to contemporary example, which was a mere vulgar rhyming, but by considering instead such questions as a measure which was not only a bond of feet but also rhythm and harmony, was able to seek an authority in poetry similar to that offered by Plato's divine sanction, but under a different guise. The heart is a potent figure in such an argument, as is clear from the section "Of Imitation", in Roger Ascham's *The Scholemaster*.

They be not wise, therefore that say, what care I for a mans words and utterance, if his matter and reasons be good. Soch men, say so, not so moch of ignorance, as eyther of some singular pride in themselves, or some special malice or other, or for some private & perciall matter, either in Religion or other kinde of learning. For good and choice meates, be no more requisite for helthie bodies, than proper and apte words be for good matters, and also plaine and sensible utterance for the best and deepest reasons: in which two pointes standeth perfite eloquence, one of the fairest and rarest giftes that God doth geve to man.

Ye know not, what hurt ye do to learning, that care not for words, but for matter, and so make a devorse betwixt the tong and the hart.[9]

The problem was not simply to induce rhythm and harmony into the measures of poetry, but to have to do so with linguistic materials which were in themselves unstable and in need of definition. Just as the Humanist scholar might look to the rhetoric of Cicero or Quintilian as a model for the achievement of eloquence in his native tongue, so he might look to classical example for his understanding of prosodic articulation. In *The Scholemaster* Ascham continues his discussion of the care of words by making an historically-conceived distinction between rhyme and verse which is analogous to the distinction made by Wills.

This matter maketh me gladly remember, my sweete tyme spent at Cambridge, and the pleasant talke which I had oft with M. Cheke, and M. Watson, of this fault, not onely in the olde Latin Poets, but also in our new English Rymers at this day. They wished as Virgil and Horace were not wedded to follow the faultes of former fathers (a shrewd marriage in greater matters) but by right Imitation of the perfit Grecias, had brought Poetrie to perfitnesse also in the Latin tong, that we Englishmen likewise would acknowledge and understand rightfully our rude beggarly ryming, brought first into Italie by Gothes and Hunnes, whan all good verses and all good learning to were destroyd by them: and after caryed into France and Germanie: and at last received into England by men of excellent wit in deede, but of small learning, and lesses judgment in that behalf.

But now, when men know the difference, and have the examples, both of the best and of the worst, surelie, to follow rather the <u>Gothes</u> in Ryming, than the <u>Greekes</u> in trew versifying, were even to eate ackornes with swine, when we may freely eate wheate bread emonges men. In deede, <u>Chauser</u>, <u>Th. Norton</u>, of Bristow, my L. of Surrey, <u>M. Wiat</u>, <u>Th. Phaer</u>, and other Ientlemen, in translating <u>Ovide</u>, <u>Palingenius</u>, and <u>Seneca</u>, have gonne as farre to their great praise, as the copie they followed could carry them; but, if soch good wittes, and forward diligence, had bene directed to follow the best examples, and not have bene caryed by tyme and custome, to content themselves with that barbarous and rude Ryming, emonges their other worthy praises, which they have justly deserved, this had not bene the least, to be counted emonges men of learning and skill, more like unto the Grecians than unto the Gothians, in handling of their verse.[10]

The Humanist contempt for rhyme derives partly from the way it covers up obscurely felt prosodic deficiencies in the line, and partly from the fact that it is associated with the rude and unlearned. Although Ascham comments on the appropriateness of various classical measures to English verse, what he has to say offers little evidence that he understands the structural parallels that are entailed in any such attempt at translation. *Carmen Heroicum* is not appropriate to English because of the preponderance of long monosyllabic words in the language. *Carmen Exametrum* "doth rather trotte and hobble, than runne smoothly in our English tong."[11] And although he believes that *Carmen Iambicum* will be naturally received by English, Ascham's remarks continue to be merely perceptive, disparaging idleness and the disinclination to labour, and admonishing men to be as diligent "in searching out, not onelie just measure in everie meter, as everie ignorant person may easely do, but also trew quantitie in every foote and sillable, as onelie the learned shalbe able to do."[12] Ascham's most discerning critical remarks occur when he discusses translations made without rhyme, such as Surrey's version of Book IV of the *Aeneid*, and it is clear that although he does not understand the phenomena he is looking for he has a sharp sense of the formal qualities at issue. "In deede, they observe just number, and even feete: but here is the fault, that their feete be feete without ioyntes, that is to say, not distinct by trew quantities of sillables: And so, soch feete, be but numme feete: and be, eve as unfitted for a verse to turne and runne roundly withal, as feete of brasse or wood be unweeldie to go well withal."[13] The metaphor of physical articulation is an indicative one, but the most interesting point in Ascham's argument is his feeling that Surrey's feet are "Not distinct by trew quantities of sillables." By "iust number" Ascham means that Surrey has observed the syllabic regularity of his lines, and from this Ascham is able to deduce the notional presence of feet, but he is unable to recognise the articulation of foot to foot, as the line progresses towards its syllabic terminus, because individually and in juxtaposition the syllables possess no distinct features as far as he can discern. Ascham is bringing two distinct standards to bear on the line of verse, one relating to the number of syllables, and the other to their aural contour, and this binary pattern underlies many subsequent Elizabethan treatises on poetry. In Ascham's case we are unable to tell what his response was to the actual phonological qualities of syllables, for whatever he heard is not testified to by the account he presents.

One of the problems facing the advocates of quantitative prosody after the classical model, was that of referring the concept to their experience of their vernacular tongue. The rules governing the determination of quantity in Latin were complex and applicable to a written language; whereas for English both orthography and pronunciation were in an unregulated condition. In a sense the patriotic and scholarly concerns of men like Ascham and Cheke only touch the fringes of poetry, and would be of little interest to the poetic theorist had they not been taken up later by men with a greater stake in the art. The advantage offered by Ascham when one comes to look at the Harvey-Spenser Letters on Reformed Versifying, for example, is that he makes clear the driving forces, formal, structural, and perceptive, which were at work behind the English hexameter craze, which might otherwise appear merely a courtly and scholarly diversion.

§ § §

In his valuable book *The Founding of English Metre* John Thompson argues that the iambic pentameter line typical to English verse was worked out in the Sixteenth Century, and that a line of development between Wyatt and Sidney marks its evolution. For Sidney, he alleges, the iambic foot was a model or imitation of the language itself.[14] The evidence for Thompson's thesis rests in the revisions of a number of Wyatt's lines made by the editor of *Tottel's Miscellany* (1557), which regularised them by introducing more obvious patterns of accentual and syllabic uniformity. For example, Wyatt's line

It was no dreme: I lay brode waking.

becomes in Tottel

It was no dreame: for I lay broade awaking.[15]

Two unstressed syllables have been introduced to regularise the line by separating previously juxtaposed pairs of stressed syllables. Historically, at least, Thompson's argument strikes me as being entirely just. What he shows is that while for the Humanist such as Ascham counted syllables offered no structural means apart from their number, the editor who revised Wyatt's lines, by engineering a natural recurrence of stressed and unstressed syllables, displayed at least an unconscious recognition of the pattern value of the stress phoneme in English, although it is difficult yet to talk about a metrical structure independent of the strict occasion of a verse, since pattern and natural stress are made to coincide exactly. Thompson goes on to argue that identity of metre and language is the prevailing norm of Elizabethan poetry until George Gascoigne in his _Certayne Notes of Instruction concerning the making of verse or ryme in English_ (1575) made it possible, by his insistence that the natural order of English words be adhered to in poetry, for poets to think of metre and speech pattern as independent of each other. Until then, especially in the long line of poulter's measure, the need to observe metrical pattern in the actual language of the poem led to such deformations of a natural word order that poets who wrote in these measures "were encouraged by the form to feel that it was not a bad thing to write verse whose sense mattered very little."[16]

Thompson's whole thesis has such an inexorable historical logic that he is able to deal summarily with the "Reformed Versifying" of Gabriel Harvey, Spenser, and Sidney in a single brief chapter devoted to what he calls "Classical Metres". This is fair enough in view of the way in which Spenser and Sidney eventually developed their prosody, but it enables Thompson to dismiss in a line or two the Campion-Daniel controversy, as though Daniel's appeal to nature was in no way ingenuous. For Thompson, attempts to write in classically derived metres were nothing more than exercises in Humanist nostalgia, performed in ignorance of the true nature of the English language. But what Campion's musical insistence suggests to us, surely, is that submerged beneath the Humanist classicising of Ascham and Harvey, and also of Sidney, is an appeal to a musical concordance between man, poetry, the structure of the cosmos, and the Divine Will, which can explain at least by naming it the nature of the expressive power of poetry. Here I anticipate the substance of my next two chapters. In order to understand the extent of Campion's achievement, and his very real and unprecedented success in achieving a genuine observance of quantity of his poems, it is necessary to consider the kind of difficulties which Harvey encountered in his attempts to write an English hexameter.

Harvey knew Gascoigne's *Certayne Notes of Instruction*; his annotated copy in the Bodleian is the source for the text printed by Gregory Smith in *Elizabethan Critical Essays*. It is worth dwelling on Gascoigne's essay, briefly, for in his urgency to maintain the coherence of his thesis Thompson crudely misrepresents Gascoigne's argument. He maintains that "The iambic foot is the only one that counts for him. The metrical pattern is absolute and admits of no variation whatsoever."[17] Thompson imputes metrical rigidity to Gascoigne (in itself no bad thing in Thompson's book) by quoting out of context Gascoigne's phrase, "We use none other order but a foote of two sillables". Although he has previously quoted the passage in which this statement occurs, Thompson does not appear to have understood its implications. What Gascoigne is saying about metre is governed by the initial precept "And in your verses remember to place every worde in his natural <u>Emphasis</u> or sound, that is to say, in such wise, and with such length of shortnesse, elevation or depression of sillables, as it is commonly pronounced or used."[18] Gascoigne then says that words should be so ordered in verse that the customary iambic metre does not distort this natural emphasis, but his acceptance of the iambic scheme as a norm is more than regretful. This whole passage is of very great interest, and indicates a man who subscribes to the Humanist values of such as Ascham, yet at the same time has a keen professional feel for the actual life of words in English poetry. This leads him to confuse the concepts of accent and quantity, and think in terms of long, short, and indifferent accent. But Gascoigne's examples make his meaning clear enough. The word "treasure", for instance, should have what he calls the grave accent on the first syllable. What we would nowadays speak of as the syllable bearing phonemic stress is clearly identified by Gascoigne, but his ability to express clearly what is at issue is undercut by Humanist propaganda about quantity. Gascoigne continues:

…whereas if it shoulde be written in this sort Treasúre, now were the second sillable long, and that were cleane contrarie to the common use wherewith it is pronounced. For furder explanation hereof, note you that commonly now a dayes in English rimes (for I dare not cal them English verses) we use none other order but a foote of two sillables, wherof the first is depressed or made short, and the second is elevate or made long; and that sound or scanning continueth throughout the verse. We have used in times past other kindes of Meeters, as for example this following:

No wight in this world, that wealth can attayne,

ùnlésse hè bèliéve, thàt áll ìs bùt váyne.

Also our father Chaucer hath used the same libertie in feete and measures that the Latinists do use: and who so ever do peruse and well consider his works, he shall finde that although his lines are not alwayes of one selfe same number of Syllables, yet, being redde by one that hath understanding, the longest verse, and that which hath most Syllables in it, will fall (to the eare) correspondent unto that whiche hath fewest sillables in it: and like wise that whiche hath in it fewest syllables shalbe founde yet to consist of woordes that have such natural sounde, as may seeme equall in length to a verse which hath many moe sillables of lighter accentes. And surely I can lament that wee are fallen into suche a playne and simple manner of writing, that there is none other foote used but one; wherby our Poemes may justly be called Rithmes, and cannot by any right challenge the name of a Verse. But, since it is so, let us take the forde as we finde it, and lette me set down unto you such rules or precepts that even in this playne foote of two syllables you wreste no woorde from his natural and usuall sounde.[19]

Even if, like his sense of quantity, Gascoigne's sense of the correspondence of lines made up of unequal numbers of syllables registers the fact that there is an equal number of stresses in such lines, rather than an actual temporal equality, Gascoigne's argument represents the advantages brought to Humanist poetics by the knowledge of a professional poet. Like the Humanists, he holds rhyme in a certain contempt, remarking "I would exhorte you also to beware of rime without reason: my meaning is hereby that your rime leade you not from your firste Invention."[20] He is traditional also in basing his advice on the rhetorical category of *Inventio*. But in his insistence on adherence to the normal pronunciation of English Gascoigne anticipates the difference between Spenser and Harvey.

The distinction felt by Elizabethan critics between rhymes and verses informs most of their writings throughout the 1580s and on into the beginning of the next decade. What controversy there was revolved around the question of the extent to which classical prosodic rules could be introduced into English, and this involved both the various writers' understanding of the classical rules, and also the extent to which they felt a necessity for introducing an equivalent structure into English verse. From Gascoigne on one discovers an increasingly sophisticated appeal to the authority of the customary usage of English poetry, coupled with the sense that the mysterious classical feet are important because they offer a means of locomotion which rhyme and syllabic regularity on their own did not offer. Thus in her important article "Passing Pitefull Hexameters: A Study of Quantity and Accent in English Renaissance Verse" G.D. Willcock says that "The question of the interior structure of the line becomes a matter of theoretical discussion with the initiation of the Quantity <u>versus</u> Rhyme controversy by that Cambridge circle of Cheke, Watson and their friends from whom Ascham derived his inspiration," and also that "to the Elizabethan the central principle of the native measures was not stress, but rhyme."[21] The extremes of controversy are perhaps represented by William Webbe on the side of classical precedent, and Thomas Nashe on the side of native common sense. Webbe's *Discourse of English Poetrie* (1586) maintains that English verse would "runne upon true quantity and those feete which the Latines use" given practice and good will.[22] New rules could be made up to make English fit a Latin pattern where the disparity between the two languages is significant.

> But some object that our words are nothing resemblaunt in nature to theirs, and therefore not possible to bee framed with any good grace after their use: but cannot we then, as well as the Latines did, alter the cannon of the rule according to the quality of our words, and where our words and theirs wyll agree, there to jumpe with them, where they will not agree, there to establish a rule of our owne to be directed by? Likewise, for the tenor of the verse, might we not (as <u>Horace</u> dyd in the Latine) alter their proportions

to what sortes we listed, and to what we sawe wold best become the nature of the thing handled or the quality of the words?[23]

Webbe's pious respect for "the nature of the thing handled" does not forestall him from concluding that "he that shall with heedfull judgement make tryall of the the English words shall not finde them so grosse or unapt but that they wyll become any one of the most accustomed sortes of Latine or Greeke verses meetely, and run thereon somewhat currantly."[24] Nashe, on the other hand, in his reply to Gabriel Harvey's *Foure Letters and certeine Sonnets*, in which Harvey wishes to be "Epitaphed, the Inventor of the English Hexameter", handles the matter with the assurance of familiarity and control.[25]

> The Hexamiter verse I graunt to be a Gentleman of an auncient house (so is many an English begger); yet this Clyme of ours he cannot thrive in. Our speech is too craggy for him to set his plough in; hee goes twitching and hopping in our language like a man running upon quagmires, up the hill in one Syllable, and down the dale in another, retaining no part of that stately smooth gate which he vaunts himselfe with amongst Greeks and Latins.[26]

Nashe's metaphorical vigour works to good purpose here. He enriches the etymological derivation of verse with his figure of the hexameter plough, and it is apparent that the characteristic of such verse for him consists in an absence of accentual feature. Implicit in Nashe's point of view is the sense that metrical rules are not arbitrary, the subject of pre-election and custom on the part of the first poets, but accord in some way to the natural limitations of language. It is in this that he stands chiefly distinguished from Webbe.

At the centre of the controversy lay the question of the verse foot. It is clear that the Elizabethan ear had great difficulty in perceiving the distinguishing qualities of individual syllables, and in fact did not expect to do so. Gascoigne's notion of emphasis applies to the pronunciation of words, and was directed at a habit which exacted, if we are to go along with Thompson, an artificial pairing of strong and weak stresses without consciously recognising the phenomenon of syllabic stress. It is not until the critical argument in favour of customary usage reaches an exceptional degree of sophistication in Puttenham that we find the conscious recognition of such a principle. In contrast to this runs the attempt of the reformed versifiers to discover the rules which would make English verses adhere to the principles of Latin quantity, by defining syllables as either long or short. Although the idea of the quantitative foot suggests an aural event, defined by actual linguistic usage, the classically-defined rules available to the Elizabethans were based not on usage but on spelling, and as Gabriel Harvey recognised in the *Letters of Reformed Versifying*, uniformity on this score could only have been attained by the application of a standard spelling convention. The way in which Harvey attaches this idea to an insistence that spelling observe the normal pronunciation of words (which Harvey calls "Prosody"—this usage is attested by his annotation of "Emphasis" in his own copy of Gascoigne's *Notes*) shows him ready to move away from the notion of quantitative hexameters.

> I am of Opinion there is no one more regular and justifiable direction, eyther for the assured and infallible Certaintie of our English Artificiall Prosodye particularly, or generally to bring our Language into Arte and to frame a Grammer or Rhetorike thereof, than first of all universally to agree upon ONE AND THE SAME ORTHOGRAPHIE, in all pointes conformable and proportionate to our COMMON NATURAL PROSODYE.[27]

One of the implications of Harvey's point of view is that if English is written as it is pronounced, rather than pronounced as it is written, then the orthographical rules for Latin quantity cannot apply to English. In his first letter to Harvey, Spenser notes that Sidney and Dyer have proclaimed "a general surceasing and silence of balde Rymers, and also of the verie beste to: in steade whereof, they have, by autho(ri)tie of their whole Senate, prescribed certaine Lawes and rules of Quantities of English sillables for English Verse, having had thereof already greate practise, and drawen mee to their faction," so that "I am, of late, more in love wyth my Englishe Versifiying than with Ryming."[28] Spenser also alludes to certain rules for English quantity formulated by Thomas Drant, which some of Harvey's verses apparently failed to observe. Harvey was obviously nettled by this, and in his reply asserts his ignorance of Spenser's "gorbellyed Maisters Rules",[29] and offers some justified censure of Spenser's own attempts at Iambic Trimeter, observing "you have in my fancie somewhat too many SPONDEES beside: and whereas TROCHEE sometime presumeth in the firste place, as namely in the second Verse, Make thy, whyche thy by youre Maistershippes owne authoritie muste needs be short."[30] The terminological confusion endemic in all attempts to discover English rules for quantity reaches its zenith, to my mind, in Spenser's answer to this.

> I like your late English Hexameters so exceedingly well that I also enure my Penne sometime in that kind: whyche I fynd indeede, as I have heard you often defende in worde, neither so harde, nor so harshe, that it will easily and fairely yeelde it selfe to oure Moother tongue. For the onely or chiefest hardnesse, which seemeth, is in the Accente; whyche sometime gapeth, and, as it were, yawneth ilfavouredly, coming shorte of that it should, and sometime exceeding the measure of the Number, as in Carpenter the middle sillable, being used shorte in speache, when it shall be read long in Verse, seemeth like a lame Gosling that draweth one legge after hir: and in Heaven, being used shorte as one sillable, when it is in Verse stretched out with a <u>Diastole</u>, is like a lame Dogge that holds up one legge. But it is to be wonne with Custome, and rough words must be subdued with Use. For why, a Gods name, may not we, as else the Greekes, have the kingdome of oure owne Langauge, and measure our Accentes by the sounde, reserving the quantitie to the Verse?[31]

I differ with Thompson considerably about how this passage should be understood. He maintains that Spenser uses the terms long and short "without any particulat thought of duration, but rather as Gascoigne used these words interchangeably with other terms for accent or stress", and that "Spenser is not proposing to change English speech: he believes we should 'measure our Accentes by the sounds.' He is talking about the adaptation of speech to the metrical pattern."[32] Thompson is surely wrong in believing that Spenser's use of the word "Accente" in this context means the same as stress or metrical accent. When Spenser talks of the accent "coming shorte of that it should" he is, possibly, not talking about real duration, but is certainly referring to the theory according to which syllables are made long by position. Unless, indeed, Spenser is using the word "Accente" in two distinct senses, he means by it something like pronunciation, so that in his final sentence, with its appeal to the notion that the Greeks had the power of election over their syllabic quantities, he is not proposing a binary principle, but identifying "sounds" and "Quantitie" as equal and determinable qualities, implying that these should govern, at least in poetry, our pronunciation. It is only on the basis of such a reading that Harvey's reply is properly intelligible. He picks up the question of the pronunciation of "Carpenter", and it is clear that, whatever the confusion that existed about stress and quantity, neither Spenser nor Harvey is simply hearing stress and calling it length, since the second syllable of the word they argue about is ordinarily both unaccented and pronounced short.

> But hoe I pray you, gentle sirra, a word with you more. In good sooth, and by the faith I bear to the Muses, you shal never have my subscription or consent (though you should charge me wyth the authoritie of five hundredth Maister DRANTS) to make your Carpēnter, our Carpĕnter, an inche longer or bigger than God with his Englishe people have made him. Is there no other Pollicie to pull downe Ryming and set uppe Versifying but you must needs correcte Magnificat: and againste all order of Lawe, and in despite of Custome, forcibly usurpe and tyrannize upon a quiet compannye of words that so farre beyond the memorie of man have so peaceably enjoyed their several Priviledges and Liberties, without any disturbance or the leaste controlment?[33]

It was probably only his attachment to the idea that English verse can be structured by using feet with *natural* proportions that kept Harvey from recognising the phenomenon of stress in English.

Just how artificial were Thomas Drant's rules we can judge from the marginal note on "The rules observed in this Englishe measured verses" attached to the eleventh poem in Sidney's *Old Arcadia* in the St. John's College manuscript. Several of the rules are taken up with special cases, and make the conventional assertions on behalf of English custom in making over words derived from Latin, so that "our language hath a special gifte in altringe theym and making theym our owne."[34] But the more general rules clearly display a notion of quantity which is orthographically dependent.

(1) Consonant before consonant allwayes longe, except a mute and a liquid (as 'refrayne') suche indifferent.

(2) Single consonants commonly shorte, but suche as have a dowble sounde (as 'lāck', 'wĭll' 'tĭll') or suche as the vowel before dothe produce longe (as 'hāte', 'debāte').

(3) Vowel before vowel or dipthonge before vowel allwayes shorte, except suche an exclamacon as 'ōh'; els the dipthonges allwayes longe and the single vowels short,

(4) Because our tonge being full of consonants and monasillables, the vowel slydes away quicklier then in Greeke or Latin, which be full of vowels and longe words; yet are suche vowels longe as the pronounciacon makes longe (as 'glōry', 'lādy'), and suche like as seem to have a dipthonge sownde (as 'shōw', 'blōw', 'dye', 'hye').[35]

From a point of view such as this English possessed many monosyllabic words which could take either long or short quantity, according to convenience. The good sense of Harvey's demand for an agreed orthography becomes obvious.

The extreme exercise of orthographically sanctioned quantity is to be found in Richard Stanyhurst's translation of the <u>Aeneid</u>, in the Dedication to which, addressed to the "Learned Reader", he claims, conventionally, that he "would not wish thee quantitie of syllables too depend so much upon thee gaze of thee eye, as thee censure of thee eare,"[36] but at the same time maintains his right to a considerable freedom of election as regards quantity

> Thee meaner clarcks wyl suppose my travail in these heroical verses too carrye no great difficultie, in that yt lay in my choise too make what word I would short or long, having no English writer before mee in this kind of poetrye with whose squire I should leavel my syllables.[37]

The kind of orthographical liberties Stanyhurst felt were available to him can only be judged from example. The following seven lines describe the activity in Carthage when Aeneas first beholds the city; my scansion is tentative, and based on Stanyhurst's own "prosodia".[38]

> Lyke bēēs / īn sūm/mār sēa/sōn, thrōugh / rūstĭcăl / hāmlĕts
> Thāt flīrt / īn sōōn/bēams, ānd / tōyle wīth / mūttĕrŭs / hūmblīng.
> Whēn thĕy do / fōorth cārr/y thēyre / yōung swārme / flēdggĭe to / gāthrīng:
> Ōr cēls / ār fārc/līng wīth / dūlce ānd / dēlicăte / hōonye:
> Ōr pōrt/ērs būrd/ēns ūnll/oāds, ōr / clūstrĕd in / hēerdswārme
> Fēaze ăwăy / thēe drōane / bēes wīth / stīng, from / māungĕr, ŏr / hīvecŏt,
> Thēe lăbŏr / hōat swēlt/rēth: thēe / cōmbs tyme / flōwrĭe bĕ/ sprīnklēth.[39]

Stanyhurst's rules are such that while they can be followed locally they constantly produce contradictory scansions of similar words; in the third line of my example, for instance, it is impossible to make "they" and "theyre" agree. It is more than likely that Stanyhurst, for much of the time, is following his sense of stress and allowing it to govern his notional quantities. Thus one might expect the rule of position to make the first syllable of "besprinkleth" long (as the first of "unloads" is long, for instance), but as Stanyhurst observes in his Dedication that word accent often shifts in compounds, this must be one of the occasions on which "thee censure of thee eare" holds sway. But at the same time the second syllable of "carry" must be made long by the exigencies of the metre. The alternative being to read the first three feet of the third line as

When they / do foorth / carry theyre

In which case one would expect the vowel in "do" to be doubled. This reading also ignores Stanyhurst's rule about length in diphthongs.

The implication of Harvey's letters to Spenser was that English could only approximate classical verse by an accentual imitation of quantitative feet. Once this is recognised the need to imitate classical feet at all, except for the sake of variety, is abolished, since the English syllabic line could at once be seen as offering an organisation of accentual iambic feet more authentic than Spenser's attempt to write iambics by orthographical rule. In his brief treatment of versifying at the end of *The Defence of Poesie* Sidney distinguishes between ancient and modern versifying, and claims that the modern type, by which he means the customary English verse, in addition to observing rhyme and number (of syllables) also observes accent "very precisely". In this he could be merely paraphrasing Gascoigne's insistence that the natural emphasis of the language be observed in English verse. Sidney's distinction is framed in terms of music: the ancient verse was written, like music, in terms of quantity, the modern, "with his rime striketh a certaine Musicke to the eare: and in fine, since it dooth delight, though by another way, it obtaineth the same purpose."[40]

In the second book of *The Arte of English Poesie* (1589), "Of Proportion Poetical", George Puttenham uses a similar parallel to control the structural distinction between classical and English poetry. Puttenham starts from the axiom that "all things stand by proportion," distinguishing three types, arithmetical, geometrical, and musical, and concludes that poetical proportion "holdeth of the Musical, because as we sayd before

Poesie is a skill to speake & write harmonically: and verses or rime be a kind of Musicall utterance, by reason of a certaine congruitie in sounds pleasing the eare."[41] Puttenham equates number of feet in classical verse with number of syllables in English.[42] For him the foot is a means of dealing with the polysyllabic character of Greek and Latin, and is therefore out of place in monosyllabic Anglo-Saxon.[43] (He later happily contradicts himself, saying that since the Norman conquest English has plenty of native polysyllables).[44] By deriving the word rhyme from the Greek <u>rithmus</u>, "a certaine musicall numerositie in utterance,"[45] Puttenham equates the two forms of harmony without depleting their force by appealing merely to analogous effect as does Sidney, "so as we in abusing this term (ryme) be neverthelesse excusable applying it to another point in Poesie no lesse curious then their <u>rithme</u> or numerositie which in deede passed the whole verse throughout, whereas our concords keepe but the latter end of every verse, or perchaunce the middle and the end of metres that be long."[46] For Puttenham the distinction between verse and rhyme is not an essential one, since both can serve identical ends of harmonious proportion. While he is eclectic enough to devote a chapter to the question "How if all manner of sodaine innovations were not very scandalouse, specially in the laws of any langage or arte, the use of the Greeke and Latine feete might be brought into our vulgar Poesie, and with good grace inough", (and it is clear that Puttenham is not really sure what the natural restraints that language places on prosody are,) he is scrupulous to distinguish in his terminology between long and short syllables and sharp and flat accents. Indeed in an easily overlooked passage discussing the Alexandrine in the chapter "How many sorts od measures we use in our vulgar" Puttenham can be said to display a sense of an accentual rhythm running "the whole verse throughout".

<u>Salomon Davids sonne, king of Jerusalem</u>.

This verse is a very good <u>Alexandrine</u>, but perchaunce woulde have sounded more musically, if the first word had bene a dissillable, or two monosillables and not a trissillable: having his sharpe accent upon the <u>Antepenultima</u> as it hath, by which occasion it runnes like a <u>Dactill</u>, and carries the two later sillables away so speedily as it seems but one foote in our vulgar measure, and by that meanes makes the verse seeme of but eleven sillables, which odnesse is nothing pleasant to the eare. Judge some body whether it would have done better (if it might) have bene sayd thus,

Robóhan Davids sonne king of Jerusalem.

Letting the sharpe accent fall upon <u>bo</u>, or thus

<u>Restóre king Dávids sónne untó Jerusalém</u>

For now the sharpe accent falls upon <u>bo</u>, and so doth it upon the
last in <u>restóre</u>, which was not in th'other verse.[47]

In Puttenham, therefore, the phenomenon of syllabic and word stress is
virtually recognised as a prosodic determinant of equivalent complexity
to classical verses as the Humanist scholar understood them. We can say
that the very simple pattern of alternating weak and strong stress which
enables the Elizabethan to discern word accent as an increment to the
syllabic number of a line, a function which, following Gascoigne, has
its basis in actual speech, led rapidly to the hypostatisation of accent as
a purely metrical phenomenon against which speech contours, brought
into verse for a second time, can be counterpointed in a dramatic fash-
ion. If we may understand the metrical contract in some such way then
an important point is to be made: the way in which the contract is ex-
pressed, and the characteristic advantages of expressive control which it
offers, stand one step removed from the terms in which the contract was
made. The convention can, indeed, be understood as a solution to the
problems of poets whose understanding of quantity in the true sense of
temporal duration was inferior to ours. Even allowing for the argument
that duration is not a significant element (not a suprasegmental phoneme,
in the terms of the structural linguists) in English syllables, not in other
words a speech quality which we have learnt to recognise as structurally
relevant, the two other suprasegmental phonemes recognised in English
in addition to stress, juncture and pitch, are not codified as stress is in the
accentual-syllabic metrical contract.

Although the Humanist hexameter knew nothing of true quantity,
deriving its rules from Latin rather than Greek sources, once poetry and
music are brought together in song real duration makes itself felt.[48] As I
have suggested, Humanist reformed versifying contains submerged within
it an ethical and expressive current based on ideas of cosmic proportion
derived from Plato and Pythagora, which is made explicit in various
attempts made by poets and musicians alike to combine their respective
arts. Sidney's quantitative poems in the *Arcadia*, although based on or-
thographical rather than aural quantity, are described as being sung to a

lute accompaniment "with suche sweetnes as every body wondered, to see suche skill in a shepearde."[49] Sidney's comments on the "ancient" art of writing poetry for music in *The Defence of Poesie* are amplified in a debate between Lalus and Dicus at the end of the First Eclogues in the <u>Arcadia</u>.

> Dicus said that since verses had ther chefe ornament, if not eand, in musicke, those which were just appropriated to musicke did best obtain ether ende, or at lest were the most adorned: but those must needs most agree with musicke, since musicke standing principally upon the sound and the quantitie, to answere the sound they brought words, and to answer the quantity they brought measure. So that for every sem[i]brefe or minam, it had his silable latched unto it with a long foote or a short foote, wheron they drew on certaine names (as dactylus, spondeus, troacheas, etc.), and without wresting the word did as it were kindly accompanie the time, so that eyther by [the] tune a poet should straight know how every word should be measured unto it, or by the verse as soone find out the full quantity of the musicke. Besides that it hath in it self a kind (as a man may well call it) of secret musicke, since by the measure one may perceive some verses running with a high note fit for great matters, some with a light foote fit for no greater than amorous conceytes.[50]

Dicus goes on to censure rhymes which only observe a rule of syllabic uniformity, saying that they do not give adequate guidance to musical setting. The precept that in setting words to music the musical notes should follow the quality of the words is a commonplace of late Sixteenth Century music. In *A Plain and Easy Introduction to Practical Music* (1597) Thomas Morley, paraphrasing Gioseffe Zarlino's *Institutioni armoniche*,[51] put it as follows.

> Now having discoursed unto you the composition of three, four, five, and six parts with these few ways of canons and catches, it followeth to show you how to dispose your music according to the nature of the words which you are therein to express, as whatsoever matter it be which you have in hand such a kind of music must you frame to it. You must therefore, if you have a grave matter, apply a grave kind of music to it; if a merry subject you must make your music also merry, for it will be a great absurdity to use a sad harmony to a merry matter or a merry harmony to a sad, lamentable, or tragical ditty.[52]

Sidney's "secret Musicke" and Morley's "framing" (which for him embraces a fully-fledged principle of visual imitation, so that the notes ascend on the musical stave when the text refers to height or heaven) can all be traced back to a passage in *The Republic*.

> "But this you are able to determine—that seemliness and unseemliness are attendant upon the good rhythm and the bad." "Of course." "And, further, that good rhythm and bad rhythm accompany, the one fair diction, assimilating itself thereto, and the other the opposite and so of the apt and the unapt, if, as we were just now saying, the rhythm and harmony follow the words and not the words these." "They certainly must follow the words," he said. "And what of the manner of the diction, and the speech?" said I. "Do they not follow and conform to the disposition of the soul?" "Of course." "And all the rest of the diction?" "Yes." "Good speech, then good accord, and good grace, and good rhythm wait upon a good disposition, not that weakness of head which we euphemistically style goodness of heart, but the truly good and fair disposition of the character and the mind."[53]

In medieval and renaissance music the study of this concordance between the soul of man and the cosmos was the sphere of a separate discipline of Speculative Music, while Practical Music dealt with such topics as the accommodation of the musical setting to a text. In its most extreme form, in the settings of the vernacular psalters with easily singable tunes designed not to obscure the intelligible pronunciation of the text, allocating a single note to each syllable, and in the reform of the Chant in the Roman liturgy, the new Humanist subservience of music to words served quasi-utilitarian ends. But in the Florentine "Camerata" of Giovanni de'Bardi, and the Academy of Jean-Antoine de Baïf, Practical Music is made subservient to the expressive needs of a text, in a Platonic fashion, for more exalted ends. The letters patent of de Baïf's *Académie de poésie et de musique* propose the following aims.

> Afin de remettre en visage la Musique selon sa perfection, qui est de representer la parole en chant accomply de son harmonie & melodie, qui consistent au choix, regle des voix, sons & accords bien accommodez pour faire l'effet selon que le sens de la letter le requiert, ou resserrant ou desserrant, ou accroississant l'esprit, renouellant aussi l'ancienne façon de composer Vers mesurez pour

y accommoder le chant pareillement mesuré selon l'Art Metrique. Afin aussi que par ce moyen les esprits des Auditeurs accoustumez et dresses à la Musique par forme de ses membres, se composent pour ester capables de plus haute connoissance, après qu'ils seront repurgez de ce qui pourroit leur rester de la barbarie.[54]

It need not matter to us that the proportions between musical intervals, the human soul, and nature, which speculative music professes to be universal and innate, might be based on a fallacious misapprehension of cultural evidence.[55] The point is that the concept of such a proportion could be applied to the very real effect, frequently pleasurable, which music has on people, and be used to underwrite a theory of textual accompaniment which would be a more coherent rendering of the conventional Horatian pairing of instruction and pleasure. For while, according to the authority of Plato, the formation of music comes from the mind by way of a man's words, it is the power of music, both in itself and in its congruence to a text, that is able to move us. In its most potent form, when music and language are indissolubly bonded together, and bearing in mind that for Plato there are also bad rhythms and bad harmonies, the description of such a process as we find it in John Case's *The Praise of Musicke* (1586) is not as circular as it might appear.

> For it cannot be but as the convenience and agreement which musicke hath with our nature, is the cause of the delectation thereof: so the pleasure and delectation is also the cause of those effects which it worketh as well in the minds and bodies of them that heare it.[56]

I think we can best understand what Campion was trying to do in his *Observations in the Art of English Poesie* (1602) which is too often written off as an anachronous final manifestation of reformed versifying controversy, if we see him as a poet whose compositional practices are deeply irradiated by the habit of setting music to words, and writing words capable of being set to music, in accordance to the concepts of speculative and practical music which I have just been discussing.

In his *Observations* Campion makes the customary Humanist comments in praise of music and in dispraise of rhyme and, in his arbitration of quantitative feet in English, as might be expected, pays heed both to native language qualities and the rule of position: "But above all the accent of the words is diligently to be observ'd, for chiefly by the accent in any language the true value of the sillables is to be measured. Neither can I remember any impediment except position that can alter any sillable in our English verse."[57] None of these ideas is particularly remarkable either for its originality or force of expression, and one infers that, like Harvey, Campion is thinking basically in terms of an accentual imitation of quantitative feet. Indeed one might question Campion's whole purpose by setting his arguments beside a statement which he made, the year before, in his preface "To the Reader" to Philip Rosseter's *A Book of Ayres* (1601).

> The Lyricke Poets among the Greekes and Latines were first inventers of Ayres, tying themselves strictly to the number, and value of their sillables, of which sort, you shall find here onely one song in Sapphicke verse; the rest are after the fascion of the time, eare-pleasing rimes without Arte.[58]

By referring the idea of artificial verse to the music of the Greeks and Latins Campion displays the influence of that strain of humanist thought initiated by de'Bardi and de Baïf. The English Air, set for a single voice with lute accompaniment, which effectively superseded the Madrigal, set in parts according to dance rhythms, marks the accomplishment of that musical revolution which John Stevens writes of, revolution being "not too strong a word to describe the change from a musical aesthetic based on 'number' to one based on 'word'—a change which tended to reverse the traditional roles of music and poetry, making the former mistress now the servant."[59] Campion's statement of intention in the preface "To the Reader" to his *Two Bookes of Ayres*, "In these English Ayres, I have chiefly aymed to couple my Words and Notes lovingly together, which will be much for him to doe that hath not power over both,"[60] suggests a union of the two arts equal to that proclaimed by the "Académie de poésie et de musique", with no pedantic insistence on one note to one syllable in the musical setting, so that it is possible to think of the music in independence, not slavishly expressing the text, but both carrying it and being coloured by the tonal quality of the words.

It is a feeling such as this for the implications of poetic quantity which makes Campion's *Observations* so interesting. His approach to the subject is not far from the traditional Humanist standpoint of art, but by way of an analogy with music, and an insistence upon the importance of proportion. In this respect Campion's approach is reminiscent of that of

Puttenham, but unlike Puttenham, who uses it largely to secure a dubious historical sanction for rhyme, Campion has his eye set on the phenomena of measure and motion. Thus Campion embeds the customary observation that syllable and note should be proportionately set in a context which substantially modifies the point behind the conventional precept.

> Number is <u>discrete quantitas</u>; so that when we speake simply of number, we intend only the dissever'd quantity; but when we speake of a Poeme written in number, we consider not only the distinct number of the sillables, but also their value, which is contained in the length or shortnes of their sound. As in Musick we do not say a straine of so many notes, but so many sem'briefes (though sometimes there are no more notes than sem'briefes), so in a verse the numeration of the sillables is not so much to be observed, as their waite and due proportion. In joining of words to harmony there is nothing more offensive to the eare then to place a long sillable with a short note, or a short sillable with a long note, though in the last the vowel often beares it out. The world is made by Simmetry and proportion, and is in that respect compared to Musick, and Musick to Poetry: for <u>Terence saith</u>, speaking of Poets, <u>artem qui tractant musicam</u>, confounding musick and Poetry together. What musick can there be where there is no proportion observed?[61]

Instead of talking about syllables in terms of an essentially ideal concept of length, but attending instead to their "waite and due proportion", Campion suggests something entirely novel about the question of quantity. Although the rules for quantity which he appends to his examples are entirely conventional, Campion's preliminary description of quantity is sanctioned by an appeal to the ear which endows it with more than merely instrumental functions.

> The eare is a rationall sence and a chiefe judge of proportion; but in our kind of riming what proportion is there kept where there remains such a confused inequalitie of sillables?[62]

The direction of quantity, as Campion understands it, is towards real time. for him the verse line is not an aggregate unit made up of separate syllabic quantities. Rather, the line itself is a unit of measured time, given contour and movement by the succession of syllables and words which it exemplifies. From this point of view the reciprocity of musical or real time and the tonal qualities of syllables and words in combination is an absolute for which the rational sense of the ear is the ultimate standard.

> I have observed, and so may any one that is either practis'd in singing, or hath a natural eare able to time a song, that the Latine verses of sixe feete, as the <u>Heroick</u> and <u>Iambick</u>, or of five feet, as the <u>Trochaick</u>, are in nature all of the same length of sound with our English verses of five feete; for either of them being tim'd with the hand, <u>quinque perficiunt tempora</u>, they fill up the quantity (as it were) of five sem'briefs;[63]

> The cause why these verses differing in feete yield the same length of sound, is by reason of some rests which either the necessity of the numbers of the heaviness of the sillables do beget. For we find in musick that oftentimes the straines of a song cannot be reduct to true number without some rests prefix in the beginning and middle, as also at the close if need requires. Besides, our English monasillables enforce many breathings which no doubt greatly lengthen a verse, so that it is no wonder if for these reasons our English verses of five feete hold pace with the <u>Latines</u> of sixe.[64]

Campion's quarrel with rhyme is not general, but with "our kind of riming". We can trust his ear for time and language to generate lines with none of the tongue-twisting and accent-wrenching of the reformed versifying, and to use rhyme to do more than merely indicate the end of a line. Campion's poems possess a formality independent of the music which he set to them, and do not depend on the musical time values for their movement and rest; Campion's argument that the Air is a type of epigram does, perhaps, influence the typically logical progression of his syntax, but the tautness of his verbal structure does not depend on argument alone. The seventh poem from *The Third Booke of Ayres* is in no way atypical.

> Kinde are her answeres,
>   But her performance keeps no day;
> Breaks time, as dancers
>   From their own Musicke when they stray:
>   All her free favors

And smooth words wing my hopes in vaine.
O did ever voice so sweet but only faine?
        Can true love yield such delay,
        Converting joy to pain?

        Lost is our freedome,
        When we submit to women so:
Why doe we need them,
        When in their best they worke our woe?
        There is no wisedome
Can alter ends, by Fate prefix.
O why is the good of man with evill mixt?
        Never were days yet cal'd two,
        But one night went betwixt.[65]

Thw whole art of this poem lies in a subtle balance or proportion of passage to passage, and this technical perfection, among other things, runs congruent both to the exposition of the poem's argument and to the argument itself, in which the broken harmony of human behaviour is healed by the invocation of the diurnal harmony of nature. Practical and speculative music, in a sense, are in control of the poem at all points. The balance of two syllabically irregular strophes (5, 8, 5, 8, 5, 8, 11, 7, 6, see footnote 65) is the immediately apparent artifice of the poem, a balance due in part, although not in its accomplishment, to a musical exigence, the Air being a strophic form in which the musical setting is recurrent from strophe to strophe. But there is a principle of balance at work within the strophe itself, the first two pairs of lines repeat a syllabic figure, which is also revealed to be a figure of alternate rhyme, and this parallelism is recapitulated in the musical setting. The syllabic figure is repeated a second time in lines five and six, without however repeating the second of the two rhymes, but the force of the repetition is undercut as it gives way to the next line which rhymes with the line which carried the second part of the now dissolved syllabic figure. This strange line of eleven syllables, framed in each strophe as a generalising question, is in a sense the logical turning point of each step in the poem's argument. The eighth line supplies us the pair-rhyme from the syllabic figure which we had expected in line six, and the strophe is brought to a close with the obtrusive rhyme from lines six and seven. Puttenham discusses proportionate rhyming of this sort, of course, but only in relation to syllabically constant lines.

If we attempt to scan Campion's lines we encounter problems which become more complex as the strophe continues. The first six lines of each strophe, if read for normal word stress, can be scanned as a version of what Campion called licentiate iambic, lines which begin with a trochaic inversion and then modulate into a standard iambic rising rhythm. From this point of view, if one runs the first two pairs of lines together as two long lines with internal rhymes, the trochaic inversion at the beginning of lines two and four is ironed out, but this does not solve the problem of the unaccented syllables which Campion so dearly loves to tack on to the ends of lines in an ametrical fashion, which are in this way merely shifted from the ends of lines one and three and given a home, with an anapaestic shuffle, over the second "her" and "their". But the final three lines of each strophe obdurately resist any clear attribution of stress pattern, partly because there are proportionately fewer words of more than one syllable, and thereby requiring stress definition, than there are in the previous lines of each strophe, and partly because of a sense of the duration of vowel sounds fostered by the absence of many defining terminal and labial consonants.

Campion's rhyme scheme, therefore, is not defined by any definite syllabic or accentual pattern. One might almost say that the rhymes were placed as they are for merely conventional reasons. This is not, in fact, the case for two reasons. The perfect rhymes, occurring as they do, help to resolve the careful attention Campion pays to the array of vowel sounds within the line (in the first strophe for instance, one might note the succession of "e" vowels, her, answers, her, per- and for-, keeps, Breaks, dancers, their, they, stray, her, free, words,, ever, sweet, true, yield, delay, Convert-, which have combined with the "r"s to draw in associated tones), and at the same time define the various pauses and enjambments which are embedded in the poem's continuous literal time, the caesura in line three, which is also an expressive pause, contrasting with the run over of lines five and six. The point I am making about this poem of Campion's, the best qualities of which are perhaps musical in an entirely different sense to that which Davie attaches to the word, is that it owes its high degree of formality to a principle of balance which is invested in the poem's structure at several different levels, syllable, phrase, and strophe, and that to accomplish this high level of art, in the Humanist sense, he has been guided by linguistic elements such as tone and juncture, in addition to normally observed stress, and been freed thereby from the ideal complexities of metrical pattern and significant variation thereupon. Campion's power to generalise does not derive from a framework of dramatic particularity, as it ought to according to Winters's arguments. The specific situation of the poem, in fact, depends on an unattached pronoun, "her", (Campion's Latin epigrams are, in comparison, much more "specifically" framed), and his generalisations are sustained by a disposition towards the coherent structure of experience, and that which is experienced, which in this case is abstract perhaps (speculative music distantly acknowledged) but not, strictly speaking, conceptual.

NOTES

[1] Dante, op. cit., p. 55

[2] For the medieval identification of poetic and rhetoric, see J.W.H. Atkins, *English Literary Criticism: The Renaissance*, London 1947, p. 69. On the Ramist reforms, see W.S. Howell, *Logic and Rhetoric in England 1500-1700*, Princeton, N.J., 1956. Rosemund Tuve, *Elizabethan and Metaphysical Imagery*, Chicago 1947, pp. 331-353, discusses the application of Ramist logic to English poetry.

[3] Richard Wills, *De Re Poetica*, translated and edited from the edition of 1573, by A.D.S. Fowler, Oxford 1958. Wills draws on Scaliger for much of his narrative; the passage quoted being derived in turn from Polydore Vergil.

[4] Ibid., p. 89.

[5] "The Defense of Poesie", *The Prose Works of Sir Philip Sidney*, ed. Albert Feuillerat, Cambridge 1912, III, p. 4.

[6] Sir Thomas Elyot, *The Boke named the Governour*, ed. H.H.S. Croft, London 1880, pp. 121-122.

[7] Sir Thomas Elyot, Of the Knowledge which maketh a wise man, London 1533. For a discussion of the controversy about the capacity of the English language for expressive purposes, see R.F. Jones, op. cit.

[8] Richard Mulcaster, *The First Part of the Elementarie*, ed. E.T. Campagnac, Oxford 1925, p. 83.

[9] Roger Ascham, "The Scholemaster", *English Works*, ed. W.A. Wright, Cambridge 1904, p. 265.

[10] Ibid., p. 289.

[11] Ibid., p. 290.

[12] Ibid., p. 290.

[13] Ibid., p. 291.

[14] See John Thompson, *The Founding of English Metre*, London 1961, p. 152.

"His achievement was to recognise the symbolic elements he worked with."
Thompson follows the Trager-Smith analysis of four degrees of English speech
stress phoneme, and maintains that the English iambic foot involves a recog-
nition of the presence of all four degrees of stress. The iambic foot therefore,
he argues, is an imitation of the essential patterns of the language, and enables
the poet to use his language as material.

[15] Both lines quoted from Thompson, op. cit., p. 15.

[16] Ibid., p. 36.

[17] Ibid., p. 73.

[18] George Gascoigne, "Certayne Notes of Instruction", in *Elizabethan Critical Essays*, ed. Gregory Smith, Oxford 1904, I, p. 49.

[19] Ibid., pp. 49-50.

[20] Ibid., p. 51.

[21] G.D. Willcock, "Passing Pitefull Hexameters: A Study of Quantity and Accent in English Renaissance Verse", MLR, XXIX (1934), pp. 1, 7.

[22] William Webbe, "A Discourse of English Poetrie", Gregory Smith, op. cit., p. 278.

[23] Ibid., p. 279.

[24] Ibid., p. 279.

[25] Gabriel Harvey, *Foure Letters and certeine Sonnets...* ed. G.B. Harrison, London 1922, p. 32.

[26] Thomas Nashe, "Strange News of the intercepting Certaine Letters...", Gregory Smith, op. cit., II, p. 240.

[27] Gabriel Harvey, "A Gallant Familiar Letter, Containing an Answer to that of M. Immerito, with Sundry Proper Examples and Some Precepts of our English Reformed Versifying", Gregory Smith, op. cit., I, p. 102.

[28] Edmund Spenser, "To the Worshipfull His Very Singular Good Friend, Maister G.H., Fellow in Trinitie Hall in Cambridge", Gregory Smith, op. cit., I, p. 89.

[29] Gabriel Harvey, "To My Verie Friende M. Immerito", Gregory Smith, op. cit., I, p. 97.

[30] Ibid., p. 95.

[31] Edmund Spenser, "To My Long Approved and Singular Good Frende, Master G.H.", Gregory Smith, op. cit., I, pp. 99-100.

[32] Thompson, op. cit., pp. 132, 133.

[33] Gabriel Harvey, "A Gallant Familiar Letter...", op. cit., p.117.

[34] These rules are printed in full in the Commentary to Poem 11 in *The Old Arcadia*, in *The Poems of Sir Philip Sidney*, ed. W.A. Ringler, Oxford 1962, pp. 389-394.

[35] Ibid., p. 391.

[36] Richard Stanyhurst, "Too thee Learned Reader", Gregory Smith, op. cit., I, p. 146.

[37] Ibid., p. 137.

[38] Ibid., p. 146.

[39] Richard Stanyhurst's Aeneis, ed. D. van der Haar, Amsterdam 1933, Bk. I, II. 434-440.

[40] The Prose Works of Sir Philip Sidney, op. cit., III, p. 44.

[41] George Puttenham, The Arte of English Poesie, ed. G.D. Willcock and Alice Walker, Cambridge 1936, p. 64.

[42] Ibid., p. 66.

[43] Ibid., p. 67.

[44] Ibid., p. 70.

[45] Ibid., p. 69.

[46] Ibid., pp. 77-78.

[47] Ibid., p. 73.

[48] The consensus of opinion appears to be that although Greek and Latin verse share the same organisation of prosodic structure, quantity was actualised only in Greek verse, and was notional in Latin, thus requiring to be defined by an orthographical convention. See James W. Halpron, et al., The Metres of Greek and Latin Poetry, London 1963.

[49] "The Countess of Pembroke's Arcadia", The Prose Works of Sir Philip Sidney, op. cit., IV, p. 75.

[50] This passage is deleted from all but two early MSS. of the Old Arcadia, and is printed in Ringler, op. cit., pp. 389-390.

[51] The relevant passages from Zarlino's Instituzioni armoniche are printed in Oliver Strunk, Source Readings in Music History, NY 1950, pp. 255-261.

[52] Thomas Morley, A Plain and Easy Introduction to Practical Music, ed. R. Alec Harmon, London 1952, p. 290.

[53] Quoted in Strunk, op. cit., p. 7.

[54] Quoted from F.A. Yates, The French Academies of the Sixteenth Century, London 1947, p. 320. See also Giovanni de' Bardi, "Discourse on Ancient Music and Good Singing", in Strunk, op. cit., pp. 290-301.

[55] See, for instance, John Hollander, The Untuning of the Sky, Ideas of Music in English Poetry, 1500-1700, pp. 15-16. Also, W.D. Allen, Philosophies of Music History, A Study of General Histories of Music 1600-1960, second (corrected edition, NY 1962, Ch. 2, "The Controversial Background".

[56] John Case, *The Praise of Musicke*, Oxford 1586, p. 54.

[57] *Campion's Works*, ed. Percival Vivian, Oxford 1909, p. 53.

[58] Ibid., p. 4. Campion contributed twenty-one songs to Rosseter's *Booke of Ayres*.

[59] John Stevens, "The Elizabethan Madrigal, 'Perfect Marriage' or 'Uneasy Flirtation', *Essays and Studies* (n.s.), II, p. 19.

[60] *Campion's Works*, op. cit., p. 115.

[61] Ibid., p. 35.

[62] Ibid., p. 36.

[63] Ibid., p. 39.

[64] Ibid., p. 39-40.

[65] Ibid., pp. 163-164. I have, however, followed the lineation given by Walter Davis in his edition of *The Works of Thomas Campion*, London 1969, printing the phrase "and smooth words" as part of l. 6 rather than as a continuation of l. 5, an emendation which clarifies the regularity of the syllabic and rhyming pattern in each strophe.

Chapter 5

The Harmony of the World and the Harmony of Verse: An Idea in Degradation

In Samuel Daniel's refutation of Campion's *Observations* we see the codification of norms of syllabic and accentual regularity, coupled with rhyme, which were to be the prevailing standard of poetic harmony in the best English verse until Coleridge wrote, in his Preface to "Christabel", that the metre of the poem was "not, properly speaking, irregular, though it may seem so from its being founded on a new principle: namely, that of counting in each line the accents, not the syllables. Though the latter may vary from seven to twelve, yet in each line the accents will be found to be only four. Nevertheless, this occasional variation in number of syllables is not introduced wantonly, or for the mere ends of convenience, but in correspondence with some transition in the nature of the imagery or passion."[1] I shall discuss in a later chapter how the notion of accent rather than syllabic regularity emerged as a prosodic determinant during the course of the Eighteenth Century. In the previous chapter I argued that a classicising Humanism, hampered by a very sketchy understanding of the nature of language, had attempted to promulgate a complex mode of verse structure in which the line was more than a division of a larger rhetorical and logical structure, marked by syllabic regularity and end rhyme; and that its appeal to a classical and quantitative structure, backed by a sense of the correspondence of poetry and music in the art of the Greeks, as witnessed by Plato, in conjunction with the essentially theological notions of speculative music, offered an explanation of the expressive powers of poetry. from this point of view poetry, music, and rhetoric are not concerned with essentially different ends, and we can understand the argument of such a commonplace writer as Henry Peacham in *The Compleat Gentleman*.

> Yea, in my opinion, no Rhetoricke more perswadeth, or hath greater power over the mind: nay, hath not Musicke her figures, the same with Rhetorique? What is a revert but her Antistrophe? her reports, but sweet Anaphora's? her counterchange of points, Antimetabole's? her passionate Aires but Prosopopaea's? with infinite other of the same nature.[2]

Peacham concludes that music is among those arts which are "the fountains of our lives good and happinesse: since it is a principall meanes of glorifying our mercifull Creator, it heightens our devotion, it gives delight and ease to our travailes, it expelleth sadnesse and heavinesse of Spirit, preserveth people in concord and amity, allayeth fiercenesse, and anger; and lastly, is the best Phisicke for many melancholy diseases."[3] These various powerful effects of music, all of them conceived primarily as performing a regulatory function, were understood as deriving from an orderly and expressive universe, the proportions of which were the subject of speculative music. Such is the universe we see assumed by John Hoskyns in his *Directions For Speech and Style.*

> The Conceipts of the minde are pictures of things and the Tongue is Interpreter of those pictures; The order of Gods Creatures in themselves is not only admirable & glorious, but eloquent, then he that could apprehend the consequence of things in their truth and utter his apprehensions as truly, were a right Orator.[4]

In this and the next chapter I shall be dealing with the breakdown of the theory that music expressed a harmony which was a key to the structure of the universe, and the effect of this idea, in its decadence, on the theory of poetry.

§ § §

It would be possible to measure the consolidation of Daniel's viewpoint by the gradual impoverishment of the idea of prosodic harmony, which for Samuel Johnson was entirely a matter of the placing of metrical accent, so that in all iambic measures "the accents are to be placed on even syllables; and every line considered by itself is more harmonious, as this rule is more strictly observed."[5] In Daniel's *A Defence of Ryme* (1603) greater care is taken to preserve the notion of harmony but, as in Puttenham, the idea is now taken to describe an effect rather than a significant structure, as is apparent from the disregard shown for the criterion of proportion which lies at the heart of the Platonic view.

> And for our Ryme (which is an excellencie added to this worke
> of measure, and a Harmonie, farre happier than any proportion

Antiquitie could ever shew us) dooth adde more grace, and hath more of delight than ever bare numbers, howsoever they can be formed to runne in our slow language, can possibly yield. Which, whether it be deriv'd of <u>Rhythmus</u>, or of <u>Romance</u> which were songs the <u>Bards</u> & <u>Druydes</u> about Tymes used, & therof were called <u>Remensi</u> as some Italians hold; or howsoever, it is likewise number and harmonie of words, consisting of an agreeing sound in the last silables of severall verses, giving both to the Eare and Eccho of delightfull report & to the Memorie a deeper impression of what is delivered therein. For as Greeke and Latine verse consists of the number and quantitie of sillables, so doth the English verse of measure and accent. And though it doth not strictly observe long and short sillables, yet it most religiously respects the accent: and as the short and the long make number, so the Acute and grave accent yeelde harmonie: And harmonie is likewise number, so that the English verse then hath number, measure and harmonie in the best proportion of Musicke. Which being more certain & more resounding, works that effect of motion with as happy successe as either the Greek or Latin.[6]

Daniel's harmony lies in the pairing of rhymes and of accented and unaccented syllables ("the Acute and grave accent yeelde harmonie"), and a primary skill in verse has to do with the correct placing of accents within the line.

> But every Versifier that wel observes his worke, finds in our language, without these unnecessary precepts, what numbers best fitte the Nature of her Idiome, and the proper places destined to such accents, as she will not let in, to any other rooms then into those for which they were borne. As for example, you cannot make this fall into the right sound of a Verse,

> <u>None thinks reward rendred worthy his worth</u> :

> unlesse you thus misplace the accent upon <u>Rendrèd</u> and <u>Worthìe</u>, contrary to the nature of these words: which sheweth that two feminine numbers (or Trochies, if so you wil call them) will not succeede in the third and fourth place of the Verse. And so likewise in this case,

5. The Harmony of the World and the Harmony of Verse

Though Death doth consume, yet Virtue preserves,

it wil not be a Verse, though it hath the just sillables, without the same number in the second, and the altering of the fourth place, in this sorte:

<u>Though Death doth ruine, Virtue yet preserves</u>.[7]

Daniel's verse examples are borrowed by Joshua Poole in *The English Parnassus: or, A Helpe to English Poesie* (1657), who adds a comment of his own. "This discovers of what consequence the exact observation of the accent is, which, like right <u>time</u> in <u>Musick</u>, produces harmony, the want of it harshnesse, and discord."[8] Poole's treatise is an interesting example of a compromise between opposed critical attitudes. He grafts on to Daniel's argument that "we are equally the children of <u>Nature</u>" his own version of the quarrel between the Ancients and the Moderns, suggesting that the powers which he attributes to poetry in the following passage, in a conventional enough fashion, are derived not from nature but from art.

> We are then to note, that as the world became more and more civilized, <u>Harmony</u>, I mean that of speech and mutual expression one to another, grew more and more into reputation. Hence it is that those languages are considered as the most refined that are most susceptible to <u>Harmony</u>, and those most savouring of incivility and <u>barbarisme</u>, wherein a man cannot express himselfe without harshnesse and discord. This harmony, in <u>prose</u>, consists in an exact placing of the accent, and an accurate <u>disposition</u> of the words; such as delighting the ear, doth in a manner captivate the passions and the understanding. Of this, strange instances might be made of the ancient <u>Orators</u>, who may be said to lead the people whither they pleased. In <u>Poesie</u>, it consists beside the aforesaid conditions of Prose in <u>measure</u>, <u>proportion</u> and <u>Rhime</u>.[9]

Harmony here is felt to be in a sense coincident with civilisation, but not identified with it, since the refinement with which Poole is concerned is something to which languages are variously susceptible. The Horatian delight, of which Sidney wrote for instance, and which was independent of the didactic purpose of a discourse, is made by Poole to be part of the process of intelligibility, since the passions and the understanding, it is implied, operate in similar ways. The ear for Poole is not in itself the rational sense it is for Campion, but a mechanical source of pleasure.

Thomas Hobbe's reply to Davenant displays more cogently still the force of customary sanction which the accentual and syllabic metrical form was acquiring. In the Preface to *Gondibert: An Heroick Poem*, addressed to Hobbes, Davenant had defended his use of an unconventional verse form.

> I shall say little, why I have chosen my interwoven <u>Stanza</u> of four, though I am not oblig'd to excuse the choice; for numbers in verse must, like distinct kinds of Musick, be expos'd to the uncertain and different taste of several ears. Yet I may declare, that I believ'd it would be more pleasant to the Reader, in a Work of length, to give this respite or pause, between every <u>Stanza</u> (having endeavour'd that each should contain a period) than to run him out of breath with continu'd <u>Couplets</u>. Nor doth alternate Rhyme by any lowliness of cadence, make the sound less Heroick, but rather adapt it to a plain and stately composing of Musick; and the brevity of the <u>Stanza</u> renders it less subtile to the Composer, and more easie to the Singer; which in <u>stilo recitativo</u>, when the song is long, is chiefly requisite.[10]

Davenant adds that the poem might be sung at village feasts, though not before monarchs, and supposes a kind of immortality thereby. "For so… did <u>Homer's</u> Spirit, long after his bodies rest, wander in musick about <u>Greece</u>."[11] In his reply, Hobbes takes up the question of Greek song, and his comments show the extent to which the issue which had inspired the Sixteenth Century Humanists had become a matter of conventional indifference.

> There is besides the grace of style, another cause Why the ancient poets chose to write in measured language, which is this. Their poems were made at first with intention to have them sung, as well Epick as Dramatick (which custom hath been long time laid aside, but began to be revived in part, of late years in <u>Italie</u>) and could not be made commensurable to the Voice of Instruments in Prose; the ways and motions thereof are so uncertain and undistinguished, (like the way and motion of a Ship in the Sea) as not only to discompose the best Composers, but also to disappoint sometimes the most attentive Reader, and put him to

hunt counter for the sense. It was therefore necessarie for Poets in those times, to write in Verse.

> The Verse which the <u>Greeks</u> and <u>Latines</u>, (considering the nature of their own languages) found by experience most grave, and for an Epique Poem most decent, was their <u>Hexameter</u>; a Verse limited, not onely in the length of the line, but also in the quantitie of the syllables. In stead of which we use the line of ten syllables, recompensing the neglect of their quantitie, with the diligence of Rime. And this measure is so proper for an Heroique Poem, as without some loss of gravitie and dignitie, it was never changed. A longer is not far from ill Prose, and a shorter, is a kind of whisking (you know) like the unlacing , rather than the singing of a Muse.[12]

Hobbes's argument that rhyme is a functional equivalent for quantity, and that it is sanctioned by the nature of the language, is conventional enough; the precedents for it are to be found in Puttenham and Daniel. What is interesting to note is the way in which the force of the customary criteria of rhythm and syllabic regularity is now sustained by an appeal to decorum and propriety, an argument which contains within itself the means for subverting any direct appeal to natural sanction for prosodic structure.

The extreme of banality which the general codification of the metrical norm which I am describing finally reached is to be seen in Edward Bysshe's very popular handbook *The Art of English Poetry*, first published in 1702, which went through many subsequent editions. Hogarth's painting "The Distressed Poet" in the City Art Gallery at Birmingham displays his subject, in a garret, searching for inspiration with a copy of Bysshe in his hand.

> The Structure of our Verses, whether Blank, or in Rhyme, consists in a certain Number of Syllables; not in Feet compos'd of long and short Syllables, as the Verses of the <u>Greeks</u> and <u>Romans</u>. And though some ingenious Persons formerly puzzled themselves in prescribing Rules for the Quantity of <u>English</u> Syllables, and, in Imitation of the *Latins*, compos'd Verses by the measure of <u>Spondees</u>, <u>Dactyls</u>, &c. yet the Success of their Undertaking has fully evinc'd the Vainness of their Attempt, and given ground to suspect they had not thoroughly weigh'd what the Genius of our Language would bear; nor reflected that each Tongue has its

peculiar Beauties, and that what is agreeable and natural to one, is very often disagreeable, nay inconsistent with another. But that Design being now wholly exploded, it is sufficient to have mentioned it.[13]

Bysshe does not explicitly insist on a principle of accentual regularity. He points out that "'tis not enough that Verses have their just Number of Syllables; the true Harmony of them depends on a dual Observation of Accent and Pause."[14] Accent for him is a linguistic rather than a metrical phenomenon, which he defines as "an Elevation or a falling of the Voice on a certain Syllable of a Word",[15] which is used as a guide for the occurrence of pause which is "a Rest or Stop that is made in pronouncing the Verse, and that divides it, as it were into Two Parts;"[16] pause being "determin'd by the Seat of the Accent; but if the Accents happen to be equally strong on the 2nd, 4th, and 6th Syllables of a Verse, the Sense and Construction of the Words must be the guide to the Observation of the Pause."

§ § §

The general tendency of the "Modern" prosodic tendency which I have been describing, which received corroboration of a sort from Boileau's *L'Art Poétique*, is to see verse as a necessary constituent of poetry. Where variation is sanctioned it is to avoid monotony and the consequent loss of the reader's attention.[17] There were few dissenting voices.[18] Milton's note on "The Verse" prefixed to *Paradise Lost* revives briefly the Humanist censure of rhyme, which he rejects chiefly for the impediment it sets between the poet and the just expression of his thought.

> The Measure is English Heroic Verse without Rime, as that of Homer in Greek, and of Virgil in Latin; Rime being no necessary Adjunct or true Ornament of Poem or good Verse, in longer Words especially, but the Invention of a barbarous Age, to set off wretched matter and lame Meeter; grac't indeed since by the use of some famous modern Poets, carried away by Custom, but much to their own vexation, hindrance and constraint to express many things otherwise, and for the most part worse than else they would have exprest them. Not without cause therefore some both Italian and Spanish Poets of prime note have rejected

5. The Harmony of the World and the Harmony of Verse

Rime both in longer and shorter Works, as have also long since our best <u>English</u> Tragedies, as a thing of it self, to all judicious eares, trivial and of no true musical delight; which consists only in apt Numbers, fit quantity of Syllables, and the Sense variously drawn out from one Verse into another, not in the jingling sound of like endings, a fault avoyded by the learned Ancients both in Poetry and all good Oratory. This neglect then of Rime so little is to be taken for a defect, though it may seem so perhaps to vulgar Readers, that it rather is to be esteem'd an example set, the first in <u>English</u>, of ancient liberty recover'd to Heroic Poem from the throublesom and modern bondage of Rimeing.[19]

Milton either ignores or rejects the argument that rhyme, according to the nature of English, is an equivalent harmony to quantity. His attachment is not to the Humanist desire to realise an English quantitative verse, but rather to the Platonic insistence that music should follow the sense of the text. Milton adheres to a syllabic norm, but "apt Numbers" and "fit quantity of Syllables" are not tautologous. For Campion to say a poem was written "in number" meant that one took account not only of the number of syllables but also their relative weights; for Puttenham, quantity in English referred to the number of syllables in a verse. What Milton means by "fit quantity of Syllables" therefore is a recognition of an orthodox norm of syllabic regularity, whereas "apt Numbers" suggests a consonance between the tenor of movement of the verse and its sense which, "variously drawn out", is not simply the employment of a principle of easy variation, but suggests a more extensive sympathetic movement between verse and argument.

The same anti-Modern spirit is displayed by Samuel Woodford in the Preface to his *A Paraphrase upon the Psalm of David*, published in the same year as *Paradise Lost*. Woodford, in the tradition of speculative music, reaffirms the connection between theology and poetry, "For if one has been lookt on as continuing the Will and Pleasure, the other no less has been reckoned the Stile, and Language of Heaven. Musick and Numbers, the chiefest of the Liberal Arts, serve but as Hand-maids to this Great and All-commanding Mistriss."[20] Woodford identifies the professions of the Divine and the Poet, they are both "Vates" in Latin. He believes in divine inspiration, and moving on from this is able to establish a requirement for flexibility of expression in verse which owes nothing to any theory of pleasing or elegant variation.

And he who finds not in himself these hidden Mines of Invention, and most happy and unaffected Facility, which only make the Poet, should never be persuaded by me to attempt the ravishing of her by force, whom by fair means he cannot allure to be his Mistriss. For to what but this may we attribute those many lame, and imperfect draughts of poems, both Originals, and Translations, which are to be seen in almost every language? Where, if they have been the Author's own, they are his bare thoughts and lifeless Prose (for I speak now especially of Modern Poesy) made worse by the uneasy shackles of confining Metre: and if versions so exactly laboured <u>ad</u> <u>verbum</u>, that what by the unlucky transposing of words, what by leaving out some little particles, wherein the grace of the sentence did consist, they lose all their former beauty, and from excellent Prose, though the language continue the same, degenerate into very indifferent and untuneable Rhyme. This has been a failing so general, that I need not seek to illustrate it by examples. But none in my opinion have been so guilty of this, as those, who have had for their argument some excellent piece of Scripture, or pious matter, which with the embellishments of Art, and the true Poet's easiness, and invention would, upon the most durable foundations, have made the fairest super-structures in the World. But how miserably have the greatest part been overseen, whilst all their pains have been bestow'd to compose a few ill-contriv'd Cadences, putting themselves to an unimaginable torture to make those conceptions intolerable by the straitness of verse, which else might have done well enough in looser Prose.[21]

The idea of lifeless prose lurking within confining metre is remarkably close to Hulme's discussion of the cosmetic nature of regular verse. For Woodford divine inspiration and the true poet's facility and easiness are still mediated by the rhetorical faculty of Invention. The purpose of verse, in this particular context, is to be singable ("tuneable"), returning inspiration to its divine source; while bad verse does not even have the virtues of prose in rendering sense. It is interesting to note that according to this theory the verse (and by analogy, musical setting) does not follow directly from the scriptural or pious text in an imitative fashion, but is related to it by art, in an apt fashion we might say, by virtue of a common derivation in Divine or poetic inspiration.

Milton and Woodford maintain into the second half of the Seventeenth Century the potency of those ideas of cosmic and human harmony which lie behind the discipline of speculative music. For them poetry is allied to music in common actions of understanding and praise which exemplify the harmonious and proportionate bonds which relate the various parts of the divine creation to one another in an orderly fashion. From such a Platonic point of view knowledge is pre-existent in the world, and made accessible by introspection and examination of the mind's processes rather than by an empirical investigation of natural phenomena. The later development of the aesthetic of the passions and the affections, in which music and poetry are allied in the sensuous influence they exert on the human frame, influencing the mind through the mechanics of associational knowledge, can only be understood when set against the breakdown of a previous theory with which it holds many terms in common.

By an historical paradox the Platonic ideal of music and verse in harmony which the Ancients wished to revive in the opposition to a complex, mathematically based polyphonic music gave rise to the very theory of expressive powers, in the passionately conceived solo Air or recitative, which brought about the disregard of traditional speculative music as musicians turned their attention exclusively to the practical mode, and loosened the voice from its affiliation to human music and the theory according to which the human voice was an instrument superior to any other. Speculative music, dealing with those proportions induced by divine reason, by which human and cosmic music were held in a metaphysical relationship, is a concept which reaches back through to the arithmetical proportions of the Pythagoreans. One of the chief sources of information concerning these beliefs for medieval and humanist scholars was Cicero's fragment *Scipio's Dream*, with its attendant commentary by the Fifth Century Latin encyclopedist Macrobius, in which Scipio the Younger is taken up among the radiant stars and the nine concentric spheres of the universe. As Macrobius states the theory, the ratios of tones were discovered by Pythagoras from the sound of hammers beaten on an anvil, and confirmed by the rates of vibration of a plucked string of various lengths, and these are the proportions which underlie the creation of the world soul and the music made by the spheres as they move.

And then the Soul had to be a combination of those numbers that alone possess mutual attraction since the Soul itself was to instil harmonious agreement in the whole world. Now two is double one and, as we have already explained, the octave arises from the double; three is one and one-half times greater than two, and this combination produces the fifth; four is one and one-third times greater than three, and this combination produces the fourth; four is also four times as great as one, and from the quadruple ratio the double octave arises. Thus the World-Soul, which stirred the body of the universe to the motion that we now witness, must have been interwoven with those numbers which produce musical harmony in order to make harmonious the sounds which it instilled by its quickening impulse. It discovered the source of these sounds in the fabric of its own composition.[22]

Every soul in this world is allured by musical sounds so that not only those who are more refined in their habits, but all the barbarous peoples as well, have adopted songs by which they are inflamed with courage or wooed to pleasure; for the soul carries with it into the body a memory of the music which it knew in the sky, and is so captivated by its charm that there is no breast so cruel or savage as not to be gripped by the spell of such an appeal.[23]

One is surely not incorrect to see in Woodford's theory of divine inspiration the remnant of Platonic belief that souls descend into human bodies from the celestial or fixed sphere, and aspire to return thither.

Boethius, writing slightly later than Macrobius, was the other major source of medieval and Humanist information about speculative music. The Micrologus of Andreas Ornithoparcus, published in 1517, and translated by the English composer John Dowland in 1609, enumerates the respective functions and motives accorded to the three main orders of music.

Of the Musicke of the World

When God (whom Plutarch proves to have made all things to a certain harmonie) had devised to make this world moveable, it was necessary, that he should governe by some active and moving power; for no bodies but those which have a soule, can move themselves, as Franchinus in the first Chapter of his first booke of Theorie saith. Now that motion (because it is the swiftest of all other, and most regular) is not without sound: for it must needs be that a sound be made of the very wheeling of the Orbes, as Macrobius in Somnium Scip. lib. 2 writeth. The like sayd Boetius, how can this quick-moving frame of the world whirle about with a dumb and silent motion? From this turning of the heaven, there

5. The Harmony of the World and the Harmony of Verse

cannot be removed a certaine order of Harmonie. And nature will (saith that prince of Romane eloquence <u>Cicero</u>, in his sixt booke <u>de Reipub</u>.) that extremities must needs sound deep on the one side, & sharp on the other. so then, the worlds Musicke is an Harmonie, caused by the motion of the stares, and violence of the Spheares. <u>Lodovicus Coelius Rodiginus, lectionum antiquarum</u> lib. 5. cap. 25. writeth, Thatthis Harmony hath been observed out of the concent of the heavens, the knitting together of the elements, and the varietie of times. Wherefore well sayd <u>Dorilaus</u> the Philosopher, That the World is Gods Organe. Now the cause we cannot heare this sound according to <u>Pliny</u> is, because the greatnesse of the sound doth exceed the sence of our eares. But whether we admit this Harmonicall sound of the Heavens, or no, it skils not much; sith certaine it is, that the grand Work-maister of this <u>Mundane Fabricke</u>, made all things in number, weight, and measure, wherein principally, <u>Mundane Musicke</u> doth consist.

Of Humane Musicke

<u>Humane Musicke</u>, is the Concordance of divers elements in one compound, by which the spirituall nature is ioyned with the body, and the reasonable part is coupled in concord with the unreasonable, which proceedes from the uniting of the body and the soule. For that amitie, by which the body is ioyned unto the soule, is not tyed with bodily bands, but vertuall, caused by the proportion of humors. For what (saith <u>Coelius</u>) makes the powers of the soule so sundry and disagreeing to conspire oftentimes with each other? who reconciles the Elements of the body? what other power doth sonder and glue that spirituall strength, which is indued with an intellect to a mortall and earthly frame, than that Musicke which every man that descends into himselfe finds in himselfe. For every like is preserved by his like, and by his dislike is disturbed. Hence is it, that we loath and abhorre discords, and are delighted when we heare harmonicall concords, because we know there is in our selves the like concord.

Of Instrumentall Musicke

<u>Instrumentall Musicke</u>, is an Harmony which is made by helpe of <u>Instruments</u>. And because Instruments are either artificial, or

natural, there is one sort of Musicke which is made with artificiall Instruments; another, which is made with natural instruments. The Philosophers call the one <u>Harmonicall</u>; the other <u>Organicall</u>.[24]

Ornithoparcus proceeds to divide these two types of instrumental music into a number of subordinate types which need not concern us here. What is interesting to note is the persistent utility of these ideas into the early Seventeenth Century. Even when the heliocentric astronomy of Galileo, Kepler, and Copernicus threatened to subvert the very physical basis of the idea of cosmic harmony, we find the idea of cosmic proportion recuperated by Kepler in his *Harmonices Mundi Libri V* (1619), in which the proportions of the spheares are related not to the planetary orbits but to their average angular velocities.[25] In Milton's public exercise *De Sphaearum Concentu*, again we find Pythagorean doctrine made to yield an allegorical interpretation. "Surely, if he ever taught the harmony of the spheres, and the circling of the heavens to the charm of melody, he wished by this wisely to signify the most friendly relations of the orbs, and their uniform revolutions for ever according to the fixed law of fate."[26] For all its bantering and ironic tone, Milton's essay finally returns on itself with genuine seriousness of moral statement, and we are reminded that his law is not arbitrary but analogous to the very harmony he has in mind.

> For how can we be made capable of grasping this celestial sound when our minds, as Persius says, are bent down towards the earth and completely empty of celestial things? But if we bore pure, chaste, snow-clean hearts, as once Pythagoras did, then indeed our ears should resound with the sweetest music of the circling stars and be filled with it. Then all things should return immediately as if to that golden age. Then, free at last from our miseries, we should lead a life of ease, blessed and enviable even by the gods.[27]

The parallel with the argument of *Paradise Lost* and *Paradise Regained* is real, and suggests the way in which a cosmology based upon a virtual relationship between the world and the soul is able to underwrite both poetic subject-matter and theory. While Milton's undergraduate exercise is composed in pagan terms, a poem like "At a solemn Musick" shows how simply these ideas could be reconciled to a Christian point of view, in which grace and salvation are seen not in personal but in collective terms. Plato's sirens are made to become "pledges of heaven's joy", their "divine sounds" wedded in voice and verse. By renewing his part in this song man can regain his home in God. Original sin is represented as a jarring of harmony in disproportion, against nature. The felt orders of cosmic proportion which inform Milton's subject at all points imply an orderliness in verse which is not predicated upon the mechanical recurrence of minor units in a pattern of abstract qualities, number simply as "discrete quantitas" in Campion's term. Behind the marriage of voice and verse, a sacramental sanction applied to the Humanist ideal of music and poetry in conjunction, one can detect the notion that motion cannot be dumb, and that parts moving together connote a harmony. However submerged the attachment of a man like Campion may have been to such a metaphysical point of view, it nevertheless colours his rejection of a purely arithmetical view of poetical numbers. The poet's consideration of the "value" of syllables is not just the exercise of an aesthetic criterion, but an act of belief and devotion.

§ § §

Speculative music falls roughly into two conceptual types of activity, dealing with the virtual relationship, sanctioned by theology, between all parts of creation and the Creator on the one hand, and with the arithmetical ratios which express these relationships on the other. One of the ways of demonstrating these ratios was by the employment of a Monochord, a single string "divided" into various lengths, the ratios of its vibrations when plucked expressing a harmony in nature. Once the two types of activity covered by the discipline of speculative music were dissociated conceptually, and the ratios of musical tones seen to be a purely natural or mechanical set, the harmony or dissonance of various tone combinations no longer felt to be ethically expressive by divine ordinance, then the conditions are established for the independent development of practical music. In a sense the demand that a musical setting allow the words to be heard, coming from whatever source, prepares the way for a sense of musical tones as independently manipulable, rather than as directly related in a virtual harmony to the spirit of the text. The process which I am very sketchily suggesting here leads, in the long run, to a new theory of aesthetic expression, obviously enough, since it is no longer possible to think of artistic activity as the direct and, in a non-empiricist sense, natural expression of the soul's participation in a universal mystery.

The shift towards an exclusively practical science of music is marked by Descartes's *Compendium Musicae* (1618), in which his point of departure is to maintain a position which runs counter to the traditional one that music's basis lies in a divine proportion.

> The basis of music is sound; its aim is to please and to arouse various emotions in us. Melodies can be at the same time sad and enjoyable; nor is this so unique, for in the same way writers of elegies and tragedies please us most the more sorrow they awake in us[28].

Descartes assumes a point of view whereby aesthetic qualities do not subsist objectively in a work, but are indicated by the nature of subjective response. This is an essentially instrumentalist view of art, and any such view entails a search for correspondently mechanical instruments of response in human beings. This is not novel in Descartes, for as G.L. Finney notes, Scaliger had been interested in the material effects of sounds, suggesting that vibrating air affecting the animal spirits, rather than any principle of sympathy, was the source of such effects.[29] Such a notion, however, is not yet a fully developed mechanical theory of musical effects. For Descartes, however, the theory of animal spirits is able to take over much of the form of the theory of virtual relationships between harmonic elements, so that, as John Hollander describes Descartes's position:

> He does feel that purely rhythmic phenomena tend automatically and almost naturally to operate on certain passions, the faster movements upon the "higher" spirits (joy, anger, etc.), the slower upon the heavier affections. Only in this does his account suggest the humoral interpretation of Humanist theories. But in general he aims at a rejection of the views that supported most of the views of imitation, "tone-painting", the emotional effects of major, minor, augmented, and chromatic chordal configurations, held by sixteenth-century theorists. And in 1630 we can find Descartes writing to Mersenne that if an auditor had only been able to listen to the lively, triple rhythms of a galliard under painful conditions, the formal elements of the dance could not help but assume a painful character.[30]

Thus when Descartes comes to speak of the power of the human voice to affect the soul it is the individual soul with which he is concerned, a soul moreover possessed with powers of association. "The human voice seems most pleasing to us because it is most directly attuned to our souls. By the same token, the voice of a close friend is more agreeable than the voice of an enemy because of sympathy or antipathy of feelings—just as it is said that a sheep skin stretched over a drum will not give forth any sound when struck if a wolf's hide on another drum is sounding at the same time."[31] It is possible to see a faint residuum of the theory of universal harmony in this passage, and as a metaphor, reinforced by classical allusions, the traditional theory continues to serve a debased function in late Seventeenth Century treatises on music. But what such writers as John Birchensha, in his translation of Johannes Alsted's *Templum Musicum: or the Musical Synopsis* (1664), and Thomas Salmon, in his A Proposal to Perform Musick in Perfect and Mathematical Proportions (1688) chiefly insist upon is a knowledge of the arithmetical proportions which, they maintain, underlie the effects of music.[32] Alsted talks about "the Order, Disposition, and admirable proportion which does occur in the Celestial, and subcelestial region," but goes on to qualify the traditional point of view, "This Harmony being such and so great, when ancient men did diligently consider it, they supposed there was like Proportion not only in Numbers and Lines, but also in the Voice," concluding of music, however, that "unless it be referred to the Glory of God, and the pious Recreation of Man it cannot but equivocally be called Musick."[33]

These are rear-guard actions, however, in the face of a general view according to which music and poetry, if combined, did so not as correspondently expressive activities, but as complementary instruments, music lending a passional or emotional quality, induced upon the human body in a mechanical fashion, to the propositional discourse of poetry. music is scarcely any longer a rational art appealing to a rational sense, but a powerful manipulative tool.

> The Force of Musick is more wonderful than the Conveyance. How strangely does it awaken the Mind? It infuses an unexpected Vigour, makes the Impression agreeable and sprightly, and seems to furnish a new Capacity, as well as a new Opportunity to Satisfaction. It Raises, and Falls, and Counterchanges the Passions at an unaccountable Rate. It Charms and Transports, Ruffles and Becalms, and Governs with an almost arbitrary Authority.

The etiolation of Milton's sense of the value of psalmody, under the pressure of such mechanical and affective theories of musical action, is aptly displayed in Sampson Estwick's St. Cecilia's Day sermon for 1696.

It may be needless to tell you that we have all been pleas'd, if not transported, whilst the skilful Performers with laudable Emulations have endeavour'd to raise and extol God's Goodness, to the utmost pitch our impair'd Faculties will allow of in this imperfect State: By the Frame of our Nature we may perceive our selves fitted and prepar'd for the Reception of Harmonious Sounds; as we are fenc'd about with Nerves, we find ourselves ready strung, and most of us tun'd for this Heavenly Entertainment: By a kind of Sympathy sometimes we tremble; we are generally pleas'd when a fitting Subject is well painted by the Composer and well breath'd and set off by the several Performers.[34]

[35]

Redemptive music has become heavenly entertainment, which as well as pleasing us, of course, also instructs. But its effect on the mind is made indirect, and the body conceived of as a sympathetic instrument merely, so that man's response is instinctive or mechanical rather than rational.

Certain theorists, however, were left with an unsatisfied curiosity about the extraordinary nature of the physical powers reported of ancient music, and drew a distinction between symphonic or harmonic music, which pleased the ear by its delightful concordances, and a non-tonic, rhythmical music, such as they supposed the art of the Greeks to have been, which had a more direct and disturbing effect on the passions.

This way of theirs seems to be more proper (by the Elaborate Curiosity and Nicety of Contrivance of Degrees, and by Measures, rather than by Harmonious Consonancy, and by long studied Performance) to make great Impressions upon the Fancy, and operate accordingly, as some Histories relate: Ours, more sedately affects the Understanding and Judgement from the judicious Contrivance and happy Composition of Melodious Consort. The One quietly, but powerfully affects the Intellect by true Harmony: The Other, chiefly by the Rhythmus, violently attacks and hurries the Imagination.[36]

That music has a therapeutic power was one of the tenets of speculative music, and this carried over also, in a mechanical form, into modern

5. The Harmony of the World and the Harmony of Verse

affective musical theory. Thus according to Richard Browne, writing in 1674, whose purpose was to show "by what Mechanism human Bodies enjoy the pleasing Effects of Singing", the effects which music brings about on the mind, through the intermediary of the animal spirits, are directed back to the body.[37]

> The Spirits also, that were before drooping, by Sympathy per <u>Prop.</u> I. will be activated and enlivened, and the Solids brac'd up to their proper Standard; and in short, the Body that before was like a lifeless Log, or a piece of inanimated Clay, will now be render'd brisk and active, and Sensation and Motion acquire their utmost Perfection.[38]

Another interesting illustration of the ramifications of outstanding questions of this sort is a contribution by Dr. John Wallis to the *Philosophical Transactions of the Royal Society of London*, in which he enquires "whence it is that these great effects which are reported of <u>Musick</u> in <u>Former Times</u>, (of <u>Orpheus</u>, <u>Amphion</u>, &c.) are not as well found to follow upon the Musick of <u>Later Ages</u>."[39] Wallis's summary of the various stages of the mechanical operations of music upon the mind is a useful account of the conventional theory.

> I must…. have discoursed of the Nature of Sounds, produced by some Subtile Motions in the Air, propagated and continued to the Ear and Organs of Hearing, and thence communicated to the Animal Spirits; which excite suitable Imaginations, Affections, Passions, &c. and these attended with conformable Motions & Actions, and according to the various Proportions, Measures, and mixtures of such Sounds, there do arise various Effects in the Mind or Imagination, suitable thereunto.[40]

Wallis concludes that the reported effects of Ancient music are hyperbolic, and owe something to the comparative rarity of music in ancient times, and something also to simplicity of manners. He refers to the effect of the fiddle or bagpipes on rustics, which "will make them skip & shake their heels notably."[41] Moreover, modern musical art is a culinary one, aimed to please the ear rather than to effect a therapeutic balance.

> If we aim only at pleasing the Ear, by a sweet Consort, I doubt not but our modern Compositions may equal, if not exceed those

of the Ancients: Amongst whom I do not find any Foot-steps of what we call several Parts or Voices, (as Bass, Treble, Mean, &c. sung in Consort) answering each other to compleat the Musick. But if we would have our Musick as adjusted as to excite particular Passion, Affections, or Temper of Mind (as that of the Ancients is supposed to have done) we must then imitate the Physician rather than the Cook; and apply more simple Ingredients, fitted for the Temper we would produce. For in the sweet Mixture of compounded Musick, one thing doth so correct another, that it doth not operate strongly any one way.[42]

Even though his notion of "compounded Musick" is strangely anachronous, suggesting polyphony rather than recitative, Wallis's summary of his musical knowledge serves as an apt conclusion to the account which I have attempted to put forward in this chapter of a transition from a metaphysical to a mechanical notion of harmony. On the one hand stands a sense of a relationship between poetry and music in which prosodic standards are underwritten by a coherent set of propositions concerning the cosmically regulated nature of poetic activity. On the other hand this view is succeeded by a theory in which the activities in which poetry and music cooperate are divided between the two arts in a specialised way. In the Eighteenth Century nostalgia for a supposed ancient union of the two arts leads to an argument designed to restore to poetry those expressive and affective powers which it had mysteriously lost, and for which it had come to depend on a separate musical adjunct. I shall deal with this in my next chapter.

Notes

[1] *The Complete Poetical Works of Samuel Taylor Coleridge*, ed. E.H. Coleridge, Oxford 1912, I, p. 215. "Christabel" was composed in 1797 and 1800, the Preface first published in 1816.

[2] *The Compleat Gentleman, the second impression, much inlarged,* (1634), reprinted Oxford 1906, p. 103.

[3] Ibid., p. 104.

[4] L.B. Osborn, *The Life, Letters, and Writings of John Hoskyns 1566-1638*, New Haven 1939, p. 116. Osborn suggests that Hoskyns's *Directions* were written c. 1599.

[5] See the "English Grammar" prefixed to *A Dictionary of the English Language*, London 1755.

[6] Samuel Daniel, *Poems and a Defence of Ryme*, ed. Arthur Colby Sprague, London 1950, p. 132.

[7] Ibid.. pp. 151-152. "These unnecessary precepts" are the "severall kinds of numbers" described in Campion's *Observations*.

[8] Joshua Poole, *The English Parnassus...*, London 1657, A5v.

[9] Ibid., A2v.

[10] William D'Avenant, "The Author's Preface to his much honour'd Friend Mr. Hobs", *Gondibert: An Heroick Poem*, London 1651, p. 18.

[11] Ibid., p. 19.

[12] "The Answer of Mr. Hobbes to Sir Will. D'Avenant's Preface before *Gondibert*", ibid., pp. 54-55.

[13] Edward Bysshe, *The Art of English Poetry*, fourth edition, London 1710, p. 1.

[14] Ibid., p. 3.

[15] Ibid., p. 3.

[16] Ibid., p. 6.

[17] Cf. Boileau, *L'Art Poétique*, Chant I, ll. 70-73:

> Voulex-vous du public mériter les amours,
> Sans cesse en écrivant varies vos discours.
> Un style trop égal et toujours uniforme
> En vain brille a nos yeux, il faut qu'il nous endorme.

[18] For a fuller account of the general acceptance of conventions of metrical regularity, see Paul Fussell Jr., *Theory of Prosody in Eighteenth Century England*, New London, Conn., 1954, Chapters 1 and 2. Fussell overlooks the emergence of the accentual-syllabic pattern in the course of the Sixteenth Century, and consequently overstates the contribution of late Seventeenth Century writers to the criterion of prosodic regularity which he describes.

[19] John Milton, *Paradise Lost*, facsimile edition, Menston 1968, no page numbers. The note on "The Verse", together with "The Argument", were prefixed to the poem in 1668.

[20] Samuel Woodford, *A Paraphrase upon the Psalms of David*, London 1667, A2r.

[21] Ibid., A3r, v.

[22] Macrobius, *Commentary on the Dream of Scipio*, translated with an introduction by William Harris Stahl, second edition, NY 1962, pp. 192-193.

[23] Ibid., p. 195.

[24] *Andreas Ornithoparcus His Micrologus, or Introduction: Containing the Art of Song*, translated by John Dowland, London 1609, B2v-Cv.

[25] For an account of Kepler's theory, see Hollander, op. cit., pp. 39-40. For a more general account of speculative music, less susceptible than Hollander to empiricist prejudices, see Allen, op. cit., pp. 3-22, 29-33.

[26] "On the Music of the Spheres", in Sigmund Spaeth, *Milton's Knowledge of Music*, new edition, with a foreword by Werner G. Rice, Ann Arbor, Mich., 1963, p. 132.

[27] Ibid., pp. 135-136.

[28] René Descartes, *Compendium of Music (Compendium Musicae)*, translated by Walter Robert, with an introduction and notes by Charles Kent, American Institute of Musicology, 1961, p. 11.

[29] Cf. G.L. Finney, *Musical Backgrounds for English Literature*, New Brunswick, N.J., 1961.

[30] Hollander, op. cit., pp. 178-179. It is interesting to note that the Preface of "The Stationer to the Reader" to the English translation of Descartes's *Compendium* (1653) rehearses many of the usual commonplaces about the magical powers of music as a charm to excite or compose the passions.

[31] Descartes, op. cit., p.11.

[32] Cf. John Birchensha, tr., *Templum Musicum: or the Musical Synopsis, of the Learned and Famous Johannes-Henricus-Alstedius, being a Compendium of the Rudiments both of the Mathematical and Practical Part of Musick*, London 1664. "But for any Musician to undervalue or speak slightly of the Mathematical part of Musick, is to reproach the Common Parent from whom the Art he professeth received a Being. I know that all Ingenuous persons who are Artists, will acknowledge that it is a more noble way to work by Rules and Precepts in any Art, i.e. to compose regularly, will be found more advantageous than any other way in these respects. For by such a way of Operation the Composer shall work more certainly, firmly, readily, and with more facility than by any other way." A7v-A8r.

Also, Thomas Salmon, *A Proposal to Perform Musick in Perfect and Mathematical Proportions*, London 1688. "This Mathematical Discourse is indeed the Anatomy of MUSICK, wherein the infinite Wisdom of the great Creator appears: How delightfully and wonderfully is it made! Marvellous are thy works, O Lord, and that my Soul knows right well.

All the best Proportions, are the best Chords of Musick, and strike the Ear with pleasure agreeable to the dignity of their Numbers. The effects of this the Sensualist is satisfied with, and desires to seek no further.

But is it not grateful to every Gentleman, who is ennobled with such a Soul as yours, to know the divine Harmony of the pleasure he enjoys? Is it not the duty and Felicity of a Rational Being to consider how the whole System of the World is framed in Consort. How Musical Instruments observe their

Arithmetical Laws, all the little Meanders of the Ear faithfully conveying the organiz'd sounds, and the Soul of man made to receive the delight, before he himself knows from whence it comes?" A2v, r.

[33] John Birchensha, op. cit., p. 11.

[34] Sampson Estwick, *The Usefulness of Church-Musick, A Sermon Preach'd at Christ-Church, Nov. 27. 1696, Upon Occasion of the Anniversary-Meeting of the Lovers of Musick On St. Coecilia's Day*, London 1696.

[35] Jeremy Collier, "Of Musick", *Essays upon Several Moral Subjects*, second edition, London 1697.

[36] William Holder, *A Treatise of the Natural Grounds and Principles of Harmony*, London 1694, pp. 127-128. The argument that Greek music owed its effects to a toneless rhythm, and that such was in general the source of musical effects, derives from Isaac Vosius, *De Poematum Cantu et Viribus Rhythmi* (1673), referred to in the notes by Dr. John Wallis annexed to Salmon's *Essay*. See also Allen, op. cit., p. 73.

[37] Richard Browne, *Medecina Musica: or, a Mechanical Essay on the Effects of Singing, Musick, and Dancing, on Human Bodies*, revis'd and corrected, London 1729, p. 14.

[38] Ibid., pp. 14-16. Browne's first proposition was that "There is a Sympathy betwixt the Soul and Animal Spirits."

[39] Dr. John Wallis, "A Letter concerning the Strange Effects reported of Musick in Former Times, beyond what is to be found in Later Ages", *Philosophical Transactions of the Royal Society of London*, XX, (1698), p. 297.

[40] Ibid., p. 297.

[41] Ibid., p. 302-303.

[42] There is an interesting poem by Wallis, annexed to his *Truth Tried: or, Animadversions on a Treatise published by the Right Honourable Robert Lord Brooke, entitled The Nature of Truth, Its Union and Unity with the Soule*, London 1643, in which traditional ideas and terms of music are deployed to suggest an expressive discord.

> But how (alas!) should I begin to speak,
> (Where all Hyperbole's will seem to weak
> To Equalize) in Measures to expresse
> What knows no other measure but Excesse?
> Or who can Bound over-abounding Tears,
> Within the streightnesse of an even Verse?
> If then perhaps I hardly weep in Rhime;
> If not in Consort; (Tears can keep no Time)
> If no melodious Harmony be shewn;
> Think but, 'Tis Hard, to put a Teare in Tune.

(Yet harder, not to Weep.—) Imperfect Tones
Serve well enough to signifie our Grones.
A Long, A Large, are all the <u>Notes</u> we know;
(Minim and sembrief <u>rests</u> are long enow)
Our Accents tuned to the Highest <u>Key</u>;
(And yet our Sighs deeper than <u>Gam</u> <u>ut</u> be:)
Nor curious are to make the consort sweet,
That all keep equall <u>Time</u>, that <u>Closes</u> meet;
None tunes his Voyce unto anothers String;
(This verse was made to Weep, and not to Sing)
All weep a <u>Part</u>, but no <u>Accord</u> can keep,
(Save only thus, That all agree to weep;)
Oft weep a <u>Sharp</u>, when our sad Thoughts be <u>Flat</u>;
If <u>Discords</u> oft appear, yet wonder not;
Some Harmony may Disproportion give,
<u>Discordant</u> Accents shew <u>Concent</u> in Grief.

An Elegie on the much Lamented Death of the Right Honorable
Robert Lord Brook, by John Wallis.

Chapter 6

Sound and Sense:
The Direct Action of Poetic Rhythm
on the Passions and the Theory of Expression

What exactly the relationship is, posited by Pope in his dictum in *An Essay on Criticism* that "The sound must be an echo to the sense" can, in a useful way, be seen as the question which underlies various contrasting theories upheld during the Eighteenth Century about the prosodic norms of poetry and their relation to music. This echoic relation of sound to sense might be understood in a straightforward imitative way (although there is nothing straightforward about the theory of imitation); or to suggest the priority of sense over sound; or, in the face of radically anti-imitative aesthetics such as that of Burke, one might look for the connectedness of sound and sense in their respective modes of operation upon the reader or auditor. Samuel Johnson's comments in the *Rambler* on Pope's exemplification of his own dictum display a critic who is sceptical of the success achieved by what he understands to be a basically imitative series of echoes.

> From the Italian gardens Pope seems to have transplanted this flower, the growth of happier climates, into a soil less adapted to its nature, and less favourable to its increase:
>
> > Soft is the strain when Zephyr gently blows,
> > And the smooth stream in smoother numbers flows;
> > But when loud billows lash the sounding shore,
> > The hoarse rough verse should like the torrent roar.
> > When Ajax strives some rock's vast weight to throw,
> > The line too labours, and the words move slow;
> > Not so when swift Camilla scours the plain,
> > Flies o'er th'unbending corn, and skims along the main.
>
> > *Essay on Criticism*, Ll. 366-373
>
> From these lines laboured with great attention, and celebrated by a rival wit, may be judged what can be expected from the most

diligent endeavours after this imagery of sound. The verse intended to represent the whisper of the vernal breeze, must be confessed not much to excel in softness or volubility; and the smooth stream, runs with a perpetual clash of jarring consonants. The noise and turbulence of the torrent, is, indeed, distinctly imaged, for it requires very little skill to make our language rough; but in these lines, which mention the effort of Ajax, there is no particular heaviness, obstruction, or delay. The swiftness of Camilla is rather contrasted than exemplifies; why the verse should be lengthened to express speed, will not easily be discovered.[1]

For Johnson the resemblance between sound and sense can be either general or particular, and in this passage he is concerned with particular resemblance. General resemblance "is to be found in every language which admits of poetry", and occurs "even without any effort of the understanding or intervention of the judgement."[2] Particular resemblance in verse is often and, from Johnson's point of view, erroneously discerned by those of an enthusiastic frame of mind. "It can scarcely be doubted that on many occasions we make the music which we imagine ourselves to hear, that we modulate the poem by our own disposition, and ascribe to the numbers the effects of the sense."[3] Johnson is absolutely clear about the constraints to which the resemblance of sense in sound must <u>naturally</u> adhere: "The representative power of poetic harmony consists of sound and measure, of the force of the syllables singly considered, and of the time in which they are pronounced. Sound can resemble nothing but sound, and time can measure nothing but motion and duration."[4] When this form of particular resemblance occurs, he argues, it is often fortuitous, often onomatopoeic; it should not be expected to occur as a matter of course, and in its occurrence it should never actually run counter to the meaning of a passage.

Johnson does not pause to discuss the idea of general representation, "consisting in the flow and structure of a whole passage taken together,"[5] once he has mentioned it, because his notion of resemblance is governed by the idea of an imitation predicated upon the particular subjects of a poetic discourse. But in his category of "general resemblance", in fact, Johnson is referring to that commonplace Eighteenth Century sense of the way music and poetry relate to each other in terms of a faculty psychology, according to which there are distinct human passions and affections which are modulated in the mind in wide bands of quasi-physiological responsiveness. "The same flow of joyous versification will celebrate the jollity of marriage and the exultation of triumph, and the same languor of melody will suit the complaints of an absent lover, as of a conquered king."[6] Johnson does not pursue this topic because he is exceptional among Eighteenth Century critics in not being primarily concerned with the nature of aesthetic effects.

Filling in some of the elisions in Johnson's discussion of the issue of the resemblance of sound to sense, I would suggest that Johnson was not really interested to discuss the category of "general resemblance" not because it was general, but because the particular ascriptive effects to which it was susceptible at the hands of many critics were personal and idiosyncratic, and not therefore the products of the operation of a natural and universal law. Johnson's apparent stance as an objective critic should not, I think, be allowed to suggest that he is concerned with the analysis of the structure of particular works, but should be understood as the strategy of a critic who is concerned to deal only with the essential effects of the works he is discussing. There is another side to Johnson's assumption about the unlawful character of many felt instances of particular resemblance, however, which sees the principle of association not as something inherently "subjective", idiosyncratic, and wayward, but as the essential mechanism by which complex emotional and intellectual responses are built up from simple, atomistic ideas. From such a point of view poetry and music are not truly imitative arts since, and here I summarise in a very rough and ready fashion, between the simple ideas to which a poem or a piece of music eventually refer and the whole work itself a whole series of mechanical associations have occurred which make the idea of any direct imitation of nature inconceivable. If, then, artistic imitation entails the imitation not of external nature directly, but of a complex mental or interior image, it becomes a matter almost of faith that the mechanics of association are the same for all normal and healthy men. Moreover, since a work of art addresses itself to the inner processes of man, it becomes possible to think that it might affect directly the mechanisms whereby man's mental processes transact themselves. The theory of the animal spirits which mediate between external events and the mind itself suggests one way in which this direct intervention might occur. In this chapter I wish to deal with two particular ideas which stem from such a normative view of association. First, that music exercises distinctive powers of expression which have a direct influence upon the passions, and a consequent modifying effect on the merely verbal meaning of poetry. Second, that there existed an original union of music and poetry, in that both sprang from similar expressive resources, which civilisation has rendered corrupt. The distinct but somewhat limited scope of these ideas can only be grasped in the context of a few generalisations about Eighteenth-Century aesthetic theory.

§ § § §

Eighteenth-Century criticism is characteristically concerned with the nature and manner of aesthetic response, and is extensively underwritten by philosophical assumptions concerning the processes of knowledge and experience which are of what M.H. Abrams calls an "elementaristic" character.[7] Writings on all the arts in this period are concerned with a complex knot of interior human processes of which I wish to distinguish three, the Imagination, the Passions, and Association, which recur constantly in discussion of both music and poetry. These are psychological rather than metaphysical or theological notions. Association suggests modes of procedure; the Passions suggest the means and the character (in as much as they are distinct from Judgement), and also supply some of the substance of an associational train; and in the Imagination is discovered a distinct and novel faculty which deals with specifically aesthetic experience. This in turn envisages a distinct category of aesthetic or beautiful objects or, equally, a distinct quality of beauty as a property of objects. (One can see in this the remnants of the theory of harmony which was discussed in the two previous chapters if one wishes).

The theory that there is a distinct inner modality of aesthetic response underlies the best theoretical criticism from Addison to Gerard and Burke. The key terms for this theory are the Imagination and Taste. Addison outlined his theory of the distinct pleasures of the Imagination in a series of papers in the *Spectator*, in which he ascribes its powers to the operations of a single sense, that of sight, which "may be considered as a more delicate and diffusive kind of Touch."[8]

> It is this Sense which furnishes the Imagination with its Ideas; so that by the Pleasures of the Imagination or Fancy (which I shall use promiscuously) I here mean such as arise from visible Objects, either when we call them actually in our view, or when we call up their Ideas into our Minds by Paintings, Statues, Descriptions, or any the like Occasion. We cannot indeed have a single Image in the Fancy that did not make its first Entrance through the Sight; but we have the Power of retaining, altering, and compounding

those Images, which we have once received, into all the varieties of Picture and Vision that are most agreeable to the Imagination; for by this Faculty, a Man in a Dungeon is capable of entertaining himself with Scenes and Landskips more beautiful than any that can be found in the whole Compass of Nature.[9]

This passage in fact anticipates Addison's important distinction between the primary and secondary imagination, the latter pertaining to art, and superior to the immediate pleasures of the primary imagination. However, "It is impossible for us to give the necessary Reason, why this Operation of the Mind is attended with so much Pleasure, as I have before observed on the same Occasion, but we find a great variety of Entertainments derived from this single Principle."[10] Addison suggests however that the power of the secondary imagination, since it is tied up with memory, derives from the way in which "any single Circumstance of what we have formerly seen often raises up a whole Scene of Imagery, and awakens numberless Ideas that before slept in the Imagination."[11] In addition, recollected pleasures appear to be more delightful. "*A Cartesian*", says Addison, "would account for both these Instances in the following Manner":

The Sett of Ideas, which we have received from such a Prospect or Garden, having entered the Mind at the same time, have a Sett of Traces belonging to them in the Brain, bordering very near upon one another; when, therefore, any one of these Ideas arises in the Imagination, and consequently dispatches a flow of Animal Spirits to its proper Trace, these Spirits, in the violence of their Motion, run not only into the Trace, to which they were more particularly directed, but into several of those that lie about it: By this means they awaken other Ideas of the same Sett, which immediately determine a new Dispatch of Spirits, that in the same manner open other Neighbouring Traces, till at last the whole Sett of them is blown up, and the whole Prospect or Garden flourishes in the Imagination. But because the Pleasure we received from these Places far surmounted, and overcame the little Disagreeableness we found in them, for this Reason there was at first a wider Passage worn in the Pleasure Traces, and, on the contrary, so narrow a one in those which belonged to the disagreeable Ideas, that they were quickly stopt up, and rendered incapable of receiving any Animal Spirits, and consequently of exciting any unpleasant Ideas in the Memory.[12]

The imagination, in other words, is an inner sense, with a quite simple mechanical mode of operation. The complete images it represents from memory are not idiosyncratic or personal because it does not store them as complex wholes but as a series of juxtaposed primary qualities, just as the senses do not present objects directly to the mind but as a collection of simple ideas.

The cultivation of the imaginative powers became one of the principal concerns of subsequent criticism, and was dealt with by the faculty of Taste. The definition given by Alexander Gerard at the beginning of *An Essay of Taste* is brief and to the point.

> Taste consists chiefly in the improvement of those principles which are commonly called <u>the powers of the imagination</u>, and are considered by modern philosophers as <u>internal</u> and <u>reflex senses</u>, supplying us with firmer and more delicate perceptions, than any which can be properly referred to our external organs.[13]

Burke added an "Introduction on Taste" to the second edition (1759) of *A Philosophical Enquiry into the Origin of our Ideas of the Sublime and Beautiful*, in which he is concerned to maintain that the standard of Taste as well as that of reason is the same for all men, his purpose, clearly, to forestall the problems of individual association which exercised Johnson in relation to particular resemblance.

It is necessary for Burke to maintain such a position as a corollary of his arguments concerning the effect of artistic representations upon the passions. I find the whole theory of the passions difficult to pin down, since it appears to deal both with the way in which the mind is affected, and a specific programme of affective tonality, as love, fear, anger, self-preservation, etc. In *An Essay on Genius* (1774) Gerard offers a definition which will serve the immediate purpose.

> A passion in strict propriety means only such an emotion as is produced by some one particular cause and directed to some one determinate object. There are several emotions, as remorse, self approbation, and the like, which may perhaps be reckoned sensations rather than passions, but our present design does not render it necessary to attend to that distinction. A passion is something different from an habitual temper or turn of mind; the latter may in some instances have derived its origin from the frequent returns or the long continuance of a particular passion;

6. Sound and Sense

but once formed, it subsists without the operation of any particular cause and without being fixed on any precise object, and produces a permanent propensity to any sentiments or passions which are congruous to it.[14]

According to Gerard's argument the Passions, as a variety of universal, exert a certain control over associative procedures; the point which concerns me here, however, is that the Passions, through the operations of the secondary imagination, are particularly susceptible to the influence of works of art. (It is a nexus of ideas such as this which, I believe, explains the general mid-Eighteenth Century rejection of the doctrine of imitation, considered in a literal way; what we might suppose to be a theory of subjective imitation, not of the thing itself but of its effect upon the mind, being more precisely distinguished as representation or expression. I shall return to this point shortly). Burke's distinction between the sublime and the beautiful is made in terms of the qualities of different classes of objects, and the passions to which they are addressed. The description he offers of the operation of beauty upon the mind can therefore stand for either kind of transaction.

> Beauty is a thing much too affecting not to depend upon some positive qualities. And, since it is no creature of our reason, since it strikes us without any reference to use, and even where no use at all can be discerned, since the order and method of nature is generally very different from our measures and proportions, we must conclude that beauty is, for the most part, some quality in bodies, acting mechanically upon the human mind by the intervention of the senses.[15]

In the fifth section of the *Enquiry* Burke considers the effect of words, and is concerned to refute "The common notion of the power of poetry and eloquence, as well as that of words in ordinary conversation... that they affect the mind by raising in it ideas of those things for which custom has appointed them to stand"[16]. He does so by discriminating three kinds of words, "aggregate words", the "simple abstract", and the "compounded abstract". He does not reject entirely the ability of the simplest, "aggregate" words to conjure up the distinct idea of the objects to which they refer, but suggests that this occurrence is very rare.

If words have all their possible extent of power, three effects arise in the mind of the hearer. The first is, the <u>sound</u>; the second, the <u>picture</u>, or representation of the thing signified by the sound; the third is, the <u>affection</u> of the soul produced by one or by both of the foregoing. <u>Compounded abstract</u> words, of which we have been speaking, (honour, justice, liberty, and the like.) produce the first and last of these effects, but not the second. <u>Simple abstracts</u>, are used to signify some one simple idea without much adverting to others which may chance to attend it, as blue, green, hot, cold, and the like; these are capable of affecting all three of the purposes of words; as the <u>aggregate</u> words, man, castle, horse, &c. are in a yet higher degree. But I am of opinion, that the most general effect even of these words, does not arise from their forming pictures of the several things they would represent in the imagination; because on a very diligent examination of my own mind, and getting others to consider theirs, I do not find that once in twenty times any such picture is formed, and when it is, there is most commonly a particular effort of the imagination for that purpose. But the aggregate words operate as I said of the compound abstracts, not by presenting any image to the mind, but by having from use the same effect on being mentioned, that their original has when it is seen.[17]

However, this argument might suggest that the power exercised by words on the mind is weak in comparison to that exercised by real objects, and that therefore poetry possesses no real power to move the passions. Burke's argument is again an appeal to experience.

We find by experience that eloquence and poetry are as capable, nay indeed much more capable of making deep and lively impressions than any other arts, and even than nature itself in very many cases. And this arises chiefly from these three causes. First, that we take an extraordinary part in the passions of others, and that we are easily affected and brought into sympathy by any tokens which are shewn of them; and there are no tokens which can express all the circumstances of most passions so fully as words; so that if a person speaks upon any subject, he can not only convey the subject to you, but likewise the manner in which he is himself affected by it. Certain it is; that the influence of most things upon our passions is not so much from the things themselves, as from our opinions concerning them; and these again depend very much on the opinions of other men, conveyable for the most part by words only.[18]

Burke goes on to maintain that there are certain ideas which can be conveyed, through the mechanism of association, by language only. However, the most important idea, in the present context, which Burke proceeds to develop, lies in the distinction he draws between clarity and strength of expression, the first of which relates to the understanding, the second to the passions. Burke here is in fact reasserting one of the means of the fifth division of rhetoric, *Pronunciato*, by which the orator influences his auditors by simulating or undergoing the emotional response he is trying to induce.[19] At this point we are able to draw into this account the issue of the effects of music. Burke however, unlike some previous writers such as Hildebrand Jacob and James Harris, is novel in ascribing to language in isolation certain powers which were generally associated with the influence of music, which was required to arouse the affections (or passions) appropriate to the ideas of the words. Jacob, for instance, suggests that poetry presents a stage in between painting and music, able to express both "the external Signs of the Operation of the Mind which are so livelily represented by <u>Painting</u>," as well as, what is proper to it, "its finest <u>abstracted</u> Thoughts, and most <u>pathetic</u> Reflections."[20] Music is a complementary adjunct to these processes, which, although it may "give the Mind no <u>Instruction</u> immediately from itself; yet it always helps greatly to <u>mend</u> the <u>Heart</u> in general, and elevate it to the doing of great and generous Actions: It disposes the Soul for the Reception of such Precepts as tend to <u>Humanity</u>, and <u>Benevolence</u>; it charms and softens us, like <u>Beauty</u> which tho' generally incapable of giving Instruction, serves to <u>refine</u> our <u>Passions</u>, and excite, and raise us to the Performance of <u>brave</u> and <u>noble</u> Exploits."[21] The argument is more concisely put by James Harris, again in an essay dealing with all three arts.

> The ideas therefore of Poetry must needs make the most sensible Impression, when the Affections, peculiar to them, are already excited by the Music. For here a <u>double Force is made to co-operate to one End</u>.[22]

In arguments of this sort asserting the complementary relation of music and poetry, of course, a distinction between instrumental and vocal music is being borne in mind. Burke's account of strong expression presents those aspects of musical expression which influence the passions (as distinct from those, that is to say, which delight the senses, an operation which is schematically prior to the effect of music on the passions) as not essentially musical, but rhetorical.

> Now, as there is a moving tone of voice, an impassioned countenance, an agitated gesture, which affect independently of the things about which they are exerted, so there are words, and certain dispositions of words, which being peculiarly devoted to passionate subject, and always used by those who are under the influence of any passion; they touch and move us more than those which far more clearly and distinctly express the subject matter. We yield to sympathy what we refuse to description. The truth is, all verbal description, merely as naked description, though never so exact, conveys so poor and insufficient an idea of the thing described, that it could scarcely have the smallest effect, if the speaker did not call in to his aid those modes of speech that mark a strong and lively feeling in himself. Then, by a contagion of our passions, we catch a fire already kindled in another, which probably might never have been struck out by the object described. Words, by strongly conveying the passions, by those means which we have already mentioned fully compensate for their weakness in other respects.[23]

Unlike Yvor Winters, Burke is not concerned to maintain any exact balance between external motive and internal emotion; for him the passions come from human nature, and are not, as are the imagination and the understanding, dependent upon objects of sense. "If the affections be well conveyed, it will work its effect without any clear idea; often without any idea at all of the thing which has originally given rise to it."[24]

Now, it is worth noting that although the proposition of writers such as Burke and Gerard is that they are pursuing a "philosophical" type of enquiry, on rational principles, in a scientifically neutral way, their descriptions of the procedures of aesthetic response carry a very definite content. The theory of the Passions amounts to a kind of affective programme, and Burke can say what the appropriate qualities are of sublime and beautiful objects. In a similar fashion, Gerard is clear in his mind about the appropriate qualities of music.

6. Sound and Sense

It is observable, that the proper and pleasing disposition of sounds in <u>melody</u> bears a great resemblance, in its principles, to that arrangement of parts which constitutes the beauty of forms. It is a succession of notes, bearing to one another a regular <u>proportion</u> in time; so <u>varied</u> in their lengths and intervals, as to relieve satiety and tediousness; and at the same time so far <u>uniform</u>, that the transitions are all in themselves agreeable, such as are taken in by the ear with ease, and are subordinate to the key which governs the whole.

The same principles are not less obvious in <u>harmony</u>; the superior delight of which springs from no other cause, but its possessing some of these qualities in greater perfection.[25]

Gerard is careful to distinguish between music's capacity to please, and a superior capacity to sway the passions. This kind of distinction, analogous to that which Burke draws between the beautiful and the sublime, although for him these both work upon the passions, although selectively, is fairly commonplace in mid-Eighteenth Century musical theory. One finds it being made by Daniel Webb, for instance, in his *Remarks on the Beauties of Poetry* (1762) where the capacity of music to transport and delight is discriminated.[26] The distinction Webb makes applies to the harmony of verse.

The sole aim of versification is harmony. To understand this properly, we must divide it into two kinds. The first consists in a general flow of verse, most pleasing to the ear, but independent of the sense: the second, in bringing the sound or measure of the verse to correspond with, and accompany the idea. The former may be called a verbal harmony: the latter a sentimental. If we consider the flow of a verse merely as music, it will then be allowed, that variety is no less necessary than sweetness; and that a continued repetition of the same movements, must be as tiresome in poetry, as it would be in music.[27]

Webb's musical analogy serves him as a means to sustain his contention that Pope's versification, especially in its placement of the caesura and its endstopped lines, is monotonous, and that blank verse such as that of *Paradise Lost* is superior, "for, the lines being made often to run one into the other, the second pause is sunk; the balance, from the equal division of each line, is removed; and by changing the pauses at pleasure, an open is given into an unlimited variety."[28] Webb's notion of a sentimental harmony is related to Burke's arguments concerning the affective powers of words. Harmony is no longer a standard, referring to what pleases the senses but does not stir the passions.

The way in which the fully developed aesthetic theory of the passions influences prosodic standards is indicated by the comments of John Mason in *An Essay on Elocution*.

> The voice must express, as near as may be, the very Sense or Idea designed to be conveyed by the emphatical Word; by a strong, rough, and violent, or a soft, smooth, and tender Sound.
>
> Thus the different Passions of the Mind are to be expressed by a different Sound or Tone of Voice. <u>Love</u>, by a soft, smooth, languishing Voice; <u>Anger</u>, by a strong, vehement, and elevated Voice; <u>Joy</u>, by a quiet, sweet, and clear Voice; <u>Fear</u>, by a dejected, tremulous, hesitating Voice, <u>Courage</u>, hath a full, bold, and loud Voice; and <u>Perplexity</u>, a grave, steady, and earnest one.[29]

Mason covers the grounds which inspired Johnson's lack of interest in general resemblance, but takes the matter in an entirely different direction. The purpose of elocution is to over-ride the expressive shortcomings of a poem's versification.

> When you read Verse, you must not at all favour the Measure or Rhime; <u>that</u> often obscures the Sense and spoils the Pronunciation: For the great End of Pronunciation is to elucidate and heighten the Sense; that is, to represent it not only in a clear but in a strong light. Whatever then obstructs this is carefully to be avoided, both in Verse and Prose. Nay, this ought to be more carefully observed in reading Verse than Prose; because the Author, by a constant Attention to his Measures and Rhime, and the Exaltation of his Language, is often very apt to obscure his Sense; which therefore requires the more Care in the Reader to discover and distinguish it by the Pronunciation. And if when you read Verse with proper Pause, Emphasis, and Cadence, and a Pronunciation varied and governed by the Sense, it be not harmonious and beautiful, the Fault is not in the Reader but the Author. And if the Verse be good, to read it thus will improve its Harmony; because it will take off that Uniformity of Sound and Accent which tires the Ear, and makes the Numbers heavy and disagreeable.[30]

6. Sound and Sense

This is the sound as an echo to the sense with a vengeance, for here sound almost leads the sense, at least by elucidating and heightening it. Mason is a crudely explicit writer, who derived many of his ideas from Samuel Say, whose *Essay on the Harmony, Variety, and Power of Numbers* (1745) I shall discuss in the next chapter. I have introduced his *Essay* at this point because it serves very well to demonstrate the way in which the passions were conceived as a very determinate set of interior senses. Mason also exemplifies a major transition in taste, however, in which Milton and Young replace Pope as the standards of harmonious composition. We may suppose that such a transition occurred at least partly in response to the theory of mechanically affected interior and reflex aesthetic senses.

§ § § §

In his essay "Of the Nature of that Imitation which takes place in what are called the Imitative Arts" Adam Smith offers a very terse summary of Charles Avison's *An Essay on Musical Expression* (1752). "To say, as Mr. Avison does, that the complete art of a musician, the complete merit of a piece of Music, is composed or made up of three distinct arts or merits, that of melody, that of harmony, and that of expression, is to say, that it is made up of melody and harmony, and the immediate and necessary effect of melody and harmony."[31] Avison's discussion of musical effects proceeds, like Gerard's, from the question of pleasure to that of influence, and it is when he comes to the second of these two effects that he promulgates his doctrine of Expression.

> If we view this Art in its Foundations we shall find, that by the Constitution of Man it is of mighty Efficacy in working both on his Imagination and his Passions. The Force of <u>Harmony</u>, or <u>Melody</u> alone, is wonderful on the Imagination. <u>A full Chord</u> struck, or a beautiful succession of <u>single Sounds</u> produced, is no less ravishing to the Ear, than just Symmetry or exquisite Colours to the Eye.
>   The capacity of receiving Pleasure from these musical Sounds, is, in Fact, a peculiar and internal Sense, but of a much more refined Nature than the external Senses: For in the Pleasures arising from our internal Sense of Harmony, there is no prior Uneasiness necessary, in order to our tasting them in their full Perfection;

neither is the Enjoyment of them attended either with Languor or Disgust. It is their peculiar and essential Property, to divest the Soul of every unquiet Passion, to pour in upon the Mind, a silent and serence Joy, beyond the Power of Words to express, and to fix the Heart in a rational, benevolent, and happy Tranquility.

But, though this be the natural Effect of <u>Melody</u> or <u>Harmony</u> on the Imagination, when simply considered; yet when to these is added the Force of Musical Expression, the Effect is greatly increased; for then they assume the Power of exciting all the most agreeable Passions of the Soul. The Force of Sound in alarming the Passions is prodigious. Thus, the Noise of Thunder, the Shouts of War, the Uproar of an enraged Ocean, strike us with Terror: So again, there are certain Sounds natural to Joy, others to Grief, or Despondency, others to Tenderness and Love; and by hearing <u>these</u>, we naturally sympathise with those who either <u>enjoy</u> or <u>suffer</u>. Thus Music, either by imitating these various Sounds in due Subordination to the Laws of <u>Air</u> and <u>Harmony</u>, or by any other method of Association, bringing the Objects of our Passions before us (especially when these Objects are determined, and made as it were visibly, and intimately present to the Imagination by the Help of Words) does naturally raise a Variety of Passions in the Human Breast, similar to the Sounds which are expressed: and thus by the Musician's Art, we are often carried into the Fury of a Battle, or a Tempest, we are by turns elated with Joy, or sunk in pleasing Sorrow, roused to Courage, or quelled by grateful Terrors, melted into Pity, Tenderness, and Love, or transported to the Regions of Bliss, in an Ecstasy of divine Praise.[32]

It is abundantly clear from Avison's argument that the theory of Expression is governed to a considerable extent by the theory of the Passions, and that the expressive is that which is able to activate the Passions which lie dormant in the human breast. An important question to which this theory gives rise concerns the nature of the connection between a mode of expression and its appropriate passion. Although the effective means are dealt with in terms of the animal spirits, or an internal reflexive sense, the question remains as to whether the connection is natural (and not entirely dependent on the physiology of man), or whether it is mechanical and conventional. An inkling of this problem is given by Webb in his *Remarks on the Beauties of Poetry*, when he makes the following comparison between accident and art.

When a man strongly affected by any passion, expresses himself in words, the natural tones of which correspond with his ideas, it may possibly be by accident. But when we observe the same co-incidence in a Poet, it is most reasonable to suppose, that it is the effect of design. For as he has time to select his images and sentiments, so he has likewise to accommodate the movement of his numbers to the nature of those ideas he means to express.[33]

Webb suggests very strongly that the expressive correspondence is artificial, and that it is sometimes possible that the tone of voice of a man naturally in a state of passionate affection will adventitiously be that which would be appropriate to it in art. William Jones of Nayland offers a clearer sense of what is at issue here in his *Treatise on the Art of Music* (1784) when he engages with the musical controversy about which of harmony and melody is dependent upon the other for its existence.[34]

The two parts essential to Music are <u>Harmony</u> and <u>Air</u>. Harmony is enlivened by Air, and Air is supported by Harmony. But as Air is the production of the fancy or imagination, some have falsely supposed that it may be left, like the Nightingale, to the wildness of Nature; and that all rules can only serve to fetter and restrain it....I am very sensible I have a difficult subject before me, and that the attempt to reconcile Air with Reason, will appear like that of giving Laws to the Wind, which <u>bloweth where it listeth</u>.[35]

Jones' figures make it sufficiently clear that the expressive correspondence can be thought of, at least, as lying in that nature which is outside the merely human frame.

Avison's own remarks on this question are directed chiefly at the abuses of musical imitation, which he careful to distinguish from expression in terms of its effects; imitation appeals to the understanding rather than "affect the Heart and raise the Passions of the Soul" as expression does.[36] Avison pursues this distinction in an interesting way.

This Distinction seems more worthy of our Notice at present, because some very eminent Composers have attached themselves chiefly to the Method here mentioned; and seem to think they have exhausted all the Depths of Expression, by a dextrous Imitation of the Meaning of a few particular Words, that occur

in the Hymns or Songs which they set to Music. Thus were one
of these Gentlemen to express the following Words of <u>Milton</u>,

> ·················.Their Songs
> <u>Divide</u> the Night, and <u>lift</u> our
>   Thoughts to Heav'n.

It is highly probable that upon the word <u>divide</u>, he would run a
<u>Division</u> of half a Dozen Bars; and on the subsequent Part of the
Sentence, he would not think he had done the Poet Justice, or
<u>risen</u> to that <u>Height</u> of Sublimity which he ought to express, till
he had climbed up to the very Top of his Instrument, or at least
as far as a human Voice could allow him. And this would pass
with a great Part of Mankind for Musical Expression instead of
that noble Mixture of solemn Airs and various Harmony, which
<u>indeed</u> elevates our Thoughts, and gives that exquisite Pleasure,
which none but the Lovers of Harmony can feel.

What then is true <u>Musical Expression</u>? I answer, it is such a
Concurrence of Air and Harmony, as affects us most strongly with
the Passions or Affections which the Poet intends to raise: And
that, on this Account, the Composer is not principally to dwell
on particular Words in the Way of Imitation, but to comprehend
the Poet's general Drift or Intention, and on this to form his Airs
and Harmony, either by Imitation (so far as Imitation may be
proper to this End) or by any other means. But this I must still
add, that if he attempts to raise the Passions by Imitation, it must
be such a chastised and temperate Imitation, as rather brings the
Object before the Hearer, as such a one as induces him to form a
Comparison between the Object and the Sound. For in this last
Case, his Attention will be turned entirely on the Composer's Art,
which must effectively check the Passion. The Power of Music is
in this Respect, parallel to the Power of Eloquence: If it works at
all, it must work in a secret and unsuspected Manner. In either
Case, a pompous Display of Art will destroy its own Intentions:
On which Account one of the best general Rules, perhaps, that
can be given for Musical Expression, is that which gives rise to
the Pathetic in every other Art, <u>an unaffected Strain of Nature
and Simplicity</u>.[37]

If the sources of expressive power are to be found in a nature which extends further than the particular instrumentalities of the human frame, the theory of the passions as a determinate series with their own discrete modalities of response is due for reorganisation, and the way is opened for a return to a theory of correspondence, this time between man and nature, in which harmony will consist not in the equilibrium of a body's elements, but in the relation of a body to other bodies. Correspondence will be between wholes rather than between parts.

§ § § §

What we see in various writers following upon Burke is a growth of interest in the powers original to works of art which make them capable of affecting men. Addison's theory of the primary and secondary imaginations does not concern itself with the nature of objects, and effectively banalises the idea of art, because it presents the essential substance of art in terms of the operations of the imagination of any man of taste, and makes art superior to experience in the same way as the pleasures of memory are superior to immediate pleasures. This is the essence of any theory of art as a mirror to nature. It seems, in fact, that it is not necessary for the critic to concern himself with the intrinsic modalities of art works more or less to the extent that he does not subscribe to a metaphysical notion of the mind. (The mind is most exactly conceived as a closed system in a purely empirical universe, in fact, for instance one in which mental activity is conceived of exclusively in terms of chemical and electrical stimulus of the brain). This Addisonian trivialisation of art meets its final rejection in the work of Archibald Alison, who recognised that a purely mechanical sense of taste, functioning upon the real qualities of objects, would lead to artistic stultification, and stand opposed to any change or improvement.[38]

The implications of the theory of expression become most acute when it deals with the association of music and poetry. In Sir William Jones's essay "On the Arts, commonly called Imitative" we encounter the conventional distinction between the beautiful and the expressive, and at the same time he deploys an idea reminiscent of Avison's "Strain of Nature",

> Now let us conceive that some vehement passion is expressed in
> strong words, exactly measured, and pronounced, <u>in a common</u>
> <u>voice</u>, in just cadence, and with proper accents, such an expression

of the passion will be <u>genuine poetry</u>; and the famous ode of <u>Sappho</u> is allowed to be so in the strictest sense: but if the same ode, with all its natural accents, were expressed in a <u>musical voice</u>, (that is, in sounds accompanied with their <u>Harmonicks</u>) if it were sung in due time and measure, in a simple and pleasing tune, that added force to the words without stifling them, it would then be <u>pure and original musick</u>, not merely soothing to the ear, but affecting to the heart, not an <u>imitation</u> of nature, but the voice of nature herself.[39]

Expression as the voice of nature, even if it is "nature herself", is not an immediately clear notion, since it is possible to suppose that the nature we are dealing with is largely a human one. Jones clarifies the matter for us in a subsequent passage. The artist works upon the passions not by an imitation of nature but by assuming its power. It is not clear whether this is a power that resides in nature which the poet channels through his work, or whether the poet is to operate by the same means as nature, assuming that nature never imitates itself.

Thus will each artist gain his end, not by <u>imitating</u> the works of nature, but by assuming her power, and causing the same effect upon the imagination, which her charms produce to the senses: this must be the chief object of a poet, a musician, and a painter, who knows that <u>great effects are not produced by minute details, but by the general spirit of the whole piece, and that a gaudy composition may strike the mind for a short time, but that the beauties of simplicity are both more delightful and more permanent</u>.[40]

If the arguments, used in this essay, have any weight, it will appear, that the finest parts of poetry, and painting, are expressive of the <u>passions</u>, and operate on our minds by <u>sympathy</u>; that the inferior parts of them are <u>descriptive</u> of natural <u>objects</u>, and affect us by <u>substitution</u>.[41]

Jones's terminology is derived, to a considerable extent, from Burke. Where he differs from Burke is in the attention he pays to the question of the modalities of the work itself. Although these are derived attributively from the nature of artistic effects, according to the conventional post-Addisonian account, it is not possible to describe the existence of a work in terms of the affections or the passions, since these are inner senses. The general nature which Jones has in mind, following hard upon Johnson's perception of the ontological difficulties involved in general resemblance, is the appropriate subject of any theory of the arts based on notions of interior passions affected in a mechanical way, because it is able to draw to itself the superior status of the powers of the secondary imagination and of the memory. The train of associations in memory which Addison describes is, in effect, a prototypical description of a hypostatised general nature derived from the functions of the mind.

The voice of nature, from this point of view, is still framed according to the functions of human physiology; external nature is the source but not the power. It is to be noted, however, that the distinctions between the passions and the understanding which is implicit in most of the theories which I have been discussing can give rise to a historical solution to the problem which occurs when the sources of expressive power can be sought neither in an artificial compact, nor in an external nature of which man has no direct cognition, and which he cannot therefore express directly. If the processes of civilization and the augmentation of the understanding can be understood to take place to the detriment of the expressive powers of the passions, then it is possible to suggest the theory that the complementary functions of musical expression and verbal specificity are the remnant of a primeval period in human culture when expression directly involved both those functions which, in their dissociated or separated form, are known respectively as poetry and music.[42] We thus discover an appeal similar to that made by the Renaissance humanists when the invoked the idea of a classical union of music and poetry, only this time we find such writers as Adam Smith appealing to the pre-civilised, as seen both in antiquity, and in the present aboriginal populations of American and the Orient. The ideas of poetry and civilisation, according to this view, become antipathetic.

> Poetry is a necessary attendant on music, especially on vocal music, the most natural and simple of any. They (savage nations) naturally express some thoughts along with their music, and these must, of consequence, be formed into verse to suit with the music. Thus it is that poetry is cultivated in the most rude and barbarous nations, often to a considerable perfection; whereas they make no attempt towards the improvement of prose. 'Tis the introduction of commerce, or at least of the opulence that is commonly the attendant of commerce, that first brings on the

improvement of prose.[43]

The idea that poetry and music are natural to man, and that general human nature is best studied in the simplest, primitive conditions of human life, recurs in Hugh Blair's *Lectures on Rhetoric and Belles Lettres* (1783; however, Blair had been delivering these lectures for upwards of twenty years), who suggests that the art of verse is a derivative of music. "The first poets sung their own Verses; and hence the beginning of what we call, Versification, or Words arranged in a more artful order than prose, so as to be suited to some tune or melody. The liberty of transposition, or inversion, which the Poetic Style, as I observed, would naturally assume, made it easier to form the words into some sort of numbers that fell in with the Music of the Song. Very harsh and uncouth, we may easily believe, these numbers would be at first. But the pleasure was felt; it was studied; and Versification, by degrees, passed into an Art."[44] Blair's position is not carefully thought out, for he assumes a normative identification of language and prose, whereas the point of the search for the natural origins of poetry in primitive man has to do with the separate modes of operation pertaining to the different ends of the passions and the understanding.

The most thoroughgoing exponent of the primitivist point of view is Dr. John Brown, the full title of whose work, *A Dissertation of the Rise, Union, and Power, the Progressions, Separations, and Corruptions, of Poetry and Music* (1763) makes his argument fairly clear. The central point of Brown's argument is that poetry, music, and the dance all have a common origin. In his statement of his "proposed Method of Enquiry" he suggests that what is "common to the whole Race of Man, will be most effectually investigated, as to its Origin and Progress, by viewing Man in his savage or uncultivated State", before "Education and Art have cast their Veil over the human Mind."[45] (It is of interest to note that the Passions which underlie the whole of Brown's argument are also found in animals.)

> By examining savage Life, where untaught Nature rules, we find that the agreeable Passions of Love, Pity, Hope, Joy, and Exultation, no less than their Contraries of Hate, Revenge, Fear, Sorrow, and Despair, oppressing the human Heart by their mighty Force, are thrown out by the three Powers of Action, Voice, and articulate Sounds. The Brute Creatures express their Passions by the first two of These; some by Action, some by Voice, and some by both united: Beyond these, Man has the added Power of articulate Speech: The same Force of Association and Fancy which gives

6. Sound and Sense

him <u>higher Degrees</u> and a <u>wider Variety of Passion</u>, gives rise to his <u>additional Power</u> of expressing those Passions which he feels.

Among the <u>Savages</u> who are in the <u>lowest Scale</u> of the human Kind, these several Modes of expressing their Passions are found altogether suited to their wretched State. Their <u>Gestures</u> are <u>uncouth</u> and <u>horrid</u>: Their <u>Voice</u> is thrown out in <u>Howls</u> and <u>Roarings</u>: Their <u>Language</u> is like the <u>Gabbling</u> of <u>Geese</u>.

But if we ascend a Step or two higher in the Scale of savage Life, we shall find this <u>Chaos</u> of <u>Gesture</u>, <u>Voice</u>, and <u>Speech</u>, rising into an agreeable <u>Order</u> and <u>Proportion</u>. The natural Love of a <u>measured Melody</u>, which Time and Experience produce, throws the <u>Voice</u> into <u>Song</u>, the <u>Gesture</u> into <u>Dance</u>, the <u>Speech</u> into <u>Verse</u> or <u>Numbers</u>. The Addition of musical <u>Instruments</u> comes of Course: They are but <u>Imitations</u> of the human Voice, or of other natural Sounds, produced gradually by frequent Trial and Experiment.

Such is the Generation and natural Alliance of these three <u>Sister-Graces</u>, <u>Music</u>, <u>Dance</u>, and <u>Poem</u>, which we find moving Hand in Hand along the savage Tribes of every Climate.

For the Truth of the Fact, we may appeal to most of the Travellers who describe the Scenes of uncultivated Nature: All these agree in telling us, that <u>Melody</u>, <u>Dance</u>, and <u>Song</u>, make up the ruling Pastime, adorn the Feasts, compose the Religion, fix the Manners, strengthen the Policy, and even form the future Paradise, of savage Man.[46]

It is the alteration of the balance of reciprocal influence between manners and music which brings about the separation of music and poetry according to Brown. His suggestions as to the possibilities of renewing the union, including the establishment of an Academy for such a purpose, need not concern us except in one respect, which indicates the conservatism of Brown's attitude to prosody. In this respect he is aligned with Johnson.

Yet there is one Circumstance, in which modern Poetry and Music, though both reduced to their full Simplicity, cannot obtain that perfect Union which they held in ancient GREECE. The Numbers of the Poem and the Measure of the Music will inevitably sometimes clash. That Variety of Feet with which the Greek Tongue abounded, gave such play to the Musician's Art, in adapting a <u>various</u> and <u>correspondent Melody</u>, as no living

Language can boast. For Want of this Variety of Feet, there is generally a <u>dead Uniformity</u> in the Structure of modern Verse. The musical Rhythm or Measure, therefore, must either want the necessary <u>Variety</u>, or must sometimes be at Variance with the poetic Numbers.[47]

In the long run, however, I think it can be argued that the central Eighteenth Century aesthetic criterion of expression, with its notion of a direct appeal to an especially subtle human sensory mechanism, and consequent enrolment of music as the characteristic mode of influence upon these senses, prepares the way for the subversion of the regularistic prosody which was discussed in the previous chapter. The very fact of referring the movement of verse to the measures of music, even if the motive for so doing was not to compare analogous structures, but to affect the intended passion in an appropriate way, opens up the possibility of analysing verse, without reference either to music or eloquence, in terms of variable movements.

Notes

[1] *The Rambler*, ed. W.J. Bate and Albrecht B. Strauss, New Haven and London 1969, II, p. 129.

[2] Ibid., II, p. 135.

[3] Ibid., II, p. 136.

[4] Ibid., II, p. 139.

[5] Ibid., II, p. 135.

[6] Ibid., II, p. 136.

[7] See M.H. Abrams, *The Mirror and the Lamp, Romantic Theory and Critical Tradition*, NY 1953, pp. 160-161.

[8] *The Spectator*, ed. Donald F. Bond, Oxford 1965, III, p. 536. The stress laid by Addison on vision has an important parallel in Locke's equation of sight and thought, in which the mind is like a dark room dependent upon exterior illumination. See E.L. Tuveson, *The Imagination as a Means of Grace, Locke and the Aesthetics of Romanticism*, Berkeley and Los Angeles 1960.

[9] *The Spectator*, op. cit., III, p. 563.

[10] Ibid., III, p. 560.

[11] Ibid., III, p. 562.

[12] Ibid., III, p. 563.

[13] Alexander Gerard, *An Essay on Taste* (1759) together with *Observations concerning the Imitative Nature of Poetry*, a facsimile reproduction of the third edition (1780) with an introduction by Walter J. Hipple Jr., Gainesville, Fla., 1963, pp. 1-2.

[14] Alexander Gerard, *An Essay on Genius*, II, iii, "Of the Influence of the Passions on Association", in Scott Elledge, *Eighteenth Century Critical Essays*, Ithaca 1961, II, pp. 895-896.

[15] Edmund Burke, *A Philosophical Enquiry into the Origin of our Ideas of the Sublime and Beautiful, the second edition, with an introductory Discourse concerning Taste, and several other additions*, London 1759, pp. 209-210.

[16] Ibid., p. 313.

[17] Ibid., p. 320-321.

[18] Ibid., p. 334-335.

[19] See M.H. Abrams, op. cit., pp. 71-72, for a discussion of the centrality of this idea to Romantic notions of expression. Also, cf. Thomas Leland's *Dissertation on the Principles of Human Eloquence*, London 1764, in which he argues against the Royal Society position, maintaining that language communicates by expression and passion as well as by conveying information.

[20] Hildebrand Jacob, "Of the Sister Arts", *Works*, London 1735, p. 381.

[21] Ibid., p. 385.

[22] James Harris, "A Discourse on Music, Painting, and Poetry", *Three Treatises*, London 1744, pp. 97-98.

[23] Edmund Burke, *A Philosophical Enquiry...*, op. cit., pp. 338-339.

[24] Ibid., p. 340.

[25] Gerard, *An Essay on Taste*, op. cit., pp. 59-60. Cf. also Adam Smith, "Of the Nature of that Imitation which takes place in what are called the Imitative Arts", Essays on Philosophical Subjects, Edinburgh 1795: "The sentiments and passions which Music can best imitate are those which unite and bind men together in society; the social, the decent, the virtuous...They are, if I may say so, all Musicall Patterns; their natural tones are all clear, distinct, and almost melodious; and they naturally express themselves in a language which is distinguished by pauses at regular and almost equal intervals; and which, upon that account, can more easily be adapted to the regular returns of the correspondent periods of a tune." P. 156.

[26] See Daniel Webb, *Remarks on the Beauties of Poetry*, London 1762, pp. 88-89.

[27] Ibid., p. 5-6.

[28] Ibid., p. 10.

[29] John Mason, *An Essay on Elocution, or Pronunciation, Intended chiefly for the Assistance of Those who instruct Others in the Art of Reading. And of Those who are often called to speak in Public*, London 1748, pp. 28-29.

[30] Ibid., pp. 32-33.

[31] Adam Smith, op. cit., p. 174.

[32] Charles Avison, *An Essay on Musical Expression*, London 1752, pp. 2-5.

[33] Daniel Webb, op. cit., pp. 34-35.

[34] The seat of this controversy was in French music, J.P. Rameau maintaining in his *Traité de l'harmonie* that melody arose from harmonic progression, and J.J. Rousseau, in his *Lettre sur la musique française*, maintaining that there could be no French music as such because of the inadequate character of the French language, and arguing for the expressive primacy of melody and measure over harmony. See Strunk, op. cit., pp. 564-574, and pp. 636-654.

[35] William Jones of Nayland, *A Treatise on the Art of Music*, Colchester 1784, p. 41.

[36] Avison, op. cit., p. 58.

[37] Ibid., p. 59-62.

[38] See Tuveson, op. cit., pp. 186-194, for a discussion of Alison's *Essays on the Nature and Principles of Taste* (1790).

[39] Sir William Jones, *Poems consisting chiefly of Translations from the Asiatick languages, to which are added Two Essays, I. On the Poetry of the Eastern Nations, II. On the Arts, commonly called Imitative*, Oxford 1772, pp. 206-207.

[40] Ibid., p. 216.

[41] Ibid., p. 216-217.

[42] Cf. James Beattie, "Of Poetry and Music, as they affect the mind", Essays, Edinburgh 1776: "Yet it is in general true, that Poetry is the most immediate and the most accurate Interpreter of Music. Without this auxiliary, a piece of the best Music, heard for the first time, might be said to mean something, but we should not be able to say what. It might incline the heart to sensibility: but poetry, or language, would be necessary to improve that sensibility into a real emotion, by fixing the fancy upon some definite and affecting ideas." p. 161.

[43] *Lectures on Rhetoric and Belles Lettres delivered in the University of Glasgow by Adam Smith, Reported by a student in 1762-3*, ed. John M. Lothian, London 1963, p. 131.

[44] Hugh Blair, Lecture 38, "The Nature of Poetry—Its Origin and Progress—Versification", *Lectures on Rhetoric and Belles Lettres*, London 1783, II, p. 316.

[45] Dr. John Brown, *A Dissertation on the Rise, Union, and Power, the Progressions, Separations, and Corruptions, of Poetry and Music*, London 1763, p. 26.

[46] Ibid., p. 27-28.
[47] Ibid., p. 227-228.

Chapter 7

Natural Rhythmic Standards
and the Demand tor Prosodic Variety

It is justifiable to regard the Eighteenth-Century theory of artistic Expression as a product of the same cast of mind which consolidated a prosody of syllabic and stress regularity. Just as the theory of Expression offers an explanation of mental qualities in terms of a chain of physiological and mechanical operations which leads back to an external world, so the rationale of syllabic and stress regularity is to organise intrinsically featureless phonological elements into numerically defined series of contrastive pairs, a mode of organisation which it is reasonable to describe as mechanical in conception, since the means of combination employed refer not to the phonological elements as such, but to their capacity to function within a numerically defined series. Paul Fussell Jr. discusses the nature of this regularistic prosodic sanction in circumstantial detail, and describes a pervasive convention of syllabic contraction to which it gave rise.[1] Paradoxically however, the theory of Expression, with its demand for a flexibility of rhythmic performance to conform with the variety of sensory motion to which the different human passions were susceptible, tended to undercut the more exclusively formal demands of a regularistic prosody which, although consolidated during the latter half of the Seventeenth Century, reaches back, as I have shown, into the Sixteenth Century. In this chapter I shall discuss attempts to establish analytical and descriptive terms capable of dealing with the sense of prosodic structure which was required as a response to the demands for prosodic variety to which the theory of Expression gave rise. Here one encounters a terminological confusion similar to that which beset the Sixteenth Century Humanist critics. However, it is to be borne in mind that although the prosodic convention of strict syllabic and stress regularity was under attack from early in the Eighteenth Century, such a convention remained the formal staple of orthodox poetic sensibility throughout the Nineteenth Century, and continues to exercise a similar function to this day.[2] It is indicative to note, for instance, Robert Bridges' description of the prosodic expectations normal to his readers, which he sought to anticipate and forestall in the Preface to his *Poems* (Third Series) in 1880. "It is left to the judgement of the reader: but the author hopes that these verses will be read with attention to the natural quantity and accent of the syllables,—for these are the interpretation of the rhythm,—and not with the notion that all accents in poetry are alternate with unaccented syllables, nor with the almost universal prejudice that when two or more unaccented syllables intervene between two accented syllables the former must suffer and be slurred over: a prejudice which probably arises from the common misuse of unaccented for short syllables."[3]

The formal qualities which were felt to inhere in numerically conceived prosodic structures, in which the whole determines the performance of the part, rather than vice versa, carried over inevitably into discussion of the standards and means of a more flexible prosody. It is such a carry-over, I think, which can best explain the characteristic early Eighteenth-Century suggestion that, in the English Language, it is accent that determines quantity. This is not the same as the notion that accent can substitute for quantity in metrical feet based on classical models. It was generally felt that the very concept of verse entailed of necessity the presence of verbal quantity, but that in verse such quantity arose not from the particular quality of this or that phonological element, but was marked, or bounded, by those accented syllables which were, to a considerable extent, thought ot be determined in turn by their occurrence in a basic prosodic unit consisting of a pair of contrasted syllables.

There existed, moreover, considerable uncertainty about the real nature of accent: whether, that is to say, it was a tonic accompaniment to vocal sounds, as its etymology strictly provided; whether it was a matter of the relative loudness or softness of the voice, akin to a purely rhetorical emphasis, which might extend over a whole phrase or sentence; or whether it was a more localised vocal impulse, with a significant function in natural language, governing the pronunciation and, in the case of homonyms, the meaning of individual words. The preoccupations of prosodic discussion of a non-regularistic type were increasingly centred on the question of accent, and led from there to the relation of the accented syllables to the other syllables in a line of verse. Considerations of this sort led in due course to a sense of verse quantity which, instead of emphasising the aggregate of quantitatively distinct syllables, in which by implication there could occur no non-syllabic quantities, suggested instead the notion of a temporal continuum of verse marked off, as in the beating of time in music, by re-iterated accents. The hegemony of regularistic prosody was first questioned by a re-distribution of the terms of the variety in uniformity principle: how much variety could uniformity bear, and what sort of ratio between the two terms provided the standard of harmony. It is worth noting that, unlike present day metrical theory, in which rhythm is a function of metre, the Eighteenth Century prosodist saw all metres as species of a generic "rhythmus", and so such questions as the substitution of a trisyllabic foot for a bisyllabic one, or the expansion of syllabic contractions (heaven for heav'n; or wandering for wand'ring—polysyllables, of course, presented special problems for the regularistic prosodist) were not earth-shaking ones. Indeed the standard of conventional taste stood opposed to the habit of elision.[4]

The kind of uncertainty which prevailed as to the relative claims of regularity on the one hand and variety on the other are typified in Henry Pemberton's *Observations on Poetry, Especially the Epic: Occasioned by the Late Poem upon Leonidas* (1738).[5] Pemberton was concerned to assert the value of harmonious verse movement as a countervailing force to extravagance of language, but sensed that the classical languages possessed a certain superiority in this respect.

> What has made many too fond of high figures, sounding epithets, and laboured constructions, I imagine is their not being duely apprized of the power of numbers; whereas a just and harmonious measure of verse will give sufficient grace or dignity to the most unaffected diction.
>
> It must be confessed, that all the modern languages fall infinitely short of the ancient in this point. Both the Greek and Latin tongues, even in discourse, assigned for the pronunciation of each syllable an exact measure of time, in some longer and in some shorter, and so variously intermixt those two different measures in the same word, as furnished means for that variety of versification, to which we are altogether strangers.[6]

The problem for Pemberton was that the regularistic prosody which he thought of as essential to modern English verse thwarted his desire for harmonious measure, which he conceived of as a function of quantity. One approach to such harmony, however, was to be found in the circumstance that "perhaps, what we commonly call smoothness of style is in part owing to something analogous, namely such a rangement of the words, whereby the syllables follow one another with a free and easy cadence."[7] Pemberton seems to be searching for a coherent theory which will allow regularity of measure to be varied without being disrupted. But although Pemberton thought of measure in terms of quantity, his criterion of regularity was an accentual one; he resolved the problem by suggesting that accent in some way generates extra quantity.

> But now, as our verse is regulated by the accent, to give our narrative five-foot verse its just and complete measure the second, fourth, sixth, eighth, and tenth syllables ought to be capable without any violence done the words of receiving some degree of emphasis, and be pronounced in a longer time than the rest; the movement of the verse being always disturbed, when such emphasis is removed from any of these syllables to any other.[8]

It is to be noted that quantity here is not a quality of the emphatic syllable, but a period of time <u>in which</u> the syllable is sounded. The theory being that "whereas the ancient accent is represented to be only a variation in the tone of voice, and had no relation to the quantity of the syllable, this is constantly attended with an emphasis, which implies greater length in the syllable."[9] It appears, that is to say, that while emphatic accent is a primary prosodic signal, its function in the prosodic system is secondary to a somewhat ideal conception of quantity. We can best understand what this meant for Pemberton in an actual verse situation when he suggests a mode of variety in which word-coherence is at variance with foot-coherence.

> And what these authors [Aristides and Quintilian] observe of the tone of voice, is equally to be regarded in relation to the movement; that as verse is distinguished from prose by disposing the words in a musical measure, so it is to be removed from the express form of music by causing the words sometimes to terminate in the middle of the feet, in order that the little pauses between the words may in a proper degree break the formality of the measure.[10]

The formality of the measure consists in the stately procession of alternately unemphatic and emphatic syllables, which Pemberton wishes to think of in terms of ideal quantity, but into which he introduces the real time of transitions between words. Pemberton's theoretical confusion nevertheless exhibits a sensibility well on the way to thinking of the integrity of the verse foot in temporal rather than accentual terms.

In the two essays published posthumously in his *Poems on Several Occasions: and Two Critical Essays* (1745) Samuel Say puts forward much more convincing arguments to underpin his demands for prosodic flexibility. In the first of these, "An Essay on the Harmony, Variety, and Power of Numbers", he makes the formal qualities of regularistic prosody, proportion, order, and so on, answer to the needs of poetic Expression, and suggests that they are in fact the functions of such an end.

> Numbers in General, to the Purpose I mean of the Present Enquiry, is but another word for ORDER and PROPORTION; the Source of HARMONY and GRACE, whether in SOUNDS or MOVEMENTS, or whatever Works of Genius of Art.[11]

Say's argument revolves around the proposition that poetic numbers are not "numerous", and do not of their nature express an equal harmony. The function of numbers is to please the ear and impress the mind, their beauty consists in their grace and propriety in adapting sound to sense, which is the basis of the well-known power of numbers. Say argues that irregularities occur naturally in impassioned speech, and refers to the work of Vergil and Milton to exhibit this contention. Prosodic variety, therefore, is necessary for two reasons. Monotony is displeasing, and variety is expressive.

> The Ear cannot long be pleas'd with One and the Same Sound continued, nor Different Impressions be made upon the Soul, by the same Motions and Percussions of the Air: Therefore Nature, or the Reason of things, has instructed the Voice in Every Language not to move by Single and Uniform Sounds, or strike forever the Same Notes, unvaried either in Tone or in Time.[12]

Say's principle of variation, like Pemberton's, is conceived of in terms of different ways of disposing a flexible number of syllables within feet which are defined by temporal regularity. Unlike Pemberton, however, Say does not offer additional pauses more or less *ad libitum*; for him the quantities are, much more directly, the functions of language itself.

> So many Sounds as may be united together in One Movement are call'd by the Name of Feet, because they seem to be the regular PACES by which the Voice moves on, or proceeds, in an equable or agreeable Manner; and therefore they are distinguish'd by different Names, according to the different Quantity or Disposition of the TIME in which we pronounce 'em, or the Stress of the Voice that is laid upon 'em.[13]

Therefore Fit Quantity of Syllables, or Sounds whose Measure of Time should be Equal or nearly Equal to one another, either in the Same or a Different Number of Syllables, were most industriously to be sought by Those who intended to write in Verse; and with the greater Exactness, Felicity, and Variety they were chosen, the Greater was the Harmony.[14]

Say's naturalistic conception of the character of the formal elements of poetry led, logically, to the view that any deformation of the natural sounds of language meant a derogation of poetic power and dignity, and that such deformation or artificiality undercut the expressive resources of poetic harmony.

But then, as in SINGING, so in RECITING, every SYLLABLE must have not only its Proper Accent, but its Just Length and Solemnity of Sound, such as different Vowels or Diphthongs, and different Emotions of the Soul, do naturally give it: And That, in whatever Place of the Verse we meet it. And This is the Great Advantage of the Admission of Different and quite contrary Movements into This kind of Verse, to adapt it to all the Endless Variety of Passions and Ideas which we propose to excite in the Mind of the Reader.[15]

Say's insistence that a syllable must receive its due natural emphasis wherever it occurs in the line of verse is the measure of the clarity of his thought, and also of his superiority as a theorist to Pemberton, for by following through the implications of his equal time theory, and by having it deal with real rather than ideal time, Say has been forced to recognise the necessity of abandoning the criterion of a regular recurrence of accent on all equal-numbered syllables. His objection to syllabic contraction for metrical regularity is stated with equal clarity.

But what Monsters of Sound would Ann'al or An-wal, Syr'an or Am'rous be? or does anyone really pronounce any otherwise than ánnŭăl, Sýrĭăn, ámŏrŏus, in three short, but distinct Syllables? why then does he suffer his Eyes to judge for his Ears? or suffer Words so agreeable in Sound to be written or printed in a manner he never pronounces? or who would dwell on a Sound naturally short? or lay the Stress of the Voice on an inconsiderable TO or THE, on pretence that the Laws of Versification require it? or, by a more amazing Inattention, drop the very Sounds, to which the whole Beauty of the Numbers is owing, and the happy Imitation of Nature itself?[16]

In his second essay, "Remarks on the Numbers in the Argument to *Paradise Lost*" Say's naturalism in linguistic matters enables him to extend the commonplace distinction between ancient and modern languages; he sees French as quite distinct in character from English, for instance, on account of its "perpetual and unwearied Monotony."[17] The English language, on the other hand, is profuse in the means with which it furnishes a principle of prosodic variety.

> For the English Language has the utmost Variety both of Time and Accent. Every Vowel with Us is sometimes Long, and sometimes Short; and we lay the Accent, indifferently, on the Last, the Last but one, or the Third Syllables from the End, and sometimes seem to draw it still more backward; or to give a kind of double Accent to some Polysyllables, one Stronger and one Fainter. For the same Reason the Verses run with the greater Fluency and Sweetness of Sound into one another; and the Ear is prepar'd either to rest at the Close of the Verse, or to be led into That which follows: And the Pauses are indifferently made, in any Part of the Verse, and on the Even or Uneven Syllables.[18]

But the most striking aspect of Say's prosodic ideas is his notion of contrast or opposition between a regular accentual system and syllabic quantity, and it is precisely this mode of variation that the most expressive effects are found. Say discovers in this principle the true meaning of Horatian formula.

> All therefore that HORACE proposed was, not either to offend or to please the Ear, but to take only the Advantage of proper Numbers to pour in upon the Mind of the Reader all the Ideas of his own Mind, with the same Evidence and Force with which they appear'd to Himself; and attended with the very same Emotions of Soul; which it is hardly possible to do in Prose; where the Reader is not under the like Necessity of giving Every Word and Every Syllable its proper Accent or Emphasis of Sound.
>   And he who has the Address, or Felicity, to join these Two, the Music I mean, and the Power of numbers together, his Works will be admir'd, wherever found.[19]

The drift of Say's argument should be clear enough in the light of the account of the Passions and the theory of Expression given in the previous chapter, but the sophistication with which Say relates music to numbers in a descriptive context drives the argument home.

The like Contrast to each other, I imagine, must be added to the many Accounts that have been given of the Pleasure which every Reader is sensible of in that celebrated Distich in Cooper's Hill, which Mr. DRYDEN has render'd so remarkable by proposing the True Reason of it as a Problem to torture the Grammarians. For nothing can be more different than the Sounds, and the Numbers or Movements in the Two Verses, as will appear to the Ear itself, and by measuring the Time in the Feet of either, that are oppos'd to the other,

Tho' deep, yet clear; tho' gentle, yet not dull:

Where the Verse moves as Slow, and Silent, or as Gentle as the River: All the Iambics, if we call 'em so, that are nearer to Spondees, excepting in one place, where it had been a manifest Impropriety.

But stronger Ideas requir'd Numbers Stronger and Fuller: and such is the following Verse,

Strong without Rage; without o'erflowing, Full.

It begins with a Trochee, which gives Motion to the River; but check'd by a Spondee of Two Very Long Times, oppos'd to the Shorter Times of That which stands in the Same Place, in the preceding Verse; as the Trochee here is oppos'd to a Spondee of Longer Sound in the Former. The Like we may observe in the True or Genuine Iambic in the Third Foot, which is oppos'd to the Gentler Spondee above it: And as the Weakest Sounds fall, as the Ideas require they should, on the Fourth and Fifth Feet in the First; so the Sounds that fill and arrest the Ear, stand in the Fourth Movement here, and yet are clos'd in the most agreeable Manner, as the Law of the Distich generally demands, with a real Iambic, or Sounds that approach the nearest to it. And the Last Half of the Former Verse has no Beauty, in My Opinion, but what is owing to this Opposition, and its Agreement with the Image it represents.[20]

Say is not employing a notational system in which accents are marked as though they are quantities; what he is concerned to show is a situation in which lines identical in number can be various in their effect. All that Say lacks is the sophisticated theory of a mechanically produced expressive power to avoid the possible accusation that the relation of sound to sense as he understands it is merely imitative.

The idea, which I have already noted, that accent determines quantity in English verse is reasserted by John Mason in *An Essay on the Power of Numbers* (1749). He maintains, like Say, that the numbers of English verse are temporal in function: "a Verse is ultimately made up of a determinate Number of Times, according to the particular Metre or Species of Verse."[21] Like Say also he refers the criterion for accent to a naturalistic sense of language.

> That which principally fixes and determines the Quantities in English Numbers is the Accent and Emphasis, and the common Manner of Pronunciation of these, as used by the best Masters of the English Language.[22]

One of the questions to which Mason pays close attention is the distinction between ancient accent and English accent; he is anxious to resist the idea of a tonic accent, since he requires the influence of an articulated accent to assure that sense of quantity which is essential to his conception of measure.

> If it be said, that among the Antients the Accent and Quantity were two different Things; that the Accent denoted the Sound of the Voice, and the Quantity the Length of the Time. Be it so (though by the Way it will be found extremely difficult to read any Greek Author by this Rule) yet I would fain know by what Principles we are obliged or even allowed to observe any such Rule in the Pronunciation of English; which is a Language of a very different Genius, and admits of a much greater Latitude in its Quantities than either the Latin or the Greek. And that it is impossible any such Distinction between the Accents and the Quantities can be observed in reading English, whether Poetry or Prose, any one may presently be convinced by making the Experiment.

The Truth is, there is a very wide Difference between the Latin and English <u>Prosody</u>. And it's in vain to think of introducing the Rules of the former into the latter; since the English Language is not so framed as to admit it. this is very plain to those who compare the Prosody of the two Languages; wherein they cannot avoid observing how they contradict each other. For Instance, one Vowel before another in English is often long, in Latin almost always short. A vowel before another in English is often short, in Latin always long. And Diphthongs which are always long in the Latin are often short in the English Tongue.

And yet to assert (as some have done) that we have therefore no certain determinate Quantities in our Language, is to sap the very Foundation of all English Verse; which is made up of Measures, as <u>they</u> are of Feet, which depends upon the determinate Quantities of the Syllables whether long or short. But if we have no such determinate Quantities, we have no certain Feet, consequently no just Measures, and therefore no Verse.

The proper Accent and Emphasis then is the chief Rule that determines the English Quantities. And it is a Rule not only more general, but more certain and unexceptionable than those that are introduced into the ancient <u>Prosodia</u>. For Common Use and Custom...will never fail to determine the Accent, and the Sense of the Period when understood, will point out the Emphasis; and where the Accent or Emphasis is thus directed to fall, that Syllable (be its natural Quantity what it will) is in that place considered as long; and those Syllables that have neither Accent or Emphasis are considered as Short.[23]

Mason's theory is by and large one in which accent is substituted for quantity, but in which the integrity of the line is conceived of in ideal quantitative terms. For all his confusion, however, it is interesting to note that one possibility which does not present itself to Mason is that of inducing artificial quantities in verse by arbitrary spelling and rules of orthographical quantity.

One of the results of the tendency to run the ideas of accent and quantity together, but to measure in terms of quantity alone, was that accent came to be thought of as a featureless event, marking time, but not occurring in any natural way in language. Commonsense recognition of emphatic articulation in normal pronunciation always resists such a development, of course, but nevertheless there was room for controversy in the Eighteenth Century. Although he starts off from the question of tonic accent in Greek, Henry Gally, in *A Dissertation Against Pronouncing the Greek Language according to Accents* (1754) is an advocate of the commonsense, realist position. He argues that accent is essential to language. "Some Accents are, and must be used in all Language. For there is no Harmony in continued Monotones."[24] Tonic accent, however, he argues, carries with it implications of stress.

> No men can read Prose or Verse according to both Accent and Quantity. For every Accent, if it is any thing, must give some Stress to the Syllable, upon which it is plac'd. And every Stress, that is laid upon a Syllable, must necessarily give some Extent to it. For every Elevation of the Voice implieth Time, and Time is Quantity.[25]

One of the circumstances which nourished confusion about the nature of accent derived from the application of the Greek terms <u>arsis</u> and <u>thesis</u>, which were effectively interchangeable in a context in which it was not clear whether the thing placed down was the foot or the hand, or whether it was the voice. Thus it was possible, by referring these terms to the voice, to make the *arsis* the accented syllable in a tonic sense. The term *ictus*, with the implied sense of beating, helped cast some light on this confusion. In John Foster we see a proponent of ideal metrical accent. His *Essay on the different nature of accent and quantity* (1761), in which the distinction is drawn between tonic and metrical accent elicited, in due course, a reply from the pen of Henry Gally, but this *Second Dissertation* (1763) added little to the controversy.

> The <u>ictus accentum</u> of which Dr. Bentley hath given us the marks in his Terence (and which have sometimes been confounded with the general accent of the language), are purely <u>metrical</u>, falling on a particular syllable of a foot, or dipodia, and marking the several divisions of the verse, according to the manner of scanning it.[26]

> I have supposed that in the metrical arsis there was an elevation of the foot or hand, but probably not of the voice. Dr. Bentley, however, speaking of this arsis, seems to think that the voice was in some way elevated too: and there are passages, I own, in the old grammarians, that appear to favour this opinion. But if the

voice was elevated, it was not to such a degree as to supercede the common syllabic accent. For if it did, the accent of their prose and verse was different (which it is difficult to suppose), the arsis on a verse coming on a syllable that had the thesis in prose, and so vice versa.[27]

But for the two sorts of confusion endemic in the use of his terminology we might feel that Foster was on the verge of discerning the principle of metrical contrast which was anticipated by Say. But Foster is not careful enough to distinguish between that tonic accent which relates to pitch on the one hand, and what he quite clearly calls syllabic accent on the other. equally he does not distinguish between his metrical sense of accent, peculiar to verse, and the accent of prose which, presumably, is more or less the same thing as that which he understands by syllabic accent.

An additional confusion lurking in Eighteenth Century prosodic terminology is aptly demonstrated by John Rice in his *Introduction to the Art of Reading with Energy and Propriety* (1765), when he explicitly connects the idea of quantity with accent.

> It is plain, that the same Quantity of Sound, or Force of Accent, may be laid upon a short Syllable as on a long one, and, vice versa, without prolonging, the one, or contracting the other. And here we have the reason why an unaccented short Syllable may, in English verse, supply the Place of a long one unaccented without injury to the Rhythmus, or Measure.[28]

Rice is a thoroughgoing accentualist, for whom accent substitutes for quantity.

> Hence it appears, that the Beauty and Harmony of English Numbers do not depend on the sole Disposition of long and short Syllables: Quantity, with us, not consisting merely of Tone or of Tune, as it is supposed to have done among the Antients: For it is very certain, that Accent supplies the Place of Time in English Verse; that is, a short accented Syllable hath the same Force, and supplies the same Place in a Foot as a long accented one. It doth not hence follow, however, that the natural Length or Time of Syllables should be neglected, or be considered as altogether the same Thing as Emphasis or Accent.[29]

For Rice the concept of Numbers is entirely detached from that of prosodic quantity, and he is able to dispense altogether with the fiction that, in English, accent is a determinant of quantity.

What is to be discovered progressively during the Eighteenth Century is the definition of the crucial but vague prosodic term accent in a way which resembles the present-day use of the word. We find such a view offered more or less as an axiom by James Monboddo in *Of the Origin and Progress of Language* (1773-1776). He maintains that accent is a relative quality, "for it is impossible to conceive a sound either acute or grave, but in relation to another sound."[30] And of rhythm in general he maintains that only two particular species need be noticed, "that which is produced by the mixture of loud and soft sounds, and that which arises from the distance or interval betwixt such sounds."[31] Metrical accent, of which Monboddo is a regularistic advocate, is clearly for him a function of real linguistic entities. "We have no more to do but to repeat any verse in English, and we shall find, that without the alternate percussion of the accented and unaccented syllable, it would not be verse."[32]

It is only when we come to Joshua Steele's *Prosodia Rationalis: or, An Essay Towards Establishing the Melody and Measure of Speech, to be Expressed and Perpetuated by Peculiar Symbols* (1779) that the generally fruitless conceptual confusion about accent and quantity comes to be clarified. Steele is a committed temporalist, and his persistence in using the term accent to refer to tonic features makes him somewhat difficult for the present-day reader to follow, but one of his major strengths is the careful evaluation he makes of five distinct attributes of sound: Accent, Quantity, Pause, Emphasis or Cadence, and Force. Moreover, Steele's grasp of the implications of his subject is such that he constantly alerts the reader to the natural and universal attributes of rhythmic activity. The technical novelty of Steele's argument is to distinguish the organisation of a verse line into syllabic feet, from the temporal organisation of the same line in what he calls bars or cadences.

> But always some <u>rests</u> or <u>pauses</u> are necessary, as being more agreeable both to the sense and to the measure; so that, including the rests, a line of nominal five feet, or ten syllables in words, occupies at least the time of six bars or cadences, as in the example following; in which the syllable <u>oh</u>! is positively <u>emphatical</u> and under <u>thesis</u>, and the syllable <u>our</u> (agreeable to the sense in this expression) is, as positively, <u>remiss</u>, and under <u>arsis</u>.

But here let it be observed, that this <u>emphasis of cadence</u> and the <u>expression of loudness</u>, are not to be considered as equivalent terms or affections of the same kind; for the <u>arsis</u>, or <u>remiss</u>, may be <u>loud</u>, or <u>forte</u>; and the <u>thesis</u>, or <u>emphatic</u>, <u>piano</u> or <u>soft</u>, occasionally. The <u>thesis and arsis</u> being periodically alternate, whether expressed or supposed; whereas the application of the <u>forte</u>, and <u>piano</u> are ad libitum, or <u>apropos</u>.[33]

What interests Steele is the way in which a continuous rhythm or cadence, invested in nature, acts upon poetic language, as well as being generated by the language. Within the established cadence we are to suppose that the rests and pauses implied of the measure of the syllables in a line are to be felt as essential, in contrast with the flexible disposition of stresses.

> Our breathing, the beating of our pulse, and our movement in walking, make the division of time by pointed and regular <u>cadences</u>, familiar and natural to us. Each of these movements, or <u>cadences</u>, is divided into two alternate motions, significantly expressed by the Greek words <u>arsis</u> and <u>thesis</u>, <u>raising</u> and <u>posing</u>, or setting down; the latter of which, coming down as it were with weight, is what we mean to call <u>heavy</u>, being the most energic or emphatic of the two; the other, being more remiss, and with less emphasis, we call <u>light</u>.[34]

The notions of heavy and light here might appear to contradict the idea that <u>arsis</u> and <u>thesis</u> are simply devices to mark the division of time; however, Steele forestalls such confusion when he makes clear that his sense of syllabic emphasis is of one which is natural to language.

> Now all speech, as well as other music, is subject to the influence of CADENCE, by <u>arsis</u> and <u>thesis</u>, or the <u>light</u> and the <u>heavy</u>, as well as of MEASURE, which determines those cadences to the <u>common</u> or the <u>triple</u>, and likewise to the affection of QUANTITY (as an inferior division of RHYTHMUS and MEASURE) by the <u>long</u> and the <u>short</u>.
> And as the <u>length</u> of syllables, as well as their particular affections to the <u>light</u> and the <u>heavy</u>, is various, according to the genius of the language; so some words and sentences must be measured by <u>common time</u>, and some by <u>triple time</u>.[35]

Steele's introduction of the notion of common and triple measures refers to the syllabic structure of individual feet. The implication of his argument is that syllabic stress occurs in verse, not as a function either of cadence (temporal measure) or of measure (number of syllables), but of the occurrence of stress in normal speech. As an exponent of the aesthetic demand, discussed in the previous chapter, that poetry and music be brought together in a renewed harmony, Steele requires that both his expressive means, pause and stress, owe their presence in verse to a natural standard, and is able to satisfy each of these, superficially contradictory, requirements by making the one answer to the constraints of a natural temporal rhythm, the other to those of natural speech pronunciation. Steele is thus, obviously, an extreme opponent of regularistic stress prosody.

> The variety of <u>loud</u> and <u>soft</u> should never be considered as (necessarily) a governing principle of <u>rhythmus</u>; because though it may, sometimes, be accidentally coincident with rhythmical pulsation, yet it would be offensive if it continued so for any considerable length of time: for the application of the <u>loud</u> and the <u>soft</u>, both in music and language, either for use or ornament, must not be indiscriminate or periodically alternate, but as occasion calls for it, whereas the rhythmical pulsation is regularly periodical and constant as the swings of a pendulum, but of itself implies no noise at all. And agreeable to this, a band of musicians are much better governed in their measures by a <u>silent</u> waving of the hand, or of anything that may catch the eye, than by the more ordinary <u>noisy</u> way of keeping time with the foot.
>
> The expression, or rather the affections of <u>heavy</u> and <u>light</u> are necessarily the governing principles of rhythmus; for they are as constantly alternate and periodical as the pulse itself, and they must be continued, by conception in the mind, during all measured rests and pauses, as well as during the continuance of either uniform, articulated, or modulating sounds.[36]

Steele's use of the terms <u>heavy</u> and <u>light</u> should not be taken to suggest anything other than an ideal division of time taking place in the mind, under the stimulus, perhaps, of a universal natural rhythm, an instance of which we possess in our pulse. Steele's notion of a constant rhythmic current of a specifically temporal nature running through the universe is, in effect, a secularised restatement of the theory of cosmic harmony which I have previously discussed. For Steele there are a number of incidental advantages in his application of such an assumption. For a start it enables him to overthrow completely the tyranny of classical quantity, which he says was both crude in its recognition of only two temporal units, and negligent in its neglect of non-syllabic quantity.[37] It also allows him to suggest that the down beat in music is not marked by any inherent emphasis in the note, and does not possess "really any pulsation or ictus, except what the mind may suppose it to have, when it makes it the leading note of the bar."[38] What the real nature is of what, for the sake of clarity, I shall now refer to as accent, in the present-day sense, Steele is in some difficulty to explain. It is distinguished from mere force or loudness, and the closest he comes to conceiving of it as a syllabic occurrence is in relation to that temporal cadence which is by definition incapable of real sound. It is something which inheres in normal speech, of course, since it is able to determine whether a measure is in double or triple time. There is no final answer to this question because for Steele what we are accustomed to think of as accent possessed no primary importance. Rhythm for Steele is a silent, temporal progression, appealing to the instincts rather than to the rational sense, expressive of man's place in the universe.[39]

The <u>instinctive</u> sense of <u>pulsation</u> gives the word and <u>idea</u> of <u>emphasis</u> and emphatic <u>divisions</u>, independent of any actual increment of sound, or even of any sound at all. But emphasis and emphatic divisions imply, that there are some sounds of a different nature; that is, that there is a discontinuance or diminution of emphasis with or without discontinuance of sound; or, in other words, independent of sound. And hence we have the mental sensation of <u>emphatic</u> and <u>unemphatic</u>, which I distinguish and represent by the words and symbols of Δ <u>heavy</u> and :: <u>light</u>. And as a common term to signify both, I appropriate the word POIZE, in like manner as ACCENT is used as the common term for <u>acute</u> and <u>grave</u> and QUANTITY for <u>long</u> and <u>short</u>.

It is the office of RHYTHMUS, aided by the <u>influence</u> of this <u>instinctive</u> POIZE, to regulate the whole duration of any melody or movement by an exactly equal and periodical pulsation, until it is thought proper to change the measure, for some other uniform pulsation, either quicker or slower.

In the time of the world, a natural day (night included) is a single <u>cadence</u>; the setting and rising of the sun the <u>thesis</u> and <u>arsis</u>; seasons and years are rhythmical clauses: the real beginning and the ending of this melody are out of our sight; but to human apprehension, the apparent are birth and death, and life is our part in the song.[40]

Steele's argument was, unfortunately, too sophisticated for his time. his system of equal temporal intervals marked by mental impulses, couple with his failure to define explicitly a natural phenomenon of syllabic stress, meant that the flexibility of a system in which words are felt as part of a larger temporal continuum failed to exercise its potential influence on poetic sensibility. It is important to note that Steele's insistence on temporal uniformity is not merely the product of an Eighteenth-Century regularistic taste, but a necessity also for a man who has no firm grasp of the phenomenon of linguistic stress. Robert Nares, for whom accent held no such difficulties, effectively wrote Steele off in a footnote to his *Elements of Orthoepy: containing a distinct view of the whole analogy of the English Language; so far as it relates to Pronunciation, Accent, and Quantity* (1784), saying "I should fear that his system is too obscure to be of general service, even if right."[41]

Nares found Steele obscure, no doubt, partly because he used the term accent in a peculiar way, which for Nares was conceptually redundant. For Nares accent is a form of stress which pertains to one syllable in a word, just as emphasis is a form of stress which pertains to a word in a sentence. Accent distinguishes one syllable "from the crowd, and brings it forward to observation."[42]

Such is the nature of accent among us. Among the ancients the term denoted a very different thing. Accent, with them, signified a musical modulation of the voice, making it higher or lower with respect to gravity or acuteness of sound. Thus προσωδια in Greek and <u>accentus</u> in Latin, the words from which our <u>accent</u> is derived, mean <u>a singing to</u>; the Latin term being a literal translation of the Greek. This has been sufficiently proved by the learned Dr. Foster, in his celebrated Treatise on <u>Accent</u>, &c.; and the long dispute upon the subject has terminated, since his time, in this conclusion: that the ancient accent was something, of which little or no traces are to be found in modern languages. It is true that we do not speak monotonously, but do frequently elevate and depress our voices, not only as to softness and loudness, but in respect of musical tone. These inflections, however, seem to affect sentences rather than single words; nor are they, as far as I can discover, directed in any degree by the accentuation of syllables.[43]

Nares's sense of accent is reaffirmed by most subsequent writers on the subject. Walter Young, for instance, in his "Essay on Rhythmical Measures" published in 1790, notes that "When I apply the term accent to syllables, I use its grammatical acceptation, to denote that superior force of articulation, and that inflection of the voice, with which we always mark in our pronunciation some particular syllable or syllables in every word."[44] Richard Roe also, with a declared debt to Walter Young in *The Principles of Rhythm, both in Speech and Music: especially as exhibited in the Mechanism of English Verse* (1823), refers to the same concept, although he uses the term pulsation in place of accent.

> Pulsation is a peculiar stress or impression of the breath, by which some one element in every syllable is maked or distinguished more than the others; which element is therefore said to be pulsated or under pulsation, and all others remiss or in a state of remission. …This elementary pulsation with a progressive augmentation of intensity, is used for the additional purposes both of distinguishing certain rhythmical intervals, and of marking all emphatic words…[45]

But although Roe's accents, or pulsations, mark a temporal rhythm of sorts, he regards pauses within the line of verse as a matter of performance only, independent of the rhythm, in fact so much a matter of discretion that their function is to break and interrupt the rhythm.[46] The crudity of this conception of variety in comparison with that displayed by Steele suggests that although Roe refers, piously one might say, to "rhythmical intervals", it is an accentual rather than a temporal rhythm to which he responds.

§ § § §

Alongside the orthodox accentual-syllabic norm of the Nineteenth Century, to which I have earlier noted Bridges's reference, equal-time and syllabically-irregular prosodies occur as a minor fact of possible prosodic theory. What I want finally to suggest, however, is a fundamental distinction within this marginal theoretical activity. In the theory of Coventry Patmore, on the one hand, is to be discerned a continuation of the strictly temporal notion of rhythm, in which accents are used to measure temporal units, but are not themselves measured. In the occasional theoretical writings of Gerard Manley Hopkins and Robert Bridges, on the other hand, the idea of a prosodic system is entertained which may be called accentual.

In the essay "English Metrical Critics" (1857), which he subsequently printed as a "Prefatory Study of English Metrical Law" in *Amelia* in 1878, Patmore cites approvingly Steele's insistence that pauses should be taken into account in the measure of verse.[47] But for Patmore, a poet more conventional in his tastes than in his technical concepts, the value of temporal measure lies in the contrast it affords to the occurrence of natural speech qualities in verse. "Meter never attains its noblest effects when it is altogether unproductive of those beautiful exorbitancies on the side of law".[48] Patmore's notion, in effect, anticipates those theories of metrical contrast which I discussed in Chapter 2, but does so in terms of a temporal matrix rather than an accentual one.

> In the finest specimens of versification, there seems to be a perpetual conflict between the law of the verse and the freedom of the language, and each is incessantly, though insignificantly, violated for the purpose of giving effect to the other. The best poet is not he whose verses are the most easily scannible, and whose phraseology is the commonest in its materials, and the most direct in its arrangement; but rather he whose language combines the greatest imaginative accuracy with the most elaborate and sensible metrical organisation, and who, in his verse, preserves everywhere the living sense of metre, not so much by unvarying obedience to, as by innumerable small departures from its <u>modulus</u>.[49]

It is important to note that for Patmore (and this applies to Steele also) metre and rhythm are not affects of language itself, but refer to a concept of rhythmical means which transcend any which might derive directly from language. Poetic language measures this absolute temporal rhythm not, primarily, by virtue of any capacity special to it, but because it can be used for this purpose by the human mind, which participates in the absolute temporal rhythm at an instinctual level. Patmore offers an impoverished version of Steele's natural metaphors for such a rhythm.

Metre, in the primary degree of a simple series of isochronous intervals, marked by accents, is as natural to spoken language as an even pace is to walking. Prose delivery, without this amount of metre, is like a drunkard's walk, the irregularity of which is so far from being natural to a person in his senses, that it is not even to be imitated without effort. Now, as dancing is no more than an increase of the element of measure which already exists in walking, so verse is but an additional degree of what metre is inherent in prose speaking.[50]

Patmore is absolutely clear about the notion that whatever marks this isochronous rhythm is not a part of the rhythm itself. Rhythmic recurrence is, properly speaking, monotonous; but since there is little charm in this for the senses, the mind tends to attribute tonic distinctions to the essentially neutral rhythmic markers. Patmore is residually aware of the notions that accent determines syllabic length in English, but his refutation of it is largely a formality, since a syllabic quantity has little function in such an extra-linguistic temporal series.

Now, it seems to us that the only tenable view of that accent upon which it is allowed, with more or less distinctness by all, that English metre depends, in contradistinction to the syllabic metre of the ancients, is the view which attributes to it the function of marking, by whatever means, certain isochronous intervals. Metre implies something measured…The thing measured is the time occupied in the delivery of a series of words. But time measured implies something that measures, and is therefore itself unmeasured; an argument before which those who hold that English accent and long quantity are identical must bow. These are two indispensable conditions of metre,—first, that the sequence of vocal utterance, represented by written verse, shall be divided into equal or proportionate spaces; secondly, that the fact of that division shall be made manifest by an "ictus" or "beat", actual or mental, which, like a post in a chain railing, shall mark the end of one space, and the commencement of another.[51]

Patmore's insistence carries with it a serious equivocation about the real or other status of accent, while at the same time insisting that accent shall, in some sense, be a manifestation. Sidney Lanier's essay *The Science of English Verse* (1880) throws some light on this question with its distinction of primary and secondary rhythms. Secondary rhythm is the produce of a tendency to arrange primary rhythmic units into subordinate groups, which, as in the case of the ticking of a clock. "the imagination will effect… when the sounds themselves do not present means for it."[52] Lanier is not clear in his mind about the distinction between accent as stress and accent as pitch, and this leads him into considerable difficulty at a later stage of his essay when he tries to argue the case that, as an alternative to temporal regularity marked by accents, one might envisage an accentual regularity employing a variety of temporal interval. But so long as accent is thought not to be a natural feature of language, temporal prosodies have to define themselves in terms of equality of rhythmical units. Hence Lanier's distinction between primary and secondary rhythms.

> It is this secondary rhythm which is usually meant by the term "rhythm" in ordinary discourse, and the variations in pitch and intensity by which we saw it effected among the clock-ticks are what is usually called "accent" in English treatises. The point to be vigorously observed here is that all secondary rhythm (in ordinary language, all "rhythm") necessarily presupposes a primary rhythm which depends upon the considerations of time or duration: in other words, that rhythm of any sort is impossible, except through the coordination of time. Time is the essential basis of rhythm. "Accent" can effect nothing, except in arranging materials already rhythmical through some temporal recurrence. Possessing a series of sounds temporally equal or temporally proportionate, we can group them into various orders of larger and larger groups, as we shall presently see, by means of accent; but the primordial temporalness is always necessary.[53]

For Lanier, then, verbal rhythm is essentially a secondary rhythm, derived from the primary or absolute temporal rhythm which other verbal functions, variable in kind we are to suppose, have defined but not created.

The counter to this is to see the authentic rhythm of poetry as a derivative of real linguistic activities. Hopkins indicates such a view as this in his notes on "Poetry and Verse", when he remarks that "Poetry is in fact speech only employed to carry the inscape of speech for the inscape's sake—and therefore the inscape must be dwelt on", and goes on to argue that repetition of sound occurs in verse in order to "detach" inscape "to the mind", so that "all poetry is either verse or falls under this or some still further development of what verse is, speech wholly or partially repeating some kind of figure which is over and above meaning, at least the grammatical, historical, and logical meaning."[54] For Bridges, equally, poetic rhythm was primary to language, and when he dispensed with the theory of syllabic regularity its place was not filled by a theory of temporal uniformity marked by notional accents, but by literal stress regularity. In *Milton's Prosody* Bridges criticises Coleridge's failure to distinguish between metrical stress and linguistic stress in some lines of "Christabel", remarking that "the primary law of pure stressed verse is, that there shall never be a conventional or imaginary stress: that is, <u>the verse cannot make the stress, because it is the stress that makes the verse</u>."[55] The laws for such verse inhere naturally in language, so that "when English poets will write verse governed honestly by natural speech-stress, they will discover the laws for themselves."[56]

The distinction between Patmore and Bridges, or between Steele and Campion, is between two different conceptions of rhythmic law. Both conceptions are naturalistic, but they differ profoundly in their conception of the way the law exercises itself in man. On the one hand man can participate in the natural laws of rhythm at a pre-rational stage, via his instincts and his pulse; on the other, human language itself is felt to be an expression of such a law, which is thus a function of reason operating through determinate units of perception. Paterian music is an exemplification of just such a concept as this. In the third chapter of his <u>Plato and Platonism</u>, "Plato and the Concept of Number", Pater offers a version of art subject to the operations of discretely realised, one might say physically exercised units of law.

Only, remember always in reading Plato—Plato as a sincere learner in the school of Pythagoras—that the essence, the active doctrine of the Pythagorean doctrine, resides, not as with the ancient Eleatics, nor as with our modern selves too often, in the "infinite", those eternities, infinitudes, abysses, Carlyle invokes for us so often—in no cultus of the infinite (το απειρου) but in the finite (το περαγ). It is so indeed, with that exception of the Parminidean sect, through all Greek philosophy, congruously with the proper vocation of the people of art, of art as being itself the finite, ever controlling the infinite, the formless.[57]

> The numerically finite enables Pater to invoke the ethical orders of that cosmic harmony which I discussed in Chapter 5, investing the idea of cosmos itself with a rational finitude, unified variety which does not controvert the Heraclitean fleeting away of things.[58]

To realise unity in variety, to discover <u>cosmos</u>—an order that shall satisfy one's reasonable soul—below and within apparent chaos; is from first to last the continuous purpose of what we call philosophy. Well! Pythagoras seems to have found that unity of principle (αρχη) in the dominion of number everywhere, the proportion, the harmony, the music, into which number as such expands. Truths of number: the essential laws of measure in time and space: —Yes, these are indeed everywhere in our experience: must, as Kant can explain to us, be an element in anything we are able so much as to conceive at all. And music, covering all it does, for Pythagoras, for Plato and Platonism—music, which though it is of course much besides, is certainly a formal development of purely numerical laws: that too surely <u>is</u> something, independently of ourselves, in the real world without us, like a personal intelligible soul durably resident there for those who bring intelligence of it, of music, with them; to be known on the favourite Platonic principle of like by like (δμοιου ομοιω) though the incapable or uninstructed ear, in various degrees of dullness, may fail to apprehend it.[59]

The suggestion that such knowledge is occulted, and the hint of metempsychosis (we remember what befell Scipio in his dream), are all beside the point of the essential proposition here, that there exists a correspondence between the facts of the cosmos, the real world without us, and the rational soul.

Notes

[1] See Fussell, op. cit., pp. 1-100, particularly pp. 68-100.

[2] Cf. the various linguistically-derived systems of metrical contrast described in Chapter 2, above; that of Yvor Winters; and also that of Robert Conquest in his introduction to *New Lines 2*, London 1963, to cite a more polemic example; and also Paul Fussell Jr. in his *Poetic Meter and Poetic Form*, NY 1965.

[3] Quoted in *The Letters of Gerard Manley Hopkins to Robert Bridges*, ed. C.C. Abbott, second (revised) impression, London 1955.

[4] Cf. for example Jonathan Swift, *A Proposal for Correcting, Improving, and Ascertaining the English Tongue* (1712), and also *The Rambler* No. 88 (1751).

[5] Fussell makes the following comment on Richard Glover's <u>Leonidas</u>: "The blank verse of <u>Leonidas</u> displays an almost total regularity of accent, with only very

occasional initial trochees and even more rare internal pyrrhics for variation." Op. cit., p. 21.

6   Henry Pemberton, *Observations on Poetry, Especially the Epic: Occasioned by the Late Poem upon Leonidas*, London 1738, p. 106.

7   Ibid., p. 106-107.

8   Ibid., p. 130. Fussell regards Pemberton as an exponent of strict stress regularity, which patently he is not, and copes with Pemberton's anomalous notion that emphasis is pronounced in a "longer time" by interpolating an exclamation mark when he quotes this passage, op. cit., p. 21.

9   Pemberton, op. cit., p. 216.

10   Ibid., p. 117.

11   Samuel Say, "An Essay on the Harmony, Variety, and Power of Numbers", *Poems on Several Occasions: and Two Critical Essays*, London 1745, p. 97.

12   Ibid., p. 101.

13   Ibid., p. 102-103.

14   Ibid., p. 120.

15   Ibid., p. 127.

16   Ibid., p. 131.

17   Samuel Say, "Remarks on the Numbers in the Argument to Paradise Lost", ibid., p. 144.

18   Ibid., p. 144.

19   Ibid., p. 154.

20   Ibid., p. 151-153.

21   John Mason, *An Essay on the Power of Numbers*, London 1749, p. 5.

22   Ibid., p. 9.

23   Ibid., p. 9-11.

24   Henry Gally, *A Dissertation Against Pronouncing theGreek Language according to Accents*, London 1754, pp. 6-7.

25   Ibid., p. 67.

26   John Foster, *An Essay on the different nature of accent and quantity*, third edition, London 1820, p. 162.

27   Ibid., p. 164.

28   John Rice, *An Introduction to the Art of Reading with Energy and Propriety*, London 1765, p. 58.

29   Ibid., p. 105-106.

30   James Monboddo, *Of the Origin and Progress of Language*, Edinburgh 1773-1776, II, pp. 272-273.

[31] Ibid., II, p. 385.

[32] Ibid., II, p. 385.

[33] Joshua Steele, *Prosodia Rationalis…*, London 1779, p. 12.

[34] Ibid., p. 20.

[35] Ibid., p. 22.

[36] Ibid., p. 68.

[37] Cf., ibid., p. 78.

[38] Ibid., p. 96.

[39] Cf., ibid., p. 78.

[40] Ibid., p. 117-118.

[41] Robert Nares, *Elements of Orthoepy…*, London 1784, p. 144.

[42] Ibid., p. 141.

[43] Ibid., p. 144-145.

[44] Walter Young, "An Essay on Rhythmical Measures", *Transactions of the Royal Society of Edinburgh*, II, (1790), p. 76.

[45] Richard Roe, *The Principles of Rhythm…*, Dublin 1823, p. 34.

[46] Ibid., p. 74-75.

[47] Cf., Coventry Patmore, "English Metrical Critics", *The North British Review*, XXVII, (1857), p. 128.

[48] Ibid., p. 131.

[49] Ibid., p. 131.

[50] Ibid., p. 132.

[51] Ibid. p. 136.

[52] Sidney Lanier, *The Science of English Verse*, new edition, NY 1909, p. 64.

[53] Ibid., p. 65.

[54] *Journals and Papers of Gerard Manley Hopkins*, ed. House and Storey, London 1959, p. 289.

[55] Robert Bridges, *Milton's Prosody*, Oxford 1901, p. 73.

[56] Ibid., p. 77.

[57] Walter Pater, *Plato and Platonism*, London 1893, p. 51-52.

[58] Cf. ibid., Ch. 1, "Plato and the Doctrine of Motion", in which Pater discusses Plato's indebtedness to Heraclitean concepts.

[59] Ibid., p. 45.

Chapter 8

Conclusion:
Free Verse and the Natural Restraints of Language

Although it is a circumstance of regret to many people, language is not a pure symbolic system, not a system of fixed fiduciary symbols, not defined by the relation of signifier to the signifies. Our words and our arrangements of words are fraught with sensible configurations of articulatory and aural activity and response. In all its aspects language possesses a tangible reality in excess of the capacity for propositional, descriptive, and interrogative transactions which it subserves. Empirically grounded arguments can never settle the question of the proper relationship of these two separable characteristics of language, the symbolic and the tangible. Some notion of the ends which language serves must be introduced prior to any attempt at such arbitration. Thus by insisting on a criterion of operational symbolic functionalism, a demand that our use and sense of language be purged of the interference of tangible verbal qualities becomes entirely rational. It is possible, on the other hand, to regard symbolic functionalism as a second-ary product of linguistic activity, and therefore as a transaction which is dependent, in ways which it is not necessary to define for the time being, on the activity of the gross and sensible, real configurations of language. Pater's sense of the discrete and finite standing over against the diffuse and infinite suggests one way in which such a notion of language as essentially a sensible presence defines a language which nevertheless can continue to be thought of as an attribute of mind. Indeed I would argue that such a view entails a superior concept of mind to that exercised by criteria of operational utility alone, to the extent that the fixed fiduciary symbol is a product only of the will, the relation between signifier and signified seen as an exclusively attributive one. If such an attributive relationship is indeed the case in language, it must follow as a matter of course that cognition and perception are pre-linguistic transactions, language furnishing simply a system of conveyance and storage of greater convenience and ease of manipulation than that, whatever kind of system it is, which initially deals with the cognitive and perceptive input. Language is thus a translation of experience made in the mind in terms of a set of tabulated equivalents. The major problem to which such a system is susceptible, of course, is that of novelty. Novel combinations of entities already tabulated for such an attributive language can be dealt with by promulgation from within the language's discrete system, of course,; but a more fundamental novelty is inconceivable unless one posits some other form of collective experience. From the point of view which I am describing, that is to say, language cannot be taken to provide such a pre-contractual collective experience. Nor can the problem of novel entities be dealt with by asking how language came to refer in the way that it does, of course, since such a question elicits the idea of a real relationship between the signifier and the signified prior to the contractual one. Once perception and knowledge are given priority over language, the system of language is closed; linguistic complexity is made an affair of compound association, in a Burkean fashion, and novelty, if it occurs at all, has to be transacted according to some other modality. It should be noted that I am careful to say that it is language which becomes a closed system, and not the world itself. The ethical implications of the closure of language, a conceptually finite world on the one hand, openness on the other hand only in terms of immediate sensory presence and various forms of extra-sensory mysticism, are of obvious interest, but do not need to be considered in the present context.

In this essay, taking Pound's "absolute rhythm" as a point of departure, and then by way of the various notions of idiom, harmony, and expression which I have discussed, I have examined various ways in which prosody has been seen, not as a purely formal (that is to say secondary) organisation of language, the essential organisation of which will have already taken place in terms of its function as a symbolising series, but rather as an organisation of those sensible configurations of language which is in some way in concordance with, correspondent to, or expressive of the meaning of the particular linguistic occasion. In other words, I have been trying to define a point of view in which prosody functions as a recognition that the sensible configurations of language are part of its meaning. These terms of relationship imply a bonding of elements which are separate or which have been dissociated, but which are, in some sense, essential to each other. Whether what we discretely call prosody is an extension of meaning, contributive to meaning, whatever the precise relationship, prosody is introduced as a significant feature of language which is not susceptible to tabulation. Whereas both words and their arrangement in grammatical sets can be posited in terms of the possible conceptual relationships between fixed fiduciary symbols, the sensible relationship of prosodic sequence is not susceptible to any such process of reduction. One of the things which should be discernible in a fully coherent theory of modern poetry, I would contend, is the abolition of any distinction between prosody and poetic meaning which makes the use of relational terms such as <u>correspondence</u> necessary. The abolition of a distinction between form and content, or their merging, is not a desideratum of a theory of aesthetic effect but of a notion of poetic ontology, only in the circumstance, however, as I distinguished in Chapter 3, in which the notion of form is referred to the description of an occasion rather than an hypostasis.

§ § § §

The influence of French *vers libre* on English free verse is not easy to define, and is bound up moreover with the influence of *Symbolisme*. It is always worth remembering, however, that someone like Pound found it necessary to insist that his work was not symbolist in the French sense, and that for him any symbolising function in a poem needed to be discharged by an object which was fully in the natural world. Pound's resistance to symbols rather than symbolising can be understood in the light of the enthusiasm of English exponents of *Symbolisme* such as Arthur Symons, in which an antagonism to criteria of operational utility in language is carried to the extreme of rejecting any referential function in language.

> There are poems of Verlaine that go as far as verse can go to become pure music, the voice of a bird with a human soul. It is part of his simplicity, his divine childishness, that he abandons himself, at times, to the song which words begin to sing in the air, with the same wise confidence with which he abandons himself to the other miracles about him. He knows that words are living things, which we have not created, and which go their way without demanding of us the right to live. He knows that words are suspicious, not without their malice, and that they resist mere force with the impalpable resistance of fire or water. They are to be caught only with guile or with trust. Verlaine has both, and words become Ariel to him. They bring him not only that submission of the slave, but all the soul, and in a happy bondage. They transform themselves for him into music, colour, and shadow; a disembodied music, diaphanous colours, luminous shadow. They serve him with so absolute a self-negation that he can write romances sans paroles, songs almost without words, in which scarcely a sense of the

interference of human speech remains. The ideal of lyric poetry, certainly, is to be this passive, flawless medium for the deeper consciousness of things, the mysterious voice of that mystery which lies about us, out of which we have come, and into which we shall return. It is not without reason that we cannot analyse a perfect lyric.[1]

There is nothing paradoxical about the way in which "words in which scarcely a sense of the interference of human speech remains" is the aim also of those for whom language is normatively a system of pure symbolic activity. Whatever life words enjoy is a function of their presence in a human context—as dissevered limbs they are quite dead. Symons's intangible and uncontaminated music is in fact the very reverse of that Platonic ethos of due and proportionate relationships which Pater cited. It is a music which hovers above rather than one which inheres in the world.

This English conception of *Symbolisme* tends to neglect the more careful precisions of *Symboliste* statements concerning verse technique such as that of Jean Moréas who, in his "Manifeste du Symbolisme" (1886), advances a point of view which could promulgate the relevance of music to poetry in an alternative fashion. "Ennemie de l'enseignement, la déclamation, la fausse sensibilité, la description objective, la poésie symboliste cherche à vêtir l'idée d'une forme sensible qui néanmoins ne serait pas son but à elle-même, mais, tout en servant à exprimer l'idée, demeurerait sujet. L'idée à son tour ne doit pas se laisser voir privée des analogies extérieures; car la caractère essentiel de l'art symbolique consiste à ne jamais aller jusqu'à la conception de l'idée en soi."[2] This subjection of form to the exigencies of an idea that can never be fully realised as idea is the basis for a relation between form and idea which is musical in the ethical sense. As Suzanne Bernard puts it in *Mallarmé et la Musique*, "C'est le désir de conférer, suivant l'expression de Verhaeren, 'à 'idée-image le droit de créer sa forme en se développant', qui aménera les Symbolistes au vers libre: modulation, dit Mallarmé, 'individuelle, parce que tout âme est nœud rythmique.'"[3]

While Moréas himself thought in terms of the refurbishing of old rhythms, constrained perhaps by a notion of "forme sensible" in which hypostasised form still played a part, a more thoroughgoing criterion of responsiveness to the inner movement of thought entailed for French poets the abandoning of the syllabic regularity of the alexandrine. Whichever of Rimbaud, Laforgue, or Gustave Kahn enjoyed the best claim to priority in the inauguration of true *vers libre* rather than *vers libéré*, the rationale was offered by Kahn in the "Preface sur le vers libre" with which he introduced his *Premiers Poèmes* in 1897. Kahn's idea was to make the verse line not a unit merely, but also a unity by joining in it a movement of intelligence and a movement of rhythm. It is in terms of such a musical unity, first of all, that he distinguishes his own innovations from those of his friend Laforgue.

> Dans un affranchissement du vers, je cherchais une musique plus complexe, et Laforgue s'inquiétait d'un mode de donner la sensation même, la vérité plus stricte, plus lacée, sans chevilles aucunes, avec le plus d'acuité possible et le plus d'accent personnel, comme parlé. Quoiqu'il y a beaucoup de mélodie dans Les Complaintes, Laforgue, se souciant moins de musique (sauf pour évoquer quelque ancien refrain de la rue), négligeait de parti-pris l'unité strophe, ce qui causa que beaucoup de ses poèmes parurent relever, avec des rythmes neufs à foison, et tant de beautés, de l'école qui tendait seulement à sensibiliser le vers, soit celle de Verlaine, Rimbaud, et quelques poètes épris de questions de césure, doués dans la recherche d'un vocabulaire rare et renouvelé. Je crois que dès ce moment, et à ce moment (surtout), mes efforts porteront surtout sur la construction de la strophe, et Laforgue s'en écartait délibérément, volontairement, vers un liberté idéologique plus grand qui le devait conduire a cette phrase mobile et transparente, poétique certes, des poignantes Fleurs de bon volonté.[4]

Kahn's definition of verse unity, which, he maintains, is applicable equally to the classical alexandrine in skilled hands which allow it to fall naturally into such subdivisions, is that "l'unité vraie n'est pas le nombre conventionnel du vers, mais un arrêt simultané du sens et du rythme sur toute fraction organique du vers et de la pensée. Cette unité consiste en un nombre ou rythme de voyelles et de consonnes qui sont cellule organique et indépendante."[5] A pause made purely for the sake of the ear, that is to say, is incapable of constituting such a verse unity. Kahn's progression from the organisation of the verse line to the organisation of the strophe takes place in terms of the formal exfoliation of germ-like thought. Rhythmical correspondence here is seen in terms of a sequential development of the relationships embodied in the leading unity of thought within a strophe.

> L'unité du vers peut se définir encore: un fragment le plus court figurant un arrêt de voix et un arrêt de sens.

Pour assembler ces unités et leur donner la cohésion de façon qu'elles forment un vers il faut les apparenter. Les parentés s'appellent allitérations, soit union de consonnes parentes ou assonances par des voyelles similaires. On obtient par assonances et allitérations des vers comme celui-ci:

Des mirages / de leur visage / garde / le lac / de mes yeux.

Tandis que le vers classique ou romantique n'existe qu'à la condition d'être suivi d'un second vers, ou d'y correspondre a brève distance, ce vers pris comme exemple possède son existence propre et intérieure. Comment l'apparenter à d'autres vers? Par la construction logique du strophe se constituent d'après les mesures intérieures du vers qui dans cette strophe contient la pensée principale ou le point essentiel de la pensée.[6]

Kahn account for these "mesures intérieures" in a fashion which is highly reminiscent of the Eighteenth-Century theory of passionate agitation.

Cet accent semblable chez tout le monde, en ce sens que chaque passion, chez tous, produit à peu près le même phénomène, accélération ou ralentissement, semblable au moins en son essence, cet accent est communiqué aux mots, par le sentiment qui agite le causeur ou le poète, uniquement, sans souci d'accent tonique ou de n'importe quelle valeur fixe qu'ils possédaient en eux-mêmes. Cet accent d'impulsion dirige l'harmonie du vers principale de la strophe, ou d'un vers initial qui donne le mouvement, et les autres vers, a moins qu'on ne recherché en effet de contraste, se doivent modeler sur les valeurs de ce vers telles que les a fixées l'accent d'impulsion.[7]

Such a theory of mechanically natural expression, as is the case also with Joshua Steele's notion of prosodic harmony, cuts right across those fine discriminations of local idiom suggested by Read and Williams, and implies a poetry of either dramatic or personally expressive modes. Rémy de Gourmont's critique of Kahn's theories, in the chapter on *vers libre* in *Esthétique de la langue francaise* discriminates between the two components of Kahn's verse unity, and insists that verse divides according to the exigencies of thought alone. "Nous sommes en présence d'une phrase coupée en fragments analytiques plutôt même que rythmiques. Ces vers sont régis par le mouvement intérieur de la pensée, et non plus par un mouvement extérieur et imposé d'avance."[8] De Gourmont rejects, first of all, the additional rhythmical organisation of Kahn's strophe, and second, the notion that rhythm follows the passions (which are, in a sense, as external to an inner principle of verse form as any *a priori* form, since the passions are accorded priority to the implementation of shape) rather than thought. We need to see the way in which de Gourmont's criterion of thought as the determinant of prosodic activity is mediated by his theory of the dissociation of ideas, according to which they are led back to those sensations whence thought originates. The interior rhythm of thinking in this sense will be that of things in the world as they are represented in the mind, language itself being the mode of such representation.

Vers libre, therefore, in the fullest sense of what can be understood by the term, was able to offer English poets not only a novel formal conception of verse, but an explanation also of the way in which verse could be made to be an exposition of the developing stages of thought and feeling within a poem, so that the real formal principle of *vers libre* was one of interior developmental structure opening out into its manifestation in language. Such an argument in favour of the rationale of *vers libre* was, and still is, open to the charge that the mode of thought implied by the asymmetries, the hesitancies and turnings of *vers libre*, is not the only mode of thought available and suggests, indeed, an inferior conception on the part of the proponents of such a point of view of what thought is capable of being. I have attempted to anticipate arguments of this sort in my first two chapters. I want now to suggest that the modes of action in the world implied by free verse, which only free verse can register properly as poetry, are not confined to mental action alone, but include also notions about the structure of the world and our experience of it. These notions will include not only the structure of the world as understood, perhaps, by natural philosophy, but the structure also of that world or that nature which includes within it mental activity as a function of nature also.

§ § §

Numerical measurement is a greatly simplified mode of pure symbolic language, able to promulgate from itself the means of describing any combinational novelty without needing to add either to its grammatical structure or to its vocabulary, requiring only the attribution of a quantity of measurement, inches, ounces, therms, or whatnot, to define the object being measured or described. It is easy in consequence to confuse the mental activity of measuring with the employment of the technical means of measurement. What measurement furnishes in fact is a very simple but comprehensive form of contact between the mind and its object. Thus Coventry Patmore's rigour when he remarks that "time measured implies something that measures, <u>and is therefore itself unmeasured</u>" is more apparent than real. That which measures, always, is the mind or consciousness. Moreover, that which Patmore excludes from measurement is not itself the standard of measure, in this case a temporal one, but that which expresses the standard.

Now, measurement is simple because it expresses a complex entity in terms of a single quality, and it is comprehensive because its numerical series can be extended or subdivided to exemplify any manifestation of that quality. But it is an axiom of modern physics that the measurement of such a complex, or such a simple, item as a sub-atomic particle is necessarily relative: the mass of such a particle cannot be measured without setting aside the question of its velocity, and vice versa. This essential qualitative relativity of measurement does not matter all that much when one constructs a table, but it is important when one is dealing with such complex entities as a particle, or, I would contend, a poem.

What, anyway, is the point of measuring a line of verse? Measurement entails the idea of a basic unit, and implies that the mind can perceive a quality before it actually measures it. But if in measuring we are also applying a standard, implying in other words that an organised series of words is or is not a line of verse according to its success in conforming to the measure we apply, then the qualities measured have their seat in the mind rather than in the hypothetical line of verse. Different systems of measurement can allow for local flexibility to varying degrees, of course. This depends, for example, in the case of measured accents, on whether what is measured is the temporal interval between recurrent accents, or the number of accents in a line. In the latter case, of course, where the line itself is the unit of measurement, then the measure carries an implicit standard in addition to its function as a description of quantity.

Prosodic measurement, therefore, is a way of enforcing the observation of patterns of recurrence upon instances of language which are intended to be poetry, and has the effect of reducing to a minimum the accountable factors of sensory configuration in poetic language. This will be the case irrespective of the extent to which the principle of metrical variation is exercised. However, by being made to serve a pattern-making function the measured sensible configurations of language will be effectively deprived of their authentically sensory character. The tendency of any principle of prosodic measurement, therefore, is not only to induce a marked regular pattern, but also to insist that, even in poetry, language is a product of the mind, with a functional modality confined to the area of the mind. Language is inexorably retained as an essentially mental experience, subject to mental laws. The senses, from this point of view, are promiscuous rather than rational.

Against such a point of view I would adduce two propositions about our knowledge of the natural world, one from the point of view of natural philosophy, the other from that of linguistics, which seem to me to sustain the view that we neither exercise language as a conceptual tool, nor, in our experience of it, can ever escape the objective character of language, of which its sensory configurations are only an aspect.

A)   If language is an exclusively mental product, its objectification as speech merely a technical convenience, then it follows that our knowledge of nature deploys itself in a modality quite distinct in kind from that according to which we derive knowledge of whatever is external to us. A.N. Whitehead rejects such a bifurcation of cognitive and descriptive functions in *The Concept of Nature*, not on the basis of a supposedly <u>perfect</u> knowledge of nature, but in terms of the way in which we know it, and the necessity that the interrelation of such knowledge be consistent.

What we ask from the philosophy of science is some account of the coherence of things perceptively known.

This means a refusal to countenance any theory of psychic additions to the object known in perception. For example, what is given in perception is the green grass. This is an object which we know as an ingredient in nature. The theory of psychic additions would treat the greenness as a psychic addition furnished by the perceiving mind, and would leave to nature merely the molecules and the radiant energy which influence the mind towards that perception. My argument is that this dragging in of the mind as making additions of its own to the thing posited for knowledge by sense-awareness is merely a way of shirking the problem of natural philosophy. That problem is to discuss the relations *inter se* of things known, abstracted from the bare fact that they are known. Natural philosophy should never ask, what is in the mind and what is in nature. To do so is a confession that it has failed to express relations between things perceptively known, namely to express those natural relations whose expression is natural philosophy.

What I am essentially protesting against is the bifurcation of nature into two systems of reality, which, in so far as they are real, are real in different senses. One reality would be the entities such as electrons which are the study of speculative physics. This would be the reality that is there for knowledge; although on this theory it is never known. For what is known is the other sort of reality, which is the byplay of the mind. Thus there would be two natures, one is the conjecture and the other is the dream.

Another way of phrasing this theory which I am arguing against is to bifurcate nature into two divisions, namely into the nature apprehended in awareness and the nature which is the cause of awareness. The nature which is the fact apprehended in awareness holds within it the greenness of the tree, the song of the birds, the warmth of the sun, the hardness of the chairs, and the feel of the velvet. The nature which is the cause of awareness is the conjectured system of molecules and electrons which so affects the mind as to produce the awareness of apparent nature. The meeting point of these two natures is the mind, the causal nature being influent and the apparent nature being effluent.[9]

The bifurcation theory is an attempt to exhibit the cause of the fact of knowledge. Namely, it is an attempt to exhibit apparent nature as an effluent from the mind because of causal nature. The whole notion is partly based on the implicit assumption that the mind can only know that which has itself produced and retains in some sense within itself, though it requires an exterior reason both as originating and determining the character of its activity.[10]

The reason why the bifurcation of nature is always creeping back into scientific philosophy is the extreme difficulty of exhibiting the perceived redness and warmth of the fire in one system of relations with the agitated molecules of carbon and oxygen, with the radiant energy from them, and with the various functionings of the material body.[11]

Whitehead's solution to this problem is to reject the scientific materialism of the two previous centuries, and make the erstwhile stable concepts time and space the generalisations of a recurring series of events, and in turn to make perception a part of such events wherever perception occurs. From this point of view nature does not exist as hypostasis but as experience, and the idea of "natural philosophy" as such is no more, or no less a quality than are "redness" and "warmth".

If what we think of as the kind and its contents are a part of nature, it follows that language is a part of any percipient event in the same degree that those objects upon which we normally think language to be predicated are part of such an event, only the category of object (a perceived entity) is now, as are time and space, the generalisation of a series of percipient events.

B)   The second proposition which I wish to draw into my frame of reference is that of linguistic relativity, as postulated by the Sapir-Whorf hypothesis, which suggests that language plays a determining role in the constitutions of the basic axioms of the universe we perceive. The natural phenomena dealt with do not differ from language to language from this point of view, but the way in which they are conceptualised or generalised does vary. Whorf adduces his argument from the study of Hopi grammar and vocabulary. Noting that Hopi has no words or tensile constructions to express our notions of time, Whorf argues that "Hopi language and culture conceals a METAPHYSICS, such as our so-called naïve view of space and time does, or as the relativity theory does, yet it is a different metaphysics from either."[12] As against our own cosmic forms of time and space, in which space is three dimensional and static, and time is divided into past present and future, Whorf describes a Hopi metaphysics in which two cosmic forces are posited which he calls the "manifested", comprising the present and the past of the physical universe, and the "manifesting, (or, unmanifest)", which comprises the future and everything which we would class as mental. Whorf goes on to explain the latter cosmic form, which he calls subjective, in detail.

If we were to approximate our metaphysical terminology more closely to Hopian terms, we should probably speak of the subjective realm as the realm of HOPE or HOPING. Every language contains terms that have come to attain cosmic scope of reference, that crystallize in themselves the basic postulates of an unformulated philosophy, in which is couched the thought of a people, a culture, a civilization, even an era. Such are our words "reality, substance, matter, cause," and as we have seen, "space, time, past, present, future." Such a term in Hopi is the word most often translated "hope"—tunátya—"it is the action of hoping, it hopes, it is hoped for, it thinks or is thought of with hope," etc. Most metaphysical words in Hopi are verbs, not nouns as in European languages. The verb tunátya contains in its idea of hope something of our words "thought", "desire", and "cause", which sometimes must be used to translate it. The word is really a term which crystallizes the Hopi philosophy of the universe in respect to its grand dualism of objective and subjective; it is the Hopi term for SUBJECTIVE. It refers to the state of the subjective, unmanifest, vital and causal aspect of the Cosmos, and the fermenting activity toward fruition and manifestation with which it seethes—an action of HOPING. As anyone acquainted with Hopi society knows, the Hopi see this burgeoning activity in the growing of plants, the formation of clouds and their condensation in rain, the careful planning out of the communal activities of agriculture and architecture, and in all human hoping, wishing, striving, and taking thought; and as most especially concentrated in prayer, the constant hopeful praying of the Hopi community, assisted by their exoteric communal ceremonies and their secret, esoteric rituals in the underground kivas—prayer which conducts the pressure of collective Hopi thought and will out of the subjective and into the objective.[13]

In another essay, "Language, Mind, and Reality", Whorf extends his argument that our language is constitutive of our reality by suggesting that nature and language are fundamentally alike in their structure. While arguing the case that there is a transcendent order of reality beyond appearance, Whorf's immediate propositions relate to the nature of language, and three of these seem to me to be of particular interest. First, that a comparatively small proportion of activity in language is taken up with reference, and that this applies as much to scientific language with its requirement of conceptual precision as it does to the casual procedures of everyday speech; that any language is subject to complex rules including morphemic rules governing the possible syllabic units that can be generated as part of the language; and that the structure of language is not to establish a requirement that thinking be done in words.

§ § § §

My observations about the relativity of measurement relate, of course, not only to the activity of prosodic measurement, but also by inference to the activity of the mind during poetic composition. What measurement reduces, that is to say, is not the object measured, or the experience measured, but the mind's conception of that object or experience. In adducing the proposition, first, that the mind should offer a unified account of natural phenomena, including those phenomena of "redness", "warmth", and so on which we have been accustomed to thinking of as separate mental qualities; and second, that the language we use is in an important sense constitutive of the universe we perceive, my purpose has been to reinforce my contention that language is not to be understood as a purely mental operation by the additional contention that to talk about the activity of the mind in poetic composition does not imply a mental activity entirely separate from the experience with which it deals, but something which is both constitutive of experience and identical in structure to the nature of experience. From such a point of view, to talk about the objects of experience as though they represented an order of reality independent of the experience of them, entails that bifurcation of nature which Whitehead argues against; yet the idiomatic force of such distinctions between the mind and its objects is so great that the nature of the relationship between language, consciousness, and reality, which I am attempting to convey here is constantly obscured by attempts at clarity of statement using the language's customary distinctions of substance. What I mean is that poetry, by the nature of its exercise of language, offers the fullest account possible of what we experience. At the opposite extreme to conscious linguistic activity as the measurement of a single quality or modality of existence, that is, poetry is an exercise of consciousness which offers an account of the complexity of experience. Here experience is offered not in the sense of a fluid <u>continuum</u> of subjective temporal awareness, but as the multiplicity of occasions participant in any <u>event</u>.

Consciousness is manifested to itself in a language which does not possess the qualities of a supposedly "pure" consciousness, but which is concretely part of the universe which informs consciousness. If we consider language from the point of view of natural philosophy we discover a system in which referential and conceptual activity occurs in conjunction with and is to a significant extent determined by the sensory configurations and structural complexity of the system, the conjunction being essential and not circumstantial, since referential and conceptual activity is understood, for reasons which I have previously gone into, not to be independent of or solely motivated by the supposed "objects" of such activity. The criteria for performances in such a system will relate to the extent to which they realise the occurrence of appropriate occasions of experience, without making such occasions submit to inappropriate restrictions on their ontological status, and will also relate to the extent to which such realisations embody a recognition of the participation of the system which makes such presentations of consciousness possible. Such criteria apply irrespective of the particular conceptual and referential vocabulary employed by consciousness; they relate to the way it is disposed in language.

I find that Zukofsky's terms "Sincerity" and "Objectification" answer fairly well to the kind of criteria I have suggested here; they confirm Pound's contention that technique is the only test we have of a poet's sincerity. Sincerity in this sense is not a personal quality in which appearance is in conformity with reality, but a condition in which language adheres accurately to the complexity of experienced reality, the product, I would maintain, of that extension of consciousness beyond or beneath the purely mental, to include the activity of the senses. Objectification, equally, will be more than the proposition that a poem be considered as an object, "a machine...made out of words", in Williams's phrase[14], or the more familiar organic sentimentality of tree or plant; objectification will entail the recognition of language as a determining presence, sensible as well as conceptual, in the poem at every level, from the syllable on through the line and phrase to the completed discourse. The observation by the poet of these determinants is in itself a feature of sincerity, as Louis Zukofsky observes in the passage which precedes that which I quoted at the end of Chapter 1.

> In sincerity shapes appear concomitants of word combinations, precursors of (if there is continuance) completed sound or structure, melody or form. Writing occurs which is the detail, not mirage, of seeing, of thinking with the things as they exist, and of directing them along a line of melody. Shapes suggest themselves,

and the mind senses and perceives awareness. Parallels sought for in the other arts call up the perfect line of occasional drawing, the clear beginnings of sculpture not proceeded with.

Presented with sincerity, the mind even tends to supply, in further suggestion which does not attain rested totality, the totality not always found in sincerity and necessary only for perfect rest, complete appreciation. This rested totality may be called objectification—the apprehension satisfied completely as to the appearance of the art form as an object.[15]

Rested totality is, perhaps, a partial definition of the achievement of a fully realised work of art; as a quality of completion it smacks rather of the theory whereby art can endure time. But clearly the criteria of sincerity and objectification, with their insistence on a more than purely mental notion of the processes of poetic meaning, demand a concept of poetic completion which is more than rest and more than conclusion; when the events mobilised in a poem reach the term of their reasonable activity we can suppose a defined complexity which is coherent without being inert.

By way of conclusion, therefore, I propose to look at a poem by Williams which Zukofsky cites as among the examples of objectification to be found in *Spring and All.*[16] Although Williams is commonly thought of as a poet for whom thought was difficult, and who therefore spent his time celebrating discrete particulars with an imagistic intensity,[17] it is surely obvious that in the following poem the specific instances of natural existence mentioned by the poet are of no individual interest, and that the primary observance of the poem is the relation between a number of things which we like to think of, perhaps, as particulars. (Where Williams's poems do appear to employ such a particular focus, it will be found that the supposed particular is something in the poem resolved from a series of actions which offset the supposed power with which the object is named; in other words in such poems no description, consequent to the nomination of a prior subject, is being offered.)

X

The universality of things
draws me toward the candy
with melon flowers that open

about the edge of refuse
proclaiming without accent
the quality of the farmer's

shoulders and his daughter's
accidental skin, so sweet
with clover and the small

yellow cinquefoil in the
parched places. It is
this that engages the favourable

distortion of eyeglasses
that see everything and remain
related to mathematics—

in the most practical frame of
brown celluloid made to
represent tortoiseshell—

A letter from the man who
wants to start a new magazine
made of linen

and he owns a typewriter—
July 1, 1922
All this is for eyeglasses

to discover. But
they lie there with the gold
earpieces folded down

tranquilly Titicaca—[18]

In the prose passage which precedes this poem Williams notes that " 'beauty' is related not to 'loveliness' but to a state in which reality plays a part."[19] In the poem the ostensible loveliness of skin quality, proclaimed by the flowers of the candytuft, an ordinary garden perennial, is a facet of the reality which is focussed both through the lenses of a pair of spectacles, and which is to be found also in the more obdurate presence of the cheap spectacles themselves seen, folded up, in the same proportional dimension as the candytuft, the dimension to which the poem returns as it concludes. The universality which draws the poet toward the disparate particulars which accomplish the poem is the mode of relationship between them all, and of others not mentioned but implicit it is to be supposed, but it is a relationship not of correspondences of appearance, no similitude except perhaps the glow which is common to petal and skin being at work. It is a relationship in which the mechanical distortions of lenses are constant with the optical equations which make the wearing of corrective lenses a possible therapy, and at the same time imposes upon a major sensory activity the coherence of a particular focus. The potential theme of appearance and reality is subsumed in the very existence of the mathematical precisions of the optician's prescription and the practical celluloid imitation of tortoiseshell, and is effectively abolished, as also is the possible distinction between the imagination and its occasions. The sophistication of the desires of the hopeful editor who only possesses a typewriter is an exemplification of the same point. What can be said about the particulars which articulate a precise point in time, July 1, 1922, is that they do not occur as discrete entities but as the definitions of a relationship between what we might falsely distinguish as the real and the imaginary, afforded a special point of view which eyeglasses exemplify. The resolution of qualitative antagonisms, to which the eyeglasses finally maintain a supreme indifference, is an instance of that imaginative transformation of local contingencies for which Williams argued, as I showed in Chapter 3, here offered as tranquillity which is modulated in the onomatopoeic suspension of Titicaca—.

The stages by which the discourse of this poem proceed are not sustained by a logical progression invested in a syntax in which the various grammatical and hence natural functions of entities are carefully discriminated and fixed. Williams' minor units of sincerity are the activation of localised and energised particles maintained in a percipient relationship by a syntax which dispenses with customary grammatical completions and re-commencements. If the quality of the farmer's presumably brawny shoulders is to be found in the accidental glamour of his daughter's skin there is no single epithet which can express the relationship, yet if the relationship be a natural one as the genetic context suggests, it can be stated as a quality of relationship equivalent to that which exists between the yellow cinquefoil and the parched places in which it grows. Trust is a major demand upon the reader here, although it is sustained and rewarded by the subtle aroma of herbs and the female skin which they can perfume, for the linguistic connections are unable to enforce themselves by any notion that the parts of the discourse are all related by class. Against the attributive weakness of a progression of perception which can be labelled pseudo-syntactic if one judges normatively of such things, however, Williams has asserted a progression of units which disrupt the sequence of imaginative construction by insisting on the realised qualities of its sensible parts. These units are neither semantic nor analytic but, by disrupting the reader's forward apprehension of what is given, retain his sensibility to the occasions of parts of a discourse. The reader's apprehension of "the quality of the farmer's // shoulders and his daughter's / accidental skin, so sweet / with clover and the small / yellow cinquefoil", with its careful deployment of "c" and "s" sounds, is entirely different from the apprehension he might have of "the quality of the farmer's shoulders / and his daughter's accidental skin, / so sweet with clover / and the small yellow cinquefoil". The arrangement of words and phrases here is not a naively expressive one, but a means of controlling the reader's awareness, the quality of related syllables made to sustain his perception of the disparate qualities which are resolved by the poem in a mood of tranquillity. Sincerity of perception, that is to say, is objectified in a regard for the powers of language to move at its own human pace.

§ § § §

Language, I have argued, can supply a function of restraint in verse which is directly creative of form where it mediates objectively with the range of experience which the poem affords. In this sense prosodic contour is absolute to the occasion of its experience, both as something contributive to the occasion and as the expression in rhythm of its experience. Implicit in this argument is the view that nature itself contains that coherence of organisation of which the theory of cosmic harmony is a particular, theologically conceived expression.

NOTES

1   Arthur Symons, *The Symbolist Movement in Literature*, second edition, revised, London 1908, pp. 86-87.

2   Jean Moréas, "Manifeste du Symbolisme", quoted from Henry Nicolas, *Mallarmé et le Symbolisme*, Paris 1965, p. 69.

3   Suzanne Bernard, *Mallarmé et la musique*, Paris 1959.

4   Gustave Kahn, *Premiers Poèmes*, Paris 1897, pp. 16-17.

5   Ibid., p. 26.

6   Ibid., p. 27.

7   Ibid., p. 30.

8   Remy de Gourmont, *Esthétique de la langue française*, second edition, revised, Paris 1904, reprinted 1955, p. 161.

9   A.N. Whitehead, *The Concept of Nature*, Cambridge 1920, pp. 29-31.

10   Ibid., p. 31-32.

11   Ibid., p. 32.

12   B.L. Whorf, "An American Indian Model of the Universe", *Language, Thought, and Reality*, Cambridge, Mass., p. 58.

13   Ibid., p. 61-62.

14   William Carlos Williams, "Author's Introduction" to *The Wedge* (1944), in *Collected Later Poems*, revised edition, NY 1963, p. 4.

15   Louis Zukofsky, op. cit., pp. 273-274.

16   Ibid., p. 276.

17   Cf. Yvor Winters, *Forms of Discovery*, Denver 1967, "He is not even an anti-intellectual poet in any intelligible sense of the term, for he did not know what the intellect is. He was a foolish and ignorant man, but at moments a fine stylist." Op. cit., p. 319.

18   William Carlos Williams, *Spring and All*, quoted from *Imaginations*, op. cit., pp. 117-118.

19   Ibid., p. 117.

Report on A. T.K. Crozier, *"Free Verse" as Formal Restraint: An Alternative to Metrical Conventions in Twentieth Century Poetic Structure*, thesis submitted in partial fulfilment of the requirement for the degree of Doctor of Philosophy of the University of Essex, September, 1972.

The thesis submitted consists of a Summary, eight chapters and endnotes (described as "footnotes") amounting to pp. iii + 333, typed in double spacing on A4 paper. The typing and presentation are neat and reasonably accurate; I have corrected a number of technical slips in the Xerox copy on which my report is based.

The work is broadly speaking a monograph arguing a critical re-definition of certain aspects of modern poetry and incorporating an historical survey of the earlier tradition of definition in these areas. It is frankly thus po-lemical in approach, argumentative rather than documentary in respect of its main thrust. Some parts of it are derived closely from what in this context may be called primary sources; some are summarising accounts of the agreed canon of relevant documents treated in a somewhat secondary way but interpreted within the argued prise de position which constitutes the work's originality of approach.

The theme is the contention in the literary theory of this century about a priori prosodic forms and their relationship to what Mr Crozier calls "the ontological status of poetry". The treatment is extremely ambitious and wide-ranging. The structure of the thesis is subject to a very consid-erable internal strain. Some of this could have been avoided or reduced, but much of it is deliberate and appropriate to his method of approach. Mr Crozier opts against supplying a stable set of terms for his analyses and correctly disassociates himself from any claimed expertise or rigour in linguistics, anthropology, and metaphysics. He determines to adhere to the more approximate language of literary history and literary criticism, accepting the problems of "a sort of conceptual no man's land". These problems prove to be very substantial; but he also retains in this way the advantages of range and flexibility and in the end these advantages prove more important than the problems.

One structural feature which demands comment is the effect of one thesis embedded within another. At the start and conclusion we concentrate on contemporary literary theory in relation to modern poetic practice; in the middle there is a long, mainly descriptive summary of the traditions of metrical theory and prosodic analysis from the Renaissance to the nineteenth century. This latter is relevant to the context which contains it by virtue of the attempt to see multiple aspects of rhythm and verbal pattern as repeatedly larger in recognised significance than the strict theories of regular prosody contemporary with these larger recognitions. But there is a very variable sense of being in primary contact with original scholarship here, and the complications of the issues which arise are often not really resolved. This is most crucially the case in Mr Crozier's analysis of the arguments about quantity and accent in Renaissance theory; he does not fully succeed in his account of this. Here he can hardly be blamed, since scholarship is in disarray (though he should give close attention to the recent Cambridge Ph.D. thesis by D. Atteridge on this subject); but this uncertainty spreads its lack of clarity, to some extent, through much which follows after.

The other chief limitation of his central historical section is his ignorance of the traditions of practical music in each period which he considers. This ignorance also affects his sections on modern theory, though to a lesser extent; note 22 to page 99 is an important discounting of physical utterance (spoken or sung) which drives a wedge of internal contradiction through his repeated emphasis on speech acts in their naturalistic settings. If the forms of poetic discourse are not centrally or importantly related to *a priori* universals or conventions, then they must contain crucial elements of non-general, occasionalistic self-instantiation. And the theoretical recognition of these elements must invoke, as with Mr Crozier it repeatedly does, some aspect or aspects of the speech situation, and to rule out any direct examination of what this literally entails seems to me to provoke severe procedural strain. In addition, Mr Crozier talks at length about musical theory, approaches to the setting of literary texts to music, and so on, without in each context as he comes to it considering at least the outline of contemporary musical practice. And furthermore this brings to light a related more general feature of his approach, which is that his account is procedurally directed against theoretical and generalised expectations of formal pattern (as reductive of the life of poetic language), and yet he attends very much more to theory than he does to contemporary practice, in poetry as well as in music. These, together with many passages of clumsy writing, are the main problems in the thesis. The advantages arise in large part out of them or despite them. Firstly he can keep a very adaptable position as regards the features he is able to register, and this enables him to sketch out a tenuous but real continuity behind what seemed the unprecedented informality of *vers libre*. This also enables him to show the wider range of poetic features than those accounted for by traditional metrics, and the existence of constraining patterns of coherence in terms of this wider range which accompany traditional prosodic norms when these are employed and which replace these norms when prosody is in conventional terms loosened or abandoned. This run of argument is subtle, accurate and mostly convincing. Secondly, he can go way towards establishing a theoretical and even philosophical context for preferring this mode of organisation, in the experience of modern literature, rather than merely defending or justifying it. It is hard to give a general account of a non-generalising activity, and Mr Crozier does not completely succeed in connecting the whole structure of intellectual and affective experience to the reading of a poem, along the lines of his attempted "naturalism" in the sense adopted from Whitehead. But he makes a very substantial advance in this direction and this constitutes an impressive achievement.

My conclusion therefore is that, despite considerable unevenness of construction and argument, this thesis deals with a difficult subject at a generally high level of intelligence. I recommend that the oral examination be waived, and that the candidate be awarded the degree of Doctor of Philosophy. I append herewith a schedule of detailed annotation on the thesis, intending thereby to suggest not that the thesis requires to be modified before it is accepted but that the candidate may wish to consider these points before revising his work for publication.

J.H. Prynne
30th April 1973

Lightning Source UK Ltd.
Milton Keynes UK
UKOW02f1339070515

251065UK00001B/23/P

9 781848 613966